Astonishments:
Stories as True as Memory

Marian Armstrong Rogers

ISBN-13: 978-1517299507
ISBN-10:1517299500

In memory of Sam, John, Bonnie Ellen
and for Laura, Catherine, Beth, Holly, Heather

As Good As a Feast

I have not traveled far, have met neither
Kings nor knaves nor the celebrity of the moment
My stories are those of a small person living a
Simple life and, some say, a hard one—
"What a saint you are," they tell me
I tell you, if I still could get on my knees to pray
I would pray God save me from sainthood!
I would not deny this frail creation that I share
With the rest of humanity—let me feel
The heat of anger, the warmth of tears coursing
Down my cheeks when I am in pain—let me rejoice
At sight of the first robin in springtime
And when I think that I am nothing much at all
An insignificant speck—let me remember
Other days when I felt as if I were standing
On top of a mountain, arms flung to the sky in
Gratitude for what I have been given, for this
Life of mine, for all that I am.
It is enough.

Marian Armstrong Rogers

CONTENTS

THE HOUSE ON THE HILL

The excursion is the same when you go looking for
your sorrow as when you go looking for your joy.
Eudora Welty

Imagine a large brown-shingled house sitting high on a hill in
the center of a golden aura, and you will be close to the way she
saw that house when she was a child. A friendly collie dog was
lying on the wide front porch, in front of which stood a cherry tree,
a thick rope with a big knot tied at its end, hanging from its
broadest branch. All the kids in the neighborhood were running,
grabbing the knot, swinging out, and dropping at the bottom of the
hill.

When she learned that Johnny—laughing, teasing, blue-eyed
Johnny—lived in that house, she was astonished. She would
wonder, many years later, if she fell in love with the boy, or with
the house, the idea of it, the story she made of it.

Johnny had caught her eye at a school assembly when he made
all the kids around him laugh. (She was so shy she hardly opened
her mouth.) The house she lived in then was new, and in the better
section of Hartsdale, New York. Now her parents had sold it, and
moved to a house just two doors away from Johnny's, near the
bottom of the hill, in the blue-collar neighborhood where they

actually belonged/.

It was the oldest house she had ever seen. In winter, she dressed before an ancient coal-stove that kept the kitchen always warm; in spring her dad raced the birds to get enough cherries from the tree in back so her mother, who hated the stove, could bake a cherry pie, which she managed to do, yelling, "Beans!" "Beans!"

It was the only curse her mother ever used, but flung into the air with such angry vehemence it could sour milk. The girl took her mother's toil for granted, just as she took for granted that her mother was asthmatic, and unable to tolerate pets, or noise, or too much excitement.

So her home was always quiet, serene actually, a place where she enjoyed books and dolls, paints and crayons, a place where a child could day-dream for hours, but not one where children full of rowdy laughter and tease came around to swing-glide from a tree, not one with a collie dog like Lassie, and with litters of kittens, and with a worn yet welcoming mother who invited her in to see the new gold fish. And Johnny had sisters who were Waves, brothers who were sailors sailing on ships she imagined rolling over the high seas like pirate ships.

Of course she had sisters, too, Jeanne, who was already married and a new mother, and Dorothy, who worked in a bank in New York City. And her brother-in-law Bill, and Dorothy's fiancé, Charles, were fighting in World War II just like Johnny's brothers, but she didn't yet count them as family. Life at her house was humdrum, she thought—no excitement, no story there.

It was a time when children played Simon Says, Hide and Seek, King of the Hill; and the hill was always the one in front of Johnny's house where the grass was half worn to dirt. There, afraid of being called, "Sissy!" she held her breath and swung into thin air from the rope on the cherry tree, as if she were as daring as the other children.

But in fact she was a cautious child, anxious when she thought of her mother's warnings and whispers—if you run with a lollypop in your mouth and fall, the stick can puncture your throat and you'll bleed to death; if you step behind a car it can back up and crush you. Once she heard her mother whisper to a friend, *her flesh is wasting away, she won't live the year. Cancer, you know.* Her mother was smart, she knew about the harm an innocent lollypop might inflict, she knew about illness so dreadful its name could not be spoken aloud, she knew about other things, too, like delicate stomachs.

In May of her eleventh year, the child caught whooping cough, a disease that often made her vomit and always made her gasp for breath. On mild days her mother bundled her up and settled her on the sun porch where she could hear the kids playing on Johnny's front lawn, where she longed to be. School was forgotten. When she learned she had missed too many lessons to be promoted to sixth grade, shocked, ashamed, and angry (it wasn't her fault, was it?), she vomited once more.

"Don't worry Dear, don't worry, you're not getting sick again," she remembers her mother telling her, "You've just had too much excitement. It's that delicate stomach of yours."

Her parents had worried that she was ill, not that she was missing lessons, and it had never occurred to them (born in the last decade of the nineteenth century as they were), that a school administrator's decision could be changed. But Charles, Dorothy's fiancé, wounded at the Battle of the Bulge and so home early from the war, visited the principal of her school, insisted she be given a chance to pass the required exams, and helped her study for them so that she passed with flying colors and was promoted with her class.

She loved Charles then, and was excited about her sister's marriage to him, which would take place in the summer on August 11th, and would make him her brother, "for real."

For the wedding, even though she wasn't a bridesmaid and Jeanne was Matron of Honor, her mother made her the most beautiful pale blue taffeta dress she had ever seen. She loved the way it rustled around her legs when the hem was being pinned up, she couldn't wait to wear it.

But as the day of the wedding drew near she began worrying about all the excitement and her delicate stomach, afraid that she would throw up again, ruining the beautiful dress, ruining the wedding, ruining everything—and in front of everybody.

The year was 1945. On August 6th an American B-29 bomber

3

dropped the first atomic bomb known to mankind on Hiroshima, Japan. On August 9th another was dropped on Nagasaki, Japan. She will never forget her father's voice, heavy with the sorrow of unshed tears, "My, God, no!" he said when the radio announcer described death and destruction beyond what the mind could fathom in that day and age, "This world will never be the same." Then it seemed he could no longer speak at all.

She had heard the radio announcer too. No thought of a dread disease, of @ bodies being crushed by a cars, of blood pouring from lollypop-punctured throats, had ever stirred a sense of horror such as she felt in that moment, Frightened, she sat on the floor near her father, leaning against his knees. He placed his hand on her head, smoke from the Chesterfield cigarette in his hand swirling around them.

As mushroom clouds rose over the two doomed cities, a pall fell over her home.

Then it was August 11th and the pall lifted as quickly as if a brisk wind blew through the house instead of breezy preparations for Dorothy's big day—her dad checking his tux and tie, her mother fussing to get Dorothy to eat something, a hurry, a flurry of happy excitement all around her as she told her mother that she felt sick to her stomach. (And maybe she really did by then.)

Her mother called the house on the hill to ask Johnny's mother if one of her daughters, also home from the war, could baby-sit. Only Johnny (twelve years old to her child's eleven), was available. "Would he do?" His mother asked.

"Yes!" her frantic mother answered.

That afternoon Johnny read to her from her Louisa May Alcott book, Under the Lilacs, occasionally stopping to rinse with fresh, cool water, the cloth her mother had placed on her forehead, then replacing it. She had never glimpsed this side of his personality: no teasing, no joking, just a tender kind of care. She may have begun to love him a little that day.

Soon after, President Truman announced that the war was officially over. All the children on the block marched up and down banging pots and pans with sticks or spoons, yelling, "The war's over! Hooray!" and "We won, we won!"

She was there, too, and as happy as if no sense of horror had ever touched her soul.

4

That summer her soul was touched in quite another way that she will always find difficult to describe: One sweltering evening after hours of play on the rope-swing, and a final game of Hide and Seek during which she lost track of how late it was getting, she raced home well past dark, clothes wet with perspiration, skin itchy from a dozen mosquito bites, and stopped at her screen door as abruptly as if an invisible hand had reached out to hold her entranced.

Inside, her mother sat leaning toward their floor-model radio, her head almost touching it because she was losing her hearing; her dad was a few feet away, newspaper on his lap, eyes closed, faint smile on his face. A nimbus of golden light from a floor lamp encircled them, and music—*such* music—spiraled into the night, a duet (Frank Munn? Jeannette McDonald?), "*If I loved you,*" they sang, "*time and again I would try to say....*"

Their voices mingled with the sultry scent of flowers, the sounds of swamp creatures, even with her body, it seemed, as she stood in that state of acute awareness longing for *something*. (Though of course there were no words to describe all this in her eleven-year-old self.)

Then the moment released her and she opened the door and ran inside to parents too engrossed in the beauty of the music to notice how late she was.

Many years later, she will wonder if she had been longing for time to stop, for her parents to be always there, surrounded by the glowing light, the perfumed night, the exquisite music, as if the child she then was had sensed time moving to fast-forward, sensed that the peace of such days would end, and quickly.

In springtime, before she contracted whooping cough, she had run from Johnny and his sling-shot, sticking her tongue out and yelling, "I hate you!"

But even then, when she saw him hopping across bogs in the nearby swamp to reach Central Avenue, she had trailed close behind, trying not to slide into the murky water and calling, "Wait! Wait for me!"

Sometimes he had waited, and they had stood together on the Avenue's verge selling bunches of the purple, white, and lavender lilacs that grew riotously behind their houses. When he was not pulling her braids or splashing swamp water at her, sometimes they had leaned over the swamp, heads almost touching, and caught pollywogs, then watched them swim in the jars they had brought.

After he babysat for her, Johnny still carried his sling-shot, still flung spit-balls at her, still pulled her braids, still spewed swamp water toward her, but she just laughed and ran out of his reach.

By September she was a cautious tomboy, hanging onto the rope-swing for dear life but soaring high and far before dropping to the ground, or scrambling up the hill through woods full of brambles that scratched, bugs that bit, poison ivy and oak that she sometimes escaped and sometimes did not--the goal was a large flat rock that, eons ago, a glacier deposited at the top of the hill. Neighborhood children dubbed it 'East Rock', though it was directly west of all their homes.

In autumn one of the boys (none over the age of thirteen), made a fire in an indentation near the middle of the rock, and they roasted hotdogs and marshmallows stuck onto branches striped of bark, the food either given to them, or stolen from their parents. Her mother gave her marshmallows coated in toasted coconut. They browned and melted all over when held over the fire (maybe she hadn't told her mother the fire part).

Strangely, considering her mother's fears, the child, when she was grown, would not recall ever being asked where she'd been during the long hours of those summer days, or in autumn when she disappeared after school, or on Halloween when in the dark she tagged behind Johnny, hanging to the shirt-tail of his tramp costume.

That night, afraid to go into a large apartment building on Central Avenue, she waited outside until he came out with bright red lips.

"You kissed someone?" she asked, shocked.

"Geeze, no!" Johnny said, looking at her with disgust.

It was blood. She never found out what he'd run into, but she would remember that Halloween when she saw the slight scar, still over his lips, on the night that he died.

Maybe there were times when her mother questioned her whereabouts, and she's simply forgotten; maybe her mother was ill, or exhausted after weeks of preparation for Dorothy's wedding.

But maybe—hating the old house, its dirt cellar that she swore made the place smell moldy, the icy chill that seeped in frost-laced windows, the coal stove that drove her to vehemently fling her one curse into the air—maybe her mother was happily anticipating a place more to her liking, and distracted by the commotion of packing.

For after only a year they were moving yet again, this time to White Plains, five miles away.

She (the child), was inconsolable; her parents were perplexed, previous moves, and there had been four, had not upset her—but she loved that old-fashioned house with its back yard full of lilacs, its huge forsythia whose blossoms in spring arced over a stone wall toward the ground like a fall of sunshine. Possibly she'd loved it in another lifetime, loved the house on the hill, and the boy who lived there, as well, been drawn to them like iron to a magnet.

And possibly the attraction was mutual. When she moved to White Plains the following spring, she answered the phone one day, and was surprised to hear Johnny's voice.

Whatever did they talk about? Probably something like:

"Hi, it's me, Johnny. What are you doing?"

"Hi. I was just going outside to jump rope. We have sidewalks here. What are you doing?"

"Oh, I'm just hanging out. There's nobody around. Hey, our cat had kittens again."

For a few weeks they telephoned each other almost every day, then it was a new summer, and she hardly thought about Johnny, who had gone upstate to work in his father's new restaurant.

As soon as he got home, he called again to invite her to an ice show at the Westchester County Center. She wore a dirndl skirt with tiny pink flowers, a white peasant blouse, penny loafers, and bobby socks—she will think of that as her first date even though someone gave Johnny's father the tickets, and his brother Jesse drove them there and back.

They were barely out of childhood when they married.

Years later, she and Johnny would live with their children in the house on the hill.

Instead of a collie dog, a German Shepard named Murphy would flop on the wide porch where she and Nellie, Johnny's mother, sat sipping tea and watching dozens of windows in an old apartment building a mile away in the village, begin to shimmer like sheets of gold, watching until the sun sank beneath the hill behind the house, and the Midas-touched windows faded to black.

Her blissful image of a story-book home with a bruised lawn and happy family would disappear as fast as those gold-struck windows when she learned that, during Johnny's childhood years, his father had come home ugly with drink.

She lives less than an hour from that house these days, but never drives by, even if she's in the area. If she looked at it now, she would see it in darkness, shadowed by the ghost of a drunken father who slept with a gun under his pillow, shadowed by the ghost of the boy she once loved, who grew into a fine man until his personality subtly, inexorably disintegrated, leading to a final devastation that would compel her to end that story and begin another.

Yet when she thinks of sipping tea with Nellie on that wide front porch, sun gilding far away windows, the scent of a stew or spaghetti sauce wafting from the dining room window; or of her children scrambling up the back hill through shrub and trees to reach "East Rock" just as she and Johnny had done when they were children; or of herself standing in the side yard, hanging wash on an autumn day, red and gold leaves against a bright blue sky, her heart lifting along with the laundry as a brisk wind suddenly blew—she is as gladdened as when she thinks of living with her parents in the old house she loved just two doors away.

Perhaps it is a gift she's been given, this ability to lift from that time and place images that comfort her when she's lonely, that reinforce the love she knew there, and not the pain. Or maybe it is simply that in her waning years she wants a happy beginning to a story that ended so sorrowfully—in which case even her dreams cooperate, the house on the hill haunting them still, but gently, pleasantly, as if it never knew a heart that ached.

HAIRPIN CURVE

"...love lay like a mirage through the golden gates of sex."
Doris Lessing, *A Proper Marriage*

It is amazing to think that a little after school job could change the course of a person's life. All the coincidences that occurred, the near-misses that happened, it was as if the whole thing was prearranged, as if her path had been determined by an unseen presence and she was powerless so say, "No, thank you," and walk in a different direction.

She was a reasonably intelligent girl, but bookish, slow, actually dull as a butter knife when it came to finding her way around in the 'outside' world. During her sophomore year of high school when ebullient friends, one by one, approached saying, "I got my working papers!" "Hey, I got my working papers!" She would tell them, "Great!" without a clue as to what working papers were, or why they made her friends so happy. She had worked for pocket money of course, baby-sitting, raking leaves, shoveling snow, but working *papers*? She wouldn't ask her friends about them, would *never* let them see her ignorance. But when they began saying, I got a job, I got a *real* job", she realized what working-papers were for, and asked her dad how she could get hers.

Her father knew where she should go, and what form she was required to complete, and in no time she had her working-papers and a job in the Cheerful Card Company. A few evenings a week she stood putting one, then another square-folded sheet of gift wrap—the two piles stacked before her on a raised wooden platform—into white boxes that moved steadily past her place at the middle of a conveyor belt. Older women stood to each side, their rubber-tipped fingers, like hers, moving the paper like well-oiled machines: one, two, one, two, one, two, the boxes moving steadily, the piles of gift wrap in front of them kept to a height of three inches or so by an unseen source. It was mind-numbing work.

One day, her hands now in tune with the rhythm of the belt, she propped a book behind her stacks of gift wrap so she could read. Suddenly Mrs. Collier, the supervisor who had always before stayed at the far end of the conveyor belt, was standing in front of her, hands on hips, glaring. The moving box before her was sliding away; she fumbled, slipping her two squares of paper in it just as it reached the person next to her.

"For the love of God, don't stop now!" Mrs. Collier yelled. Then she paused and said, "Well I'll be damned!"

Silent, near tears, she (the girl) kept going. She wonders now how she managed to do that, but she did, sure that Mrs. Collier would fire her on the spot as soon as she got another woman to replace her. Suddenly Mrs. Collier demanded, "Go on read! Let me hear you!"

So, fingers continuing to move, her voice barely above a whisper, she read aloud and after a minute or so heard Mrs. Collier say, "Well okay; if you can do both more power to you," or words to that effect.

She could hardly believe her ears; she had been given permission to read while standing and collating paper into boxes.

After that she read at work all the time: *Gone with the Wind*; *Drums along the Mohawk,* and the hours raced by. The older women, likely because she was the youngest among them, didn't seem to mind her escape into books. On evenings when they sat together at long tables, tying tiny satin bows and gluing them onto greeting cards—which to her was like play: paper, glue, and the trick of tying narrow ribbon into perfect tiny, flat bows—the women were as friendly with her as they were with each other.

When she was a junior in high school, sixteen, nearly seventeen, she began to come into her own. Never really popular (are shy people ever popular?), she was nevertheless a member of Sigma Kappa Delta sorority, with its teas and parties, and of the Tigerettes, who marched and danced in precision formations at football games where boys collided while trying to catch the flying ball, and ran for touchdowns while spectators roared, cheerleaders cheered, and the band belted out songs of victory. It was hard for her to believe that she was an integral, if infinitesimal, part of that exciting scene; sometimes she felt like a shining star.

Other times, especially if a boy she liked never once glanced her way, she felt invisible.

That year, with money from her job at the Cheerful Card Company, she bought sweaters at The Black Sheep, and shoes at The French Boot Shop, stores that would now be called "high end" where her friends shopped. More confident, she walked with lightness, her head high. Boys began asking for dates—boys other than Johnny from her old neighborhood, that is, who had been her steady date when no other boys were asking.

It seemed that she had known Johnny forever. In the summer of her fifteenth year they had double or triple-dated, grabbing a bus for Playland Park in Rye, New York, where they swam all afternoon in the pool, unless they had somehow gathered among themselves enough money for the amusement park.

When she baby-sat for her nephews, Johnny took two buses to her home, then they walked (sometimes carrying the boys who were only two and three years old), to the Bronx River for a picnic—in those days the water was as clear as polished glass and full of minnows and other tiny creatures that the boys loved to watch.

Later the soothing sound of the shallow river spilling over pebbles and rocks like a bubbling brook, eased the toddlers, tired after that long walk, into naps on the big plaid blanket they'd brought. Then she and Johnny would sit next to the sleeping children and "neck". That was the thing in those years: "necking" or "petting" (but good girls didn't pet).

11

By the time she began working at the Cheerful Card Company, Johnny, who went to a Catholic high school, had faded from her mind. Yet he was never entirely out of the picture; when a date took her to a show at the RKO movie theater where Johnny worked as an usher, her phone would ring a day or two later and that familiar voice would say:

"Saw you with that short guy last night," or, "When did you cut your hair?" or, "Who was that creep you were with?"

One night, in a phony 'poor me' tone of voice Johnny said, "I see you're going out with college-Joes now, I guess I'm not good enough for you anymore."

"Don't be silly," she told him, laughing.

Her conversations with Johnny were short now. He didn't ask her out, and, busy with homework, girlfriends, work, and dates with other boys, she didn't miss him.

Still, she was glad he had seen her with the older boy and glad that it had bothered him. (It had to have been a wild guess on his part, but her date that night *was* a college freshman, the brother of one of her friends.)

Then, once again, newspaper headlines were screaming WAR! The government called it a "police action", but it was war in a country she had never heard of called Korea. And just as his brothers and sisters had done at the beginning of World War II, as soon as Johnny was old enough he enlisted in the Navy. Excited, he called that evening to tell her what he'd done, and that there would be a photograph of him with a few other new recruits in *The Reporter Dispatch*, the local paper.

"Long time no see," Johnny began the conversation, "Guess what? I finally joined up. I'll be leaving for training soon."

"Where is training? Where are you going? She asked.

"To Pensacola, it's in Florida," he told her, "And I'd really like to see you before I leave. Would Saturday be okay? A movie? Or we can just get an ice-cream sundae like we used to at Doc's. For old time's sake, you know?"

So she had a date for Saturday night with Johnny. And she was excited; it had been ages since she'd seen him, and the few times he had called they hadn't talked about anything at all. He didn't know that she had a job, or that she was in a sorority, or that she was a Tigerette, which was as good as being a cheerleader. Now she would brag a little. She knew he would, too. After all, he had joined up to fight a war.

That Saturday night she wore a navy blue pleated skirt, with a brand new aquamarine angora sweater and her mother's borrowed pearls. Her legs, skinny sticks when they were children, had grown shapely and were in stockings and heels instead of socks and penny-loafers; her brown hair had developed natural highlights and waves, and now fell to her shoulders.

She remembers her dad smiling when he told her how pretty she looked, remembers him with his head buried in his newspaper, trying to act as if nothing was wrong as she jumped up and ran to the window every time she heard a car coming down the road. It must have been agonizing for him, too, but he never said a word. Finally she ran upstairs, flung herself on her bed, and dissolved in tears, humiliated to have been stood up, and by Johnny of all people!

Fiercely angry, she called him the next day. He had been out with Joyce, a girl she remembered from their childhood.

"It was just a mix-up," Johnny told her, "I thought our date was *next* Saturday. It was just a mix-up, why are you so mad?"

He was out with Joyce? Not for one second did she believe he'd mixed up the days. "Just because you're wearing a uniform, don't think you're such a big-shot that you can stand me up!" She yelled, slamming the receiver down.

Johnny didn't call back, as she had expected. Instead a letter arrived a few days later. In it he wrote, "You can insult me if you want, but not the uniform I'm wearing."

As if she had done that, as if he had no clue about what had upset her. *I don't need a jerk like that in my life,* she thought as she crumpled the letter and threw it in the garbage.

Several months later, hurrying to her evening job at the Cheerful Card Company, schoolbooks held to her chest as usual to hide what she considered her too large breasts, she saw Johnny's older brother Jesse standing near the building where she worked.

"Hi, what are you doing here?" he asked, walking over.

"I work here now," she answered, smiling.

"Well so do I," Jesse said, "What building are you in?"

"This one, the factory, and I have to hurry or I'll be late for work," she told him, wanting to avoid a long conversation, "But it's good to see you," she added, "say hello to the family for me."

"Sure, good to see you, too," Jesse said. As she walked away he called, "Hey, by the way, Johnny's home on leave. I'll tell him to give you a call."

"Great," she said.

But she knew Johnny wasn't going to call, and she didn't care. She wouldn't have cared if she never heard his voice again.

By the time she got home she had forgotten about meeting Jesse, about Johnny being on leave, about everything but the ton of homework ahead of her. She ate the supper her mother reheated for her, then went to her room and dug into her books.

A few days later she answered the phone and, yes, it was Johnny. This time he said, "Listen, I'm sorry. I was a fool. I miss our friendship. Can I stop by to see you on Sunday after Mass?"

Oh sure, she thought, *after Mass, so that I'll think 'what a good guy'*. But then she smiled, her lingering anger replaced by an agreeable sense of familiarity, of fondness—Johnny had been her childhood playmate, her first sweetheart. Still, she hadn't forgotten the painful night of the 'date that never was'.

"No, I can't see you on Sunday, I'm busy. Saturday afternoon is the only time I'm free," she coolly lied.

Then can I come over around two o'clock on Saturday?" Johnny asked.

"Okay, I guess so," she said, trying to sound indifferent.

That Saturday she opened the door expecting a slouching boy wearing dungarees and a rugged jacket, and saw instead a young man in uniform, standing straight and tall, a dark tan making his blue eyes look even bluer, a jaunty white hat on his head.

Oh that sailor suit! That middy, those sexy bell bottom trousers. God but he was handsome.

It must have been spring, that season that can grab a heart and squeeze. Yes, now she remembers tulips—and essays due, exams to study for, a sorority dance, a surprise party for a friend. There was so much ahead of her. But by the time Johnny returned to the Brooklyn Navy Yard at the end of those two weeks, it was assumed that one day they would marry.

That November, as if there were not another thing of importance in her life, she joyfully marched to the band, and danced and cheered while her high school football team played against their greatest rival on Thanksgiving Day, and won.

And that November, on weekend leave from his ship, Johnny asked her father for her hand in marriage, as was proper then.

When her father asked her what she loved about Johnny, she wasn't exactly sure. "He makes me happy, he makes me laugh," she told him. Her father seemed pensive, even reluctant, but nevertheless he liked Johnny, and gave his consent. (He had always told his daughter that she would make some man a terrific wife. It was considered a high complement at that time, in that blue-collar family, and, after all, no date was set, there was plenty of time yet, plenty of time.)

In December, Johnny learned that the aircraft carrier he was assigned to, the Oriskany, would sail for San Diego, California in the early spring or summer, and from there to Korea.

Movie images of World War II 'goodbyes' played in her mind; she imagined herself on a dock kissing Johnny goodbye, imagined waving as the ship pulled out to sea.

On Christmas day, Johnny was at sea, his ship on maneuvers. But under the glittering Christmas tree in her living room, she discovered a small, equally glittering diamond ring bedded in white satin. Her mother had helped Johnny arrange for that gift. (Having suffered her oldest daughter's elopement, she was determined that everything be done "properly" for her youngest, so there would be no "talk".) The engagement was announced to family and friends.

She and Johnny would be married on a Friday so that not one day of his leave would be wasted. Since they were Catholic, fish would be served at their reception. The wedding date was set for the second of May. Her class would graduate in June.

The summer after her junior year, in blistering sun, or pouring rain, she walked the long, long way from the public bus stop to the school she loved—a school that looked like a castle on a hill—so she could earn the last six credits required for her high school diploma.

The following September, instead of beginning her senior year in high school, she was working for the telephone company and saving most of her paychecks for her marriage, and the trip to California.

In the 1950s it was not unusual to marry young, but not quite as young as they were: she was three months into her eighteenth year, and therefore considered by the law to be old enough to marry. But a boy had to be twenty-one, or his parents were required to complete a form granting their permission, and Johnny was only nineteen.

The poor parents, what could they do? It was either permission to marry or these children were headed for trouble, which was narrowly defined in that age (before birth control pills, before the rampant use of illegal drugs), as sex without benefit of clergy, and the shame of out-of-wedlock pregnancy that would most certainly follow. (Of course in her mother's eyes, the shame of an elopement would have been trouble enough.)

She has no memory now, of when the bans were announced in church, or when and where she and Johnny got the required blood tests, but she clearly recalls both of them sitting before a priest who lectured them about the holy sacrament of marriage, the sin of any form of birth control, the necessity of raising children born of their union, in the Catholic faith. He sternly requested—as if they were learning the catechism of their childhoods—that they repeat what he had said point by point, so he could be sure they understood the Church's position on their marriage, and their obligation to adhere to that position.

A singer of that time crooned a popular song that went: *"They tried to tell us we're too young, too young to really be in love...."* It should have become 'their song', but since they had known each other since grade school, Johnny chose another: *"It Had to Be You"*. It was what he told her over and over.

So she missed being a high school senior, missed performing at football games, planning teas and dances with her sorority sisters, going on dates with boys who had finally begun to notice her. She missed the senior prom, the graduation ceremony, the caps and gowns (caps joyfully flung into the air at the end of the ceremony), missed the parties, the promises friends made to stay in touch.

And she is astonished, now, to recall that she never gave all that a single thought. She wonders if she even told her friends about her plan to marry.

Then suddenly she remembers showing them her diamond ring, recalls her sorority sisters giving her a wedding shower at which they told her to close her eyes and reach into a paper bag holding a big fat frankfurter; she hears a far echo of squeals and screams and laughter, sees herself opening gifts of lacy nightgowns, negligees, sets of glasses and dishes.

And yes, now she recalls her telephone company friends, too, Bea and Anne and Jean (whose nickname was Zuffy), giving her a special lunch and presenting her with an expensive mix-master that she would use for more than thirty years. So there was that: she had good friends who wished her well. Yet she kept in touch with none of them. It was as if she turned a hairpin curve and never looked back.

In August she was speeding west on Route 66 with another navy wife, Jeannette, whose husband was on the same ship as Johnny, and with whom she would share an apartment in California while their men were in Korea.

Off and running headlong, she was, with little thought to where, exactly, she would land.

But it was magic, you see.

That's what she and John (no longer Johnny), would tell their friends in California: *God pulled the strings as if He were a magician*, they would say, and then they would repeat their litany:

> - What if Jesse had not been standing outside of her building at the Cheerful Card Company when she arrived that day—she never saw him there before that, or after.

- What if she had been late for work, or out sick?

- What if Mrs. Collier had fired her instead of letting her continue to read her books? (*That* certainly was magic!)

- What if Johnny had been at the end, instead of at the beginning, of his two-week leave from the Navy?

Yes, she thinks now, and what if there had not been a Korean war? What if she had opened the door to Johnny in his same old dungarees and jacket, instead of tall, and tanned, and looking all grown up in that sexy bell-bottom uniform—God but he was handsome.

And what if, when he kissed her at the end of that afternoon, she had not experienced a physical sensation deep inside that she had never known before: disturbing, demanding, compelling.

Ah those hormones, raging in an age when sex outside of marriage was a mortal sin that would doom a soul to hell for all eternity.

She knew books, and from the books she read she knew about romance, excitement, love. Now those things were hers. Now, enveloped in the simmering energy of that most wondrous of all things, she knew exactly what love felt like.

Didn't she?

SOMEONE WHO KNEW CYNTHIA

The best thing about the future is that it
only comes one day at a time
Source unknown

I don't know where Cynthia and I first met, but the year that
Cliff Scholl's accordion band was preparing to give a concert we
were surprised to see each other at the first practice session. The
band would be performing an ambitious classical piece, and Cliff
Scholl was an exacting conductor, so Cynthia and I had little time
to say more than "Hi," to each other before we got down to
business—she sitting on one end of the stage, and I on the other.

At the high school, we would exchange a wave, a smile, a word
or two if we passed each other on our way to or from a class, and
once we played an accordion duet at an assembly—but we were
never pals, we never went to a movie, or the beach, or on a double
date, never sat at a lunch table in the cafeteria giggling over boys.
No spark kindled that sort of friendship. Given time it might have,
but time was something neither of us had.

`Only for a season, did I think of Cynthia as a friend.

Today, she has come alive in my memory. It is the autumn of
1950 and we are with a bevy of girls walking in a large circle
around the recently shellacked and shining floor of the school

gymnasium where Mrs. Rose, the gym teacher, is pointing to one girl, then another and another, each girl dropping out until there are only about thirty left. These thirty will be members of the Tigerettes in this year of the drill team's inception at White Plains High School. And we are among the chosen, Cynthia and I.

Shy, and usually reticent, I can hardly believe I am one of these jubilant, squealing girls, while Cynthia, self assured, outgoing, vivacious, seems to never have had a doubt that she would be selected. I see her smiling serenely. She exudes confidence.

When our uniforms arrive, we try them on while chattering like a flock of starlings. They are made of soft wool the color of vanilla ice-cream, the bodices trimmed with orange satin and black braid, our school colors. The skirts reach to our knees, the sleeves, to our wrists. When we march at the football games, tiny hats will perch on our heads, white leather boots will cover our feet, and we will carry white wooden guns that the boys are making in their shop classes.

That autumn, anyone in the vicinity of the gym will hear Mrs. Rose yelling, "Kick higher, higher! Keep those backs straight! Keep those legs straight! Keep those heads up! "Why are you frowning? Smile, smile! Tighten that formation! Okay, that's better, that's better. Now do it again!"

And we do each number again, and yet again, until we can hardly stand. We learn to perform intricate precision formations with more skill than we ever dreamed we had.

Cynthia and I are friends now, and often talk before or after practice. We're more proud of being Tigerettes than anything else, even grades that place us both on the school's honor roll. Laughing, only half-joking, we agree that we're as good as the Rockettes who dance at Radio City Hall in New York City.

A photographer takes a group picture of the Tigerettes for the 1951 White Plains High School year book, the *Oracle*. When I see the picture I am, as usual, in the back row. Cynthia, short, attractive, her dark hair styled in a becoming pageboy, and a bright smile on her face, is front row center.

We perform at every football game, the last on a cold Thanksgiving Day when the clouds are heavy and gray and flurrying large flakes of snow that land like feathers on the band, the cheerleaders, and we Tigerettes who—with our backs straight, kicks high, steps synchronized—march and dance into one formation after another. Is the game against New Rochelle High? I think so, and they are our great rival. But our team wins, they win all the time, and on the way back to White Plains our triumphant cheers rock the bus. We sing Ninety-nine *bottles of beer on the wall…* riotously, over and over. Cynthia and I sit next to each other, loving the rollicking, madcap joy. We always sit next to each other on the bus when the game is away from our high school..

Outside of the Tigerettes, since each of us is engaged in different activities with different friends, Cynthia and I seldom see each other. So I am surprised to receive an invitation to her birthday party.

At a small gathering at Cynthia's home, her mother serves a superb German-style dinner with hot potato salad. I don't think I will like hot potato salad but I do. "This is delicious," I say, glancing at Cynthia's mother.

"Good, I am so glad you like it, she says, smiling.

As 1951 begins, the Korean War is raging. That September I don't return to school. Instead, having taken summer courses to earn the required credits for my high school diploma, I am working for the telephone company, saving money, and waiting for my eighteenth birthday so I can marry John, whom I've known since childhood. He is a year older than I, and in the navy, and I want to be with him in California before his ship sails for Korea.

Caught in the flurry of wedding plans, it is as if high school happened in another lifetime, it has simply disappeared from my consciousness; I forget to order my year book (the Class of 1952 Oracle), Forget Cynthia and the Tigerettes whose pictures surely grace its pages.

When John and I marry in May of 1952, Cynthia is neither bridesmaid nor guest.

In August, I am on my way to California with Jen, a navy wife with whom I will live while John, and her husband Bill, are in Korea. The back seat and trunk of her car are loaded with our belongings. I think it is over a hundred degrees, and air-conditioned cars are only a dream; the car-windows are down, hot air swirling inside, blowing the dry earth in our eyes, in our hair.

I don't care, we're on our way! We tool along Route 66 unaware that it will one day be famous. Jen does the driving, I follow the map, calling out the next town we will arrive at if we are on course. The world of school is far, far behind.

Later, I will learn that when Jen and I were settling into the tiny old house we rented in San Diego, Cynthia was on her way to Wesleyan University in Ohio.

On a Sunday a year or so later (our husbands now in Korea), Jen and I have been to Mass at St. Joseph's Cathedral, then stopped at a little café in the city for a lunch of the homemade chicken-pot-pies we love, and now are settled in our living room for a quiet, lazy afternoon at home. In the paper I'm reading a story called The Red Slipper Mystery. "The victim," I read, "...whose mutilated body was found on a lonely country road near Upper Sandusky, Ohio, was wearing only a blue flannel nightgown and red slippers that were purchased at The French Boot Shop in White Plains, New York."

"Hey, I bought *my* ballerina slippers at the same store where this murdered girl bought hers!" I exclaim to Jen.

I read on, and suddenly I'm reading about Cynthia: ". . .Cynthia A. Pfeil, of White Plains, New York, who left home August 24th for a reunion with the boyfriend she met last year when they were freshman classmates at Wesleyan. . . ."

"Oh no!" I gasp.

"What? What's the matter?" Jen asks.

Though I can barely speak for the shock and horror I feel, I tell her my friend has been murdered, blinking away tears so I can keep reading, anxious to know how such a thing could have happened to Cynthia.

I learn that her body was identified by tracing the red ballerina slippers she wore when she was found, to the French Boot Shop in the city where she lived.

I learn that her sweetheart, Roy Schinagle, is an ROTC cadet who belonged to a fraternity and was planning on going into the ministry. According to the story, he confessed to strangling Cynthia when he flew into a rage over something minor. "We had planned to be married," he sobbed, after confessing to the crime.

The story also says that Cynthia was pregnant, and I wonder if the "something minor" that triggered the boy's rage had to do with that fact: it is 1953, sex out of wedlock is an acutely shameful and sinful act, and Roy Schinagle, studying for the ministry, is surely expected to behave in an exemplary manner. He is only nineteen years old, as was Cynthia.

I read the story over and over, unable to believe that Cynthia, high-spirited, full of life Cynthia, with whom I'd shared a glorious autumn only two years before, marching, cheering, singing with joyful abandon, is dead, murdered. I am stunned, sickened.

A year and a half later, back in New York and expecting my first child, I'm in White Plains shopping for items for the baby's layette. The summer day is brutally hot. Even in a light-weight cotton skirt, and loose maternity top, I am sweaty, and tired, and walking more slowly than usual along the sidewalk on Main Street when a woman going in the opposite direction steps directly in my path. "Oh," she says, with an intake of breath.

Startled, and mildly alarmed, I see that the woman's face has suddenly turned white, and she is looking at me with a peculiar expression. I'm about to ask if she's alright when she says,

"I'm Cynthia's mother. She would be your age now." She glances at my stomach, then quickly away. "You heard what happened to Cynthia?" she asks.

"Yes," I tell her, "I heard. And I'm so…I'm so *very sorry*," I stammer.

I don't know what else to say, what to do, I feel a strange and terrible emotion akin to shame because I am alive and pregnant and standing before this woman whose only daughter, and future grandchild, were murdered. I want to be someplace, *anyplace,* else. I want to disappear.

Cynthia's mother must have sensed my acute discomfort. Perhaps she hastened to ease it with words, or quickly moved along with a farewell smile, for these many years later, remembering that day, I sense her kindness, as well as her grief and pain at our chance encounter which surely reminded her of all she had lost.

And I remember, regretfully, that when I was in San Diego and read about the Red Slipper Murder, and learned who the victim was, I never sent a note or a card of condolence to the kind woman who had introduced me to hot German potato salad; I never told her how—for one *splendid* season—her beautiful Cynthia was my friend.

The story has not ended. *The Transcript* (a college newspaper 10/23/2010) mentions a book called *Ghosts of Historic Delaware Ohio,* by John Ciochetty. In it he refers to a person ". . . who said the female ghost of the 1953 Red Slipper Murder still walks Henry Street to this day, her image disappearing as vehicles pass the spot where she was murdered."

I prefer to think of Cynthia's soul, and that of her unborn child, now with the grieving woman I once met on a White Plains sidewalk, and at peace, serene.

BACK WHERE WE STARTED FROM

But that time was spent in happiness, wasn't it? ....
That's been lived. It can't just be turned into unhappiness."
James Salter, *Last Night*

In those days, John and I never discussed owning our own home. Own a house? We were still kids. Anyway, we were already living in a house, the upstairs of one on the street where we had played when we were children. It had three bedrooms, one quite large, and a living room, kitchen, and bath. From the kitchen I could see the hill, and the roughly terraced back yard, each tier only about seven feet wide.

On the top tier was a swing-set that I worried would topple over, which it did one day as I watched out the window, flinging our oldest daughter Laura two tiers below. (She was unharmed, unlike my frayed nerves.) Oh, but it was a fine place to live, it really was.

My friend Florence lived in the downstairs apartment. When I was eleven and she was ten, we had fought over John, rolling in the dirt of his front yard, pulling hair, scratching each other like little cats. Now we shared maternity clothes, our toddlers played together. When I had a miscarriage, Florence came upstairs, gathered together my dirty laundry, and returned it clean and folded.

There were parties, life was fun. I remember lying in bed one winter night as snow pelted the slightly open window—the indescribable scent of it in the air as I fell asleep anticipating morning when I would take our toddlers sledding—I was so happy I could have hugged myself.

Then too, there were times when a black cloud fell over me, and I had no idea why I felt so wretched. It would lift a week or so later, and be forgotten. I blamed New York; I might love snowstorms, but I hated the otherwise cold and dreary winters.

John and I had planned on settling in sunny southern California when he was discharged from the Navy, but first decided to drive to New York (for an unspecified time), to visit with our families. I had resigned from my job at the Bank of America in San Diego but the bank manager said he would welcome me back if I changed my mind, and John, always optimistic in those days, was sure he'd find work there as soon as we returned.

About two weeks into our vacation a doctor confirmed what I had suspected but not dared believe: I was pregnant. I'd expected to be pregnant by the time John left for Korea but it hadn't happened. Now it had, and we were ecstatic. California was forgotten. "I'm going to be a dad!" John bragged to everyone in sight.

By the time our daughter Laura was born, John was working in Grand Central Terminal in Manhattan, and we were living in a small apartment in Mt. Vernon, New York. When she was six weeks old, he developed shadows on his lungs. The doctor, after confirming that he had no deadly disease, suggested underground work might be the cause, and John resigned from the railroad.

We moved in with his parents until Laura was eleven months old when an opening at the local post office, and simultaneously an upstairs apartment in the newly converted two-family house next door, became available—John grabbed the post office job, we grabbed the apartment, and we were content. Content, that is, until our friend Harry telephoned from California.

Laura was almost six years old when that call—a major event in that time of rare, expensive, long-distance phone calls—came, but

Harry *had* to call, he said; he *had* to tell us to get our asses out there right away because houses were going up all over the place, and we could get one with only a few hundred dollars down. "Don't let any grass grow under your feet," he said, "Why wait? Come on out."—at least that was the gist of the conversation John and Harry had.

By then we had a second daughter, Bonnie, and John had a good steady job. We couldn't just pick up and go, but we began reminiscing about our days in San Diego, began thinking of owning a home for *only a few hundred dollars down*! Began dreaming a dream we'd never had.

It was the first time I felt the way a starving man must feel when he looks through the window of a busy restaurant at all the people eating delicious meals, and he hasn't a penny to his name— suddenly I was *starving* to live in a home that belonged to us. And the houses we could afford to buy were three thousand miles away where, I joyously recalled, sunshine brightened every day into perfect warmth, nights were deliciously cool, and rain was so rare that I ran outside to see it.

John began accumulating vacation time. He explained to his postmaster that he hoped to find a California post office that would accept a transfer, and was granted leave for six weeks.

We gave our landlord notice, sold furniture, packed clothes, linens, dishes and kitchenware, put the cartons in the trunk of the White Cloud (as we called our car), loaded the back seat with toys, games, and pillows for Laura and Bonnie, put a cooler on the floor their feet didn't yet reach, and were on our way singing, "California here we come, right back where we started from. . ."

Our girls were born travelers, uncomplaining in that cramped back seat, enjoying the novelty of the trip, learning about the States we passed through, each one unique, in those days. We sang old favorites: *You Are My Sunshine; Red River Valley; Oh Susanna,* and laughed out loud when Bonnie, a few months past her forth birthday, belted out an Irish ditty she'd heard on the radio: "Haitch, Aaaa, double R I, G A N spells Harrigan. . ." We watched for amusing Burma-Shave rhymes, the words posted a few at a time on billboards planted along major highways—Don't take/ a curve/ at 60 per/ we hate to lose/ a customer/ Burma-Shave.

Every few hours we stopped to exercise, gobble peanut butter and jelly sandwiches, and sip Tang (that appallingly sweet vitamin C drink), filling the gallon thermos with the orange powder, and what we hoped was clean water, whenever we could.

There were no food franchises, no McDonalds from one end of the country to the other, so we ate our one hot meal of the day at truck stops, which were known for their cheap, wholesome food. The truckers were friendly; when we passed them on the road they would wave, and the girls, tickled, would wave back.

Still in our twenties, loving the freedom of the road, John and I almost forgot why we were traveling through state after state after state. It was pure fun.

Fun, that is, until one January evening when—having gone just a *little* farther, and a *little* farther—we found ourselves driving in a remote area of Texas, in freezing rain, in the dark, on a road of solid ice. An excellent driver, John knew to keep the car moving slowly, not to use the brakes at all, if possible.

The car inched forward on a two-lane highway blessedly empty, local drivers likely having been forewarned that an ice storm was approaching. Then we spotted a motel sign. "Thank God," John said. *Thank You, God,* I silently echoed, taking a deep breath. So relieved were we that we never noticed the lights on the motel sign were turned off.

John edged the car into a driveway in front of a house that appeared to be the main building (motels in those days being comprised of several small cabins set farther back on the land). He got out of the car, walked up a short path, and knocked on the door. A man answered. I remember tired eyes, grizzled hair, worn dungarees or maybe overalls, a frayed sweater; he looked as if he'd been sleeping.

We need a place for the night, John probably said. When I saw his shoulders slump, I opened the car door, and the man, who had just told John the place was closed up for the winter, noticed me and the children. "Uh, wait, wait here," I heard him say as he hurried off, coming back a minute later with a woman I assumed was his wife. She gave us the once-over, and I think gave a slight nod to the man.

"Well y'all can stay the night," he said, "but ah'm afraid there's no heat, no water eitha. Y'all can go ahead and use the toilet anyway," he added, handing John the key to the nearest cabin.

Slowly, we drove down a slippery lane to the row of cabins in back. We hadn't had dinner, but with us were the jars of peanut butter and jelly, half a loaf of bread, and the thermos with a bit of Tang that wasn't frozen. We ate quickly, and were about to join the girls, who had scrambled under the summer-weight blanket on the double bed (all of us wearing our heavy winter jackets), when there was a knock at the door.

Alarmed, John and I looked at each other—*Who would be out on such a night? Someone looking for trouble?* He opened the door a crack, and there stood the motel owner and his wife who had driven down the treacherous icy lane to bring us comforters, a kettle of hot cocoa, and tin cups to put it in—"to warm your cold bodies," the woman said. (The thought of their kindness warms me still.)

The next morning we left at sunrise, putting the key in our hosts' mailbox, as he'd asked us to, along with a note of thanks that I scribbled on a page torn out of my journal. The world was transformed: clear water trickled on roads washed clean, trees still coated with ice sparked diamonds into a flawless sky. I remember feeling *everything is right with my world,* elation, a strong sense of promise.

But when we got to California, we learned there had been a dip in the economy. There was no opening for John in the San Diego post office or those in nearby towns, no jobs of any kind anywhere.

We weren't particularly bothered, after a year imagining ourselves in that fondly remembered city we found, in fact, that we didn't much like it anymore. The pleasant two-story garden apartment we'd lived in was gone, a freeway in its place. Foothills and canyons we had once hiked now had homes crawling up one side and down the other, and the houses we could afford were built so close together you could reach an arm out of one window, and tap the glass of the one next door.

So we visited with Harry and our other friends, visited with John's sister Peg and her family (who lived near San Diego, and with whom we'd been staying). And then, in a vacation frame of mind, we decided to head for Florida for a visit with my parents, who had rented cottage in Gulfport.

While there, we looked at brand new *very* reasonably priced homes and found one we loved. But when John went to post offices in the area, they had no job openings either. So we scurried back to New York, and his family home (our former apartment in the two-family house having been rented to others), until John, who still had his post office job in town, found us a place that would accept children: three rooms in a garden-apartment complex we called "the white apartments." John always found us a place to live.

The apartments in that u-shaped white building were all exactly the same: a very large living room with a small 'L' of a dining area, a bedroom, small kitchen, and bath.

John and I bought a Castro convertible couch to sleep on, a dresser, a small chest, and a hutch to put on top of it so it looked like a room divider in front of the dining area. He also managed to get a portable washing machine (a blessing), in the tiny kitchen, leaving about a foot of space between it and the sink.

The living room was plenty large enough for the girls to play, for a bridge table for crafts, or jigsaw puzzles, or my sewing machine, and for a big tree at Christmastime. The bedroom, also large, belonged to the children. Before we knew it we were adding a crib for another baby.

Early on, I was sure I would miscarry as I had done three times after Bonnie was born (we were Catholics, you see, young and randy, and rigid in following the Church's rules). But this time, to my great joy—which may be hard to believe considering the limited space we were living in—but yes, to my great joy a third daughter would arrive in July, 1962. We would name her Catherine.

Since we had used our savings for the trip to California, the new furniture was bought on credit. John worked two, even three jobs (if you count bartending at a local gin-mill when the usual bartender was out), to pay off the debt. He must have been exhausted, yet in my memory he is always whistling, which he did when he was happy.

I see us with friends at barbecues; at St. Patrick's Day dances at our church; at Memorial Day parades, Bonnie marching with the Brownies, Laura with the Girl Scouts, the fire department handing out free beer and Carvel ice-cream sandwiches.

I also see a frozen turkey flying through the air directly for John's head while he is standing in front of the large living room window. Below the window a neighbor is tossing a ball to his small son; John's arms reach out and catch the bird as if it were a football, "You could have *killed* someone if that thing went through the window!" he bellows at me. But he is proud of his catch, and now we are both laughing, the tempest over as quickly as a summer thunderstorm.

On another day (it must have been after Catherine was born), a five pound jar of Vaseline hurtled through the air toward the same target. I might have *killed* John with that raging temper of mine.

Years later, that rage, and the black cloud that accompanied it, which always occurred a week before my period, was recognized as premenstrual syndrome, PMS. Still, I wonder if that fury simmered like molten lava, deep in my subconscious, during the rest of the month.

I don't know. I only recall the events, not the triggers. And I recall, regretfully, that at such times I was a bitch of a mother to my two older girls.

But there was far more happiness while we were there, while we were young, than anger.

Early in 1962, my brother-in-law Bill telephoned. He owned an offset printing business called Photonews, in Long Island, where he and my sister Jeanne lived. The conversation went something like this:

"I'm expanding the business, Marian, opening two new branches, one not far from where you live. I want you to come and work for me as a paste-up artist, and..."

"*A*s a *paste-up artist?* Bill, I don't even know what a paste-up artist does! And you know the baby is due in August, I can't possibly ..."

"I know, I know, but listen, listen a minute. You'll be trained during the day while the girls are in school. Then after the baby is born you can work when John's home, seven to eleven P.M., except for one night a week when I've got a big one, and the paper won't be put to bed until one or two in the morning. Look, just think about it, you don't have to give me an answer now. Think about it, talk to John, and then call me," he said. "By the way," he added, "I'll be grooming you for a supervisory position."

Like every woman in my stratum of society, I was expected to stay home once the children arrived, and I *liked* being at home, it was a vocation I took seriously. (Those were the days when it was said, "The hand that rocks the cradle rules the world"). I had enjoyed a feeling of independence when I worked for the telephone company, and then the Bank of America, but now that I had children? No.

In spite of myself I thought about it, couldn't *not* think about it: *if I worked John could quit his second job; I love drawing and painting and I would be a paste-up* artist! *But I don't know a thing about paste-up, what if I'm no good at it? I'm good at running a home, decorating, sewing, baking, and my God, I'm pregnant! No, I can't take the job. Oh, but what an opportunity!*

By the time John got home I wanted that job. I knew he would be fine with taking care of the girls while I worked, he always helped when he was at home, and besides working evenings I'd have everything done before I left: homework, dinner, baths. But I was sure his ego would not allow it, that he would consider my working outside of the home a reflection on his ability to provide for us.

But, "Well why not?" he said when I told him about Bill's offer. (I suspect that offer arrived at a perfect moment, John must have been sick to death of working two and three jobs.)

"You can train for the job now," he told me, excited, "and if you don't like it, quit when the baby comes. Well, you'll have to quit then anyhow."

Oh no I won't, I thought, but I let it go, it was still winter, the baby wasn't due until August.

So I accepted Bill's offer of a job, and at Photonews one night, in the middle of the fuss of putting a newspaper together, that newly-minted dream of ours took form as magically as Cinderella's pumpkin turned into a coach: there was a house meant for us right in our home town, where we were again contentedly settled—a house, and all we had to do was reach out and grab it.

First, though, I almost quit my new job.. I liked paste-up, the trouble was I couldn't seem to do it. As I perched on a high stool in front of a slanted table with a big white sheet of heavy paper called a "flat" on it, my mind went blank, my eyelids drooped, I fought to simply keep sitting on the stool, awake.

One day Bill walked in, talked to the supervisor who was training me, came over to where I was sitting, and said in a pleasant voice, "Come on Marian, I'm taking you to lunch."

I won't have to quit, he's going to fire me, he's taking me to lunch to soften the blow, I thought. (His way with me was always that of a kind older brother.)

I remember a warm spring day, a restaurant where businessmen wore suits, women good dresses, and I, hugely pregnant wore a light blue wrinkled cotton maternity outfit (they were always wrinkled), damp with perspiration, and with a spot of glue from work on the skirt. Horribly embarrassed, I was nevertheless pleased at being taken someplace special, as I thought of it then, not to a diner or hamburger joint.

I heard Bill say the expected words: "I know the job hasn't been going well," and then, "But it will; you need to relax, you have to be patient with yourself."

I was so tired, so pregnant, so discouraged that I don't know if I was relieved or dismayed that I still had a job.

(Oh, but how good it is to now recall that lunch with Bill in a treat of a restaurant; it's a memory as light and sweet as the lemon sherbet that's served to clear the palate between courses of a heavy meal.)

And Bill was right. As if deliberately held in abeyance until Catherine was born (almost a month early), every piece of the job that puzzled me fell into place when I began working the evening shift. I was a paste-up artist, and a good one.

The "big one" that Bill had spoken of was *The Citizen Herald* of Walden, New York, a newspaper that won awards for excellence. The night we put it together, a Thursday I believe, it often wasn't ready for print until three or four in the morning. I would arrive home totally exhausted, yet energized, exhilarated, and with a tremendous sense of competence and accomplishment.

It was on one of those busy nights that Mabel, a friend who had visited John and me in our small apartment, rushed over to where I was sitting. She had begun working at Photonews when her husband, minister of the Seventh Day Advent church in our town, died. Excited, she said, "Our church is selling the house that my husband and I lived in, for only $15,000! and they want it to go to a family who needs a home. It will be *perfect* for you!"

The price was well below that of houses in Westchester at that time, and it *was* perfect—there were three large bedrooms, a formal dining room, a fireplace in the living room, and it was near our church, the children's school, and the post office where John worked. We were told that it was ours, if we wanted it, and boy did we want it!

But the bank required a twenty percent down payment, and having saved nothing after our California trip, we didn't have three thousand dollars.

The money magically appeared in the form of an unsolicited, interest-free loan from the parents of another friend (parents we had never even met). Then we learned we would need about nine hundred dollars for closing costs. John explained the situation to Bill and asked for a loan.

"Sure," Bill said, "Just give me a couple of days; I'll cash in a certificate."

When you marry at eighteen and nineteen years of age you're ignorant of many things, at least John and I were. We didn't know what a "certificate" was (a certificate of deposit), or that my brother-in-law might have to pay a penalty for early withdrawal, and would lose future interest on that amount. That knowledge would have troubled us if we had known.

But as it was, everything had fallen into place in a most astonishing manner, and we were ecstatic—we would have a home of our own; our girls would grow up in a house just as we had, *Oh God, thank you, thank you, thank you,* I said probably twenty times a day.

I called my parents in Florida to tell them the wonderful news.

"Oh but Perky," my mother said, calling me by my nickname, and sounding worried, "Perky, you don't *know* what a *burden* a

house is. And buying it with all that *borrowed* money! What
you do if the roof leaks, or the hot-water heater breaks down,
the furnace? How will you even afford oil for the furnace?"

Those are almost exactly my mother's words, and they were all
it took; the seed of fear, always just under my skin, sprouted, grew
wild, and smothered every joyful, optimistic feeling we had had.
For if I was afraid, so was John, if he was afraid, so was I.

With all arrangements in place, we backed out of the deal.

That house had appeared as if Mabel were a fairy godmother
who had tapped us with a magic wand. It was as if a miracle had
been bestowed upon us, and even now, a lifetime later, it is hard to
remember passing up a miracle. I used to blame my mother, but it
was my fear that gave her such power. If we had bought that house
of course there would have been unexpected expenses, there
always are, and the taxes would have gone up year after year, but
so did the rent we paid. John and I would have managed, we
always did.

On the other hand, there are unanticipated events that have
nothing to do with unexpected expenses.

Bill called me at home several months later, and the news was
bad. His business accountant had stolen money, taxes had not been
paid. Overnight the government had locked up the two new
branches of Photonews (the one in White Plains, where I worked,
and one in Maryland), confiscating machinery and supplies. Bill
had tried to raise the necessary money but hadn't been able to. He
hated to tell me, but my job was gone.

"What about you and Jeanne?" I asked, worried about them
(three of their eight children were as young as Laura and Bonnie).

"Don't worry, we'll be fine, the main office is okay," he told
me, sounding exhausted.

A few days later, the editor of *The Citizen Herald* called to ask
if I'd like to move to Walden and work for them. For a brief
moment I thought John and I might still have that dream of ours,
and, excited, we drove to that then idyllic Norman Rockwell town,
where homes were still in our price range. But the tiny Walden
post office had no opening, and the distance was too great for John
to commute.

life was busily full, and the next half empty, as
en abruptly sliced off. After the children were
it, I wandered around the living room, dining
if I'd forgotten something, as if there were
lo. Then, slowly life regained its former shape,
John working a second job, me busy with church, and the
children's school, and friends—our dream of owning a home as
lost to us as night-dreams are in the morning when you rush to the
kitchen, pop bread in the toaster, put jam and butter on the table,
and tell the children to hurry so they won't be late for school.

While the shape of my world was shifting, so was that of the
world at large—the Bay of Pigs fiasco happened in April 1961; in
August, Russia's Iron Curtain took form with construction of the
Berlin Wall; in October 1962, the Cuban Missile Crisis threatened
nuclear destruction. (I was working, but I remember watching
television for the latest development every chance I got, terrified at
the thought of a holocaust); and in November 1963, President
Kennedy was assassinated and the whole country, the whole world,
was in shock and disbelief that such a thing could happen in
America.

John and I were among the stunned when those events occurred,
yet for me the small lived life seems to dominate, for I've tucked
memories of major world crises—the horror, the terror, the
shock—far beneath those of our fun-filled cross-country trip to
California; beneath Hallmark memories of barbecues, church
dances, Memorial Day Parades; beneath memories of the world
outside opening to me, and then closing, of a house soon to be
ours, and then not.

ALWAYS, SOME MERCY

When your dreams tire they go underground
And out of kindness, that's where they stay
Libby Houston

The train conductor pulled one of the seats back so we could face each other, my mother, me, Catherine, and Beth, my six week old baby. My memory is of Catherine, who was four years old, sitting beside me while the baby slept in a canvas car-bed placed on the floor between my mother and us. But that can't be right, there wouldn't have been enough room to get in and out to the ladies lounge on the long trip from Florida to New York, so the baby must have been in my arms or lying next to me, and Catherine, I guess, sat next to my mother.

It was a relief to be traveling toward my husband John and our two older daughters, Laura, almost twelve, and Bonnie, ten, who had left a month earlier so the girls wouldn't miss the start of school in September; but, if relieved, I was also tense and anxious and numb with fatigue, and I can't remember details like our seating arrangement, like how we managed in the dining car with the baby. Did we take turns, my mother and I? Not likely. She was not herself and wouldn't have wanted to dine alone, or to be left with the baby while Catherine and I dined. My one sure memory is of laying my head against the window, the baby sleeping, Catherine on my lap, and watching autumn colors change in one scene after another like chips of colored glass in a kaleidoscope.

Thinking about that October day, it's no wonder my memory is hazy, considering all that had happened since April of that year, 1966. We had moved to Florida to buy a house; we dreamed of one with a big yard, and a tall tree that John would hang a piece of wide rope on so the children could swing-glide, as we once had in front of his childhood home.

We'd dreamt the same dream six years earlier, driving across the country to California when a friend telephoned to tell us that homes were "going up like crazy," all over San Diego and could be had with little money down. John, a postman, had been unable to find a job, and the trip had turned into a jolly adventure. Still young, we'd returned to New York, and a three room apartment, undismayed, our dream of owning a home not gone, but rising only occasionally, like a ghostly haunt.

Then I'd gotten a job, and we'd almost done it, almost moved into our own place. When we let that chance slip through our fingers, we never quite got over it.

A few years later, John came home from work in a state of high excitement. "Perk," he said, "Mo bought the old house next to his, and he's renting the downstairs. He says we can take a look at it. Come on, let's go before he changes his mind, oh, and if we want it the rent will be the same as it is here. That is, if we're willing to fix it up." (Mo owned a shop in town).

We went to see the house immediately, friends in the apartment across the hall watching our daughters. Mo told us a couple in their nineties had lived in the old house alone until their deaths, the upstairs (at some point converted to an apartment), empty. *They must have had no family*, I thought, imagining children dying before them, perhaps sons in the First World War.

The place looked as if it had died long before the old couple, the floors, fireplace, and curtains gray and grimy, lace panels at the living room windows so friable that one disintegrated at my touch. In the kitchen, the ceiling had a large ragged hole, the sink stood on legs, and the shelves in a walk-in pantry were strewn with mouse-droppings. But the stove was gas, not coal, and there were wonderful tall windows, a small front porch, and a large back yard. We wanted it.

Mo let us fix the place up before we actually moved in. We pulled down curtains, and washed windows whose glass sparkled the way glass these days never will. We scrubbed and waxed floors, and polished the non-working marble fireplace. John's uncle repaired the kitchen ceiling, and helped us paint. Having learned to hang wallpaper when I lived with another Navy wife while John was in Korea, I bought paper for the living room walls, a light unobtrusive pattern in a soft mauve hue. This was before the days of pre-pasted paper, so John set up a table made from a door and two saw-horses. I mixed the paste, laid the strips of paper over the makeshift table, and slathered them with paste as thick as mucous.

I can still see Catherine, who was two and a half, playing nearby with blocks on the day I lifted a heavily glued sheet of paper toward the crown molding, and it slipped and wrapped itself around my head, body, and the ladder.

"Oh, Mommy," she squealed, folding over in laughter as I broke out of the paper straightjacket.

I smile, now, but then—my shoulders and neck sore, paste in my hair, and eyes, and mouth—I was mad as a wet hen (the cliché spot on in this case), and squawking at having to quit and go home to shower when there was still so much to do.

The last thing I did was to sew pleated, double tiers for the windows, out of floor-length drapes that we had used in the apartment. When the room was finished—walls papered, windows sparkling, tiers hung, furniture in place—it looked so fine that I would stand for minutes just gazing at it. I don't think I've ever again felt quite that way. It was as if we had brought the house back to life.

We moved there in December, and could hardly believe it when Florence, a childhood friend with whom we had shared a two-family house before we went to California, moved into the upstairs apartment. Her daughters and ours were about the same ages. I have a photograph of all six taken the following Easter morning, they're wearing new bonnets and dresses, dainty white anklets, patent leather shoes, and even white gloves on Laura and Susie, the two oldest.

In my mind I see the circular garden behind where they stand, a profusion of purple and yellow irises unfolding through a carpet of weeds; I see my daughters eating breakfast at a kitchen table in front of the window that framed that view; in the dining room I see beautiful furniture: a table, chairs, and china closet (bought second hand for four hundred dollars). Mom and Dad, visiting from Florida, are sitting with us at the table, eating roast chicken dinner, and, for dessert, my three layer coconut cake with lemon filling. It's summertime now; maybe it's someone's birthday: Dad's, Catherine's, Bonnie's.

By January I will be pregnant again, and by the next summer, in fact before the next Easter, we will be gone from there.

When we were living in the white apartments, as we referred to the place where our three-rooms were, my dad had telephoned to tell us he'd bought a brand new two-bedroom bungalow in Gulfport, Florida for only six thousand dollars. I remember his excited voice, "Only *six thousand dollars*! Can you believe it, Perky?"

Now, hearing that I was pregnant once again, he and Mom began encouraging us to move to that more affordable State. John and I were not enthusiastic about the idea, not at first; we'd worked hard to restore the downstairs of the old house we lived in, now it felt like our own. And we'd barely settled in.

But with another baby coming, and no room for a crib in the girl's bedroom, as there had been in the white apartments where Catherine was born, we began envisioning a place with room for a growing family, began talking, once again, about *owning* a home, began dreaming of what it would be like to live in Florida with its sunny skies, warm breezes, white-sand beaches, a place where John needn't trudge through ice and snow to deliver the mail.

Soon the cartons came out and we were packing to move yet again.

The drive to Florida was as different from our California jaunt as tears are from laughter. Our new Nash Rambler car was less spacious than the White Cloud (as we called our old Ford), had been, and now three children were crowded into the back seat.

Halfway there, Bonnie came down with chickenpox. Catherine got car-sick. John was a bundle of nerves (is it any wonder?), and I, three months pregnant, was uncomfortable, irritable, and as impatient to reach our destination as our poor miserable girls were.

And then we were there—balmy air, intense blue sky, billowing mountains of cumulous clouds on the horizon—and our spirits soared; even Bonnie, still quite ill, brightened.

This time we knew we would stay because, unlike our attempt to relocate to California, this time John had been able to arrange a transfer to the St. Petersburg post office. In his pocket was a copy of the letter Ed, his postmaster, had sent to the postmaster in Florida, a glowing recommendation, "John is responsible, reliable, intelligent, congenial," he wrote. I remember John's slow smile when he read it. I remember how eager and confident he was when he began his new job.

For just seventy-five dollars a month, my father had rented for us a tiny cottage in Gulfport, which is near St. Petersburg. It sat haphazardly among other cottages on the scant, sandy grass, all of them looking as if they'd tumbled like toy blocks from a giant child's hand. I recall John's dismay upon seeing it.

My dad must have been there when the moving men arrived because our familiar furniture (minus the beautiful dining room set which we had sold for a third of what we paid), was appropriately placed in the living room and bedrooms.

Easter arrived soon after we did. I see the living room crammed with unpacked boxes, and, on the couch, Bonnie, still recovering from chickenpox, propped on a pillow, with a box of new Crayola crayons and a new coloring book in her lap, while the rest of us leave for Easter Mass. But could that be right? She was only ten years old. Didn't I stay with her?

I don't know. And I don't know where she and Laura finished the school year. I can't recall registering them, or seeing them off each morning, or helping them with homework.

But I see myself pouring orange juice in the small kitchen at breakfast time, cleaning up, making beds, Catherine following me around with her little miniature broom. I see us at Gulfport beach, which we walked to every day as soon as the older girls were home from school. Sometimes we brought with us a light supper—tuna and macaroni salad, potato chips, soda—so John could join us when he came home. Then we'd stay until the sun went down. Gulfport beach was gorgeous in those days, surrounded by scrub pines and not a condominium in sight.

Often we'd see my father, and my mother—who to my knowledge had never before set foot on sand nor toe in water—sitting in a cabana in the middle of the sandy beach, playing bridge or canasta with their friends. It was a marvelous sight. When they saw us walking toward them they would swell with delight. Then the girls and I would swim, splashing each other and laughing; they would build sand castles; I would read; in late afternoon John would arrive, and at day's end we'd return home wonderfully sleepy, and deeply contented.

I think John was happy when we lived there. Although one day, sounding disgusted and angry, he said, "I feel like we're white trash, living with an oil burner in the middle of the living room!"

"But we're not living here forever, we're going to move soon," I retorted, surprised at his outburst.

On June 6th, when Hurricane Alma blew through Florida, we were still living in the quirky cottage near the ocean. Homes there had to be evacuated, so we drove farther inland to my parents' place, where we listened to weather updates on their portable radio: *All Florida battened down and waiting; 93 miles per hour winds; Car blown off a bridge between Tampa and St. Petersburg; Phantom jet fighters leave McGill Air Force Base in Tampa, for Columbus Air Force Base in Mississippi.* I remember feeling excited, not afraid. When it was over, we returned to find the Gulfport cottage exactly as we'd left it, except for wind-blown debris in the yard.

Here my memory fails me. I wonder if we had already bought our house that day; if so, how many did we look at before buying it? When? Where? Did we look at any in Gulfport, which I knew and liked?

And when we finally moved into that dream of a home of our own were we overjoyed? Or had we just settled for what we could get. I don't remember feeling joy—though possibly there were a few blissful moments, grains of sand in a sandcastle of disparate images lost to a tide of exhaustion.

I was exhausted every day that summer. I am exhausted just thinking about it.

The house was in St. Petersburg, and cost eleven thousand dollars with not a cent down. There were large yuccas bordering the attractive entrance, and in the back a large yard where the children could play (but no tree suitable for a rope-swing). Inside were a large kitchen, fair-sized living room, and three bedrooms. All had terrazzo floors, and jalousie windows.

We must have bought it *sometime* in June, because I see us celebrating my father's seventy-third birthday on July 9th—Steak broiled outside on a grill; a birthday cake decorated with too many melting candles; John and Dad laughing together; the girls handing their grandpa birthday cards they had made for him; Mom watching all of us with great pleasure; and me, hugely pregnant again, tired and wrung out from the heat, but happy.

Was it that day that John was suddenly called into the bathroom where, overcome with weakness, Dad was holding for dear life to a sink full of blood? No. Impossible. I remember him enjoying that meal, feeling fine, all of us happy. It could not have been that day. But it did happen.

(In my earliest years it was my father who took me for walks, naming the flowers and bugs that we saw. He took me to see *Bambi, Dumbo,* and *Pinocchio* at Radio City Hall, to the circus at Madison Square Garden. Mom always stayed home, either because she was losing her hearing, or because she simply didn't enjoy such occasions. She loved Jeanne, and Dorothy, and me. Our father cherished us.)

When John and I were living in the Gulfport cottage, we had basked in a perfect combination of warm sun and gulf breezes. Almost every day, I walked to the beach where my mother and father played a game of cards with their friends.

Now my father was dying. And now we lived inland in St. Petersburg, where the temperature was in the 90s with 90% humidity every hour of every day, after day, after day. There were no gulf breezes. There was no beach close enough to walk to, and John needed the car. In every room, fans blew air that fell against our skin like wet cobwebs. The girls didn't mind the heat and humidity, but it clobbered John. It clobbered me. I would hear our next door neighbor's air conditioner humming (a big one, jutting out of a window on the side of their house), and long to sit in a cool kitchen with the woman who lived there, chatting and sipping iced tea.

One day Laura and Bonnie ran in visibly upset, "Mommy, what's orgies?" Laura asked, near tears.

"Wild parties," I answered (leaving out the sex, and wondering where the question came from). "What's the matter, Honey?

"The kids won't play with us because we're Catholics. They said we have orgies every weekend. They said we're the devil's spawn," she said, indignant.

I ran after those misinformed children of ignorant parents, I screamed at them, shook them by the scruffs of their collars, and....

No of course I didn't. But I *burned* with a desire to run after them, to bang on their parents' doors (as if I knew what doors to bang on), and try to enlighten their locked minds. No, I just hugged my girls and offered them that tired truth: "They don't know any better."

My daughters quickly regained their equilibrium, but I no longer anticipated friendship with other mothers on the block, wondering if they really believed orgies took place in the quiet home where the pregnant woman lived with her husband and children, or if it was just the nasty teasing of a few children.

I was too timid to find out. If no neighbor said 'Hi', if none acknowledged our presence in any way at all (and none did), then neither would I smile or wave at them. Miserable, I circled the wagons.

Maybe it was then that I began silently crying at night after John collapsed into sleep. Or maybe it was when Dad, weak and badly burned from radiation treatments, could barely stand, or when things went bad for John at the post office. (And maybe those things all happened at once.)

I've often wondered if John was really asleep, or if he heard me weep and could find no words of comfort. If so, the weight of my tears must have exponentially increased the weight he already carried, for he *hated* working at the St. Petersburg post office.

As the newest hire, he knew he would be a 'floater', covering other postmen's routes when they were off, but he had expected cheerful repartee when the men were in the office, like there had been at home. There was none. John decided the men were prejudiced against him because he was a Yankee (a conclusion that may or may not have held some truth).

If he or any of the men, needed to go to the bathroom in the morning while they were sorting mail, a permit slip requesting permission was required, a senseless rule that riled John anew each morning before he left to deliver mail. "I feel like I'm in kindergarten," he said. Sometimes he had to cover a bicycle route. Since he was not used to riding a bicycle, and was always soaked with perspiration, he developed a painfully irritated groin.

One day he parked the bicycle against a tree at the beginning of each block, and quickly delivered the mail on foot, as he had done at home. A woman saw him walking with the mail instead of riding his bicycle, and, perhaps fearing he was an imposter bent on some nefarious act, called the postmaster.

Once John would have seen that as hilarious, but in St. Petersburg it was no joking matter—when he got back to the office he was reprimanded and a report was filed saying that he had abandoned government property, and was guilty of dereliction of duty. At dinner that night he was not able to eat. "Dereliction of duty," he kept mumbling, as if he could not believe it.

He became edgy, jumpy, began looking over his shoulder when we were on the beach or shopping; began leaning toward me to whisper things like, *They're watching me, you know, they hate me here. They're always watching.*

"That's not funny, John," I said at first, thinking he was joking about the "spying" woman who had called the post office. But he wasn't.

"Stop imagining things!" I yelled one day. John looked at me with a half a smile, then shook his head the way you might shake your head at someone who *just didn't get* something that was perfectly obvious.

He changed in other ways as well—usually relaxed at the

beach, and enjoying the sight of our youngsters splashing and swimming in the ocean, now he constantly yelled at one or another to "Get back in here!" "Didn't I tell you not to go out so far?" "Do you want to drown? Get in here right now!"

It was as if he expected disaster at any moment, from any quarter, an expectation that included the certainty that he would soon be fired.

I was dizzy with fear. I saw myself, and my girls, and a baby not yet born, as totally dependent on a man who was falling apart. I saw myself as helpless, and regarded what was happening to John not as a problem to be addressed, but as weakness. Sometimes I hated him.

There were distractions, like Sunday dinners with my folks. Dad could eat very little now, but he enjoyed his grandchildren, and Mom, even in that brutal heat, baked oatmeal or molasses cookies; after dinner we munched on them in their Florida room where there was always a warm but wonderful gulf breeze.

On those short visits John and I acted as if not a thing in the world was troubling us.

(Oh my God, Carol! I only now remembered Carol—how could I have forgotten her?

About my age, and with two boys a little younger than Laura and Bonnie, Carol and I had become friends years earlier when she lived in the bungalow next to my parents'.

The summer that John and I were living in St. Petersburg, she and her husband had moved to a larger house farther away, so I hardly saw her. But it was Carol who took care of my girls when I went into labor with my forth child, and Carol who cared for them, and the new baby, throughout the ordeal of my father's death.

She was a blessing, a good friend, and I let her fade from mind as if she were of no importance at all. Oh these sore regrets in my late years.)

In September, when my father lay dying in a Tampa hospital, my sisters flew in from New York, and Illinois, to be with him. If one can speak of "a good death," his qualifies—each evening a gentle, smiling nun came to bathe him, dress him in clean pajamas, and help him sit up against his pillow.

I remember Dad's peaceful face, his anticipation as a gentle bell echoed in the hall, signifying a priest's imminent arrival to offer the sacrament of Holy Communion. By then the small wafer of bread, and sips of water, were all he could tolerate. (The water, unless asked for, at other times withheld by those compassionate nuns, so as not to prolong the painful process of dying.)

On September 13th, our fourth daughter was born in that same hospital. On the day of my discharge, an attendant wheeled me to my father's room so he could meet his new granddaughter. Dad's eyes were huge in an emaciated face, and he had little strength, yet he managed to reach out and gently cup the baby's head.

"I named her Elizabeth Ann, after your mother," I told him.

"I won't get to see this one grow up," he replied.

When he died a week later, my sisters and mother were with him; I was at a doctor's office getting a shot of cortisone for a face hugely swollen from crying and hives.

But the night before, as my mother, sisters, and I walked down the hall on our way out of the hospital, I had impulsively turned and walked back to see my father once more. He was watching the door, "I knew you'd come back, Perk," he said.

Even before Beth (as we call Elizabeth Ann), was born, even before my father died, I had begged John to call Ed, his old postmaster, and ask if he could return to his job in our home town. John refused. "Do you want everyone to know that I'm a failure?" he said, furious.

I didn't care what people thought. I *longed* to go back to New York. I was sure if we could just get back to our home town John would be fine. Everything would be fine.

Shortly after Dad died, a woman appeared at our door with a noodle casserole. (John was at home, so it may have been a Sunday.) I invited her in, thinking she was a neighbor, but she wasn't. As we sat around the kitchen table sipping coffee or iced tea, the woman told us a story:

At the end of a bright day of sailing fun, she and her seven children had watched as her husband was crushed to death between their boat and the dock in Tampa Bay. She had survived the tragedy, she said, only because of the help and comfort she'd received from countless people in the area. And now she wanted to bring comfort to others. This good woman, whose name is lost to me, had read in the *St. Petersburg Times* that my father's death, and my baby's birth had occurred within a week of each other, and had "impulsively," she said, decided to bring us a casserole and tell us her story.

Birth, and death from illness, being normal, if sorrowful occasions, she couldn't have known how discomfited John and I actually were—that beyond those stressors, our life was quickly, unraveling. So it is astonishing that she arrived when we needed something to lift us from despondency close to despair. Her story was grim, but she was not; we visited and laughed all afternoon. It felt so good to laugh again.

Soon after that visit (perhaps because of it), John gave in and called Ed, his old postmaster. When Ed said he'd be glad to have him back, John gave notice to his current postmaster, and was on the road to New York with Laura and Bonnie by the time Beth was three weeks old.

I search my memory to see when my sisters left Florida, when we helped my mother go through Dad's things, and clean out her home, when Mom decided she would move back to New York and live with John and me. Nothing.

But I see Mom, in what had been Laura and Bonnie's room, going through boxes and boxes of letters, recipes, newspaper clippings, sad remnants of her recently lost life.

I see myself packing our belongings in carton after carton, day and night, until I can barely stand on my feet.

I see the baby in a canvas car-bed next to my double bed, so I can reach out and rock her if she fusses when I finally lie down for a few hours of sleep after her night feedings.

And I see Catherine crawling in bed to cuddle with me in space now empty of John.

My mother, lost to grief and a fathomless fear, doesn't help me at all. As soon as it's dark, she drapes a blanket over the large front window so no evil men will see two women alone, she braces chairs under the knobs of the front and back doors. She will not stay alone with the baby, and will not come with me to the supermarket (I have Dad's Chrysler, it will be sold when we leave).

In need of food, and more and more empty cartons, I drive to the store with Catherine sitting next to me, and my infant in the canvas car-bed on the back seat.

Years before, Mom had helped whenever a child was born to me, or my sisters. She had shown me how to hold my first infant while bathing her in the kitchen sink, had sent five or ten dollars of what she called "apron money", because "A woman needs a little independence." All my life she had been a comforting presence. Now I didn't recognize her.

What she needed was help, a sedative, and I never thought to call a doctor.

What she needed was reassurance, and I never gave it, never said, *Don't worry, we're going to be fine; don't worry, everything's going to be alright.*

Exhausted, I nagged her to finish fussing with those damn useless papers. "You're driving me crazy!" I yelled.

But I knew she couldn't hear me because she had removed her hearing aids, as she did whenever she wanted peace, which also drove me crazy when I needed to talk to her. (Without them, she was profoundly deaf.)

Near the end of October I woke to the whisper of dry leaves stirred by a somewhat brisk breeze. With a mild shock, I realized I was still in Florida, and there really was a cool autumn breeze rustling the fronds of the palm tree outside of my bedroom window. Just that suddenly the oppressive heat disappeared, and every day was as exquisite as when we'd arrived less than a year before.

By then our realtor had found a young couple to take over our mortgage, John had found a large four room apartment in our home town, and I had set a date for our departure, called a moving company, and called the railroad to arrange for our trip home.

For fourteen years, wherever John and I had lived—in the tiny

Gulfport cottage; in the downstairs of the old house we'd fixed up;, even in a three room apartment, with three children—we had been reasonably happy.

When we finally got our dream—a home of our own—that dream had turned into a nightmare of hellish heat, loss, despair.

John was never the same after Florida. When that train carrying me, my two youngest daughters, and my mother, pulled into New York's Pennsylvania Station, he was standing on the steamy platform, tears streaming down his face.

And that train-ride home? Oh, what a mercy it was! I know that now.

For if I was exhausted and tense over all that had happened, if I was anxious over what lay ahead—for long, long hours I was also adrift in that peaceful space between—without a thought, without a care, without a wisp of a dream for anything at all.

REMEMBERING

There is something in the pang of change
More than the heart can bear
Unhappiness remembering happiness
Euripides

The image startles me. It is of John, who at that time was my
husband of almost twenty years, and he is not laughing at
something he heard or overheard, not joking (he was always joking
if he wasn't depressed, usually with an edge), but relaxing in an
easy chair, gently smiling, finally at peace.

Other images follow, one on top of another, a Slinky of
memories tumbling down from some dark corner of my brain,
good memories that I had completely forgotten: friends, so many
friends, and John humming, whistling, singing; our daughters
reveling in their parents' new-found joy (or more likely in the
effect it had on the atmosphere in our home). And Nellie, my
mother-in-law, too, I hear her saying, *Ah, and I'm so glad for it.* I
think those were her exact words, spoken with the hint of an Irish
accent.

These past months I have summoned memories of early years—
early, that is, in relation to the eighty I have lived—an attempt, I
suppose, to knit the disparate halves of my life together. But these
new images astound me, I question them. Was there ever such a

time? Was John ever in so great a state of peace that every spot of psoriasis (a skin condition he'd suffered for years), disappeared? It seems impossible.

But yes, there really was such a time, and memories of it flew from my mind as quickly as birds fly from the smoke of a house on fire. We were living in John's family home when that happened, that flight.

Eight years earlier, John's self-esteem had been shaken to the core by a failed attempt to relocate to Florida. Upon our return we lived in a four room apartment on the forth floor of a tall building for several months, and then moved in with Nellie, an arrangement beneficial for all—we paid reasonable rent, took care of heat, utilities, and upkeep, and Nellie could live comfortably in her own house. There were five bedrooms, plus an extra one downstairs next to a tiny den with a fireplace—plenty of room for the seven of us. Most of the furniture was ours, and could be arranged however I chose; the only immovable objects being Nellie's chair and the television in the living room.

I was delighted. I loved the house, and loved Nellie. But for John the move back to the home of his childhood must have seemed a further, and permanent, failure.

It was 1968—the year Martin Luther King Jr. was assassinated, and then Robert Kennedy, another year when it felt as if the world were spinning off its axis—when one day John came home from the post office where he worked from 7 A.M. to 3 P.M. several hours late.

Usually you could set your watch by when he left for work and arrived home, but that day four o'clock passed, five o'clock, six. At first I thought he'd stopped at Doc's to pick up cigarettes, met a friend, and was gabbing. Then I began worrying: *maybe the post office asked him to work overtime. But then why hasn't he called? My God, could he have been hit by a car while he was walking home? But then someone would have called from the hospital.*

Anxiety, fear, fury: *Damn him! Where the hell is he!?*

Nellie and I finally sat down to dinner with the girls, though I couldn't eat, and, sensing trouble, and probably also worried about John, she soon went up to her bedroom, her refuge.

I stayed at the table until the girls finished eating, then, while the older two did the dishes, I bathed the younger two, got the baby settled in her crib, and Catherine in her cot, read the expected bedtime story—and went back downstairs and drank coffee and chain-smoked Winston cigarettes and ran to the window every time I heard a sound.

Finally there were footsteps on the porch. I rushed to the door. "Where were you?" I furiously demanded as John walked in. Then I saw his ashen face, his clouded, red-veined eyes, and caught myself, caught my breath.

He answered my question in a faltering voice: "I just, I just drove to the Tappan Zee Bridge. . . I, I stood there. I wanted to jump, but I…I didn't have the *guts*."

At Family Services of Westchester, where I made an appointment for him, a caseworker determined that John suffered from deep-seated rage (I had never seen a sign of it).

A psychiatrist was recommended and he began treatment, hating every second of every fifty-minute hour of what he said was total silence, "Christ, what a waste of money," he told me, which might be why he snapped out of depression so quickly, or at least seemed to, staying in treatment only a couple of months.

In no time, it seems, the Tappan-zee Bridge crisis was far behind us and we were again fully engaged in home-town life—family get-togethers; Memorial Day parades; trips to Manhattan with friends to dine at Top of the Sixes, Lindy's, and a club from which I have a mug that says "Gaslight Speakeasy."

Good friends. Good times.

And John and I enjoyed working around Nellie's house, painting, papering. We mixed cement and put together rough stone steps so I could climb the steep hill in back, and plant mountain-pink that eventually poured over the rocky land like a pastel waterfall. Weather permitting, I'd be up in that garden, weeding and transplanting slips of plants, every morning as soon as the children left for school.

I was happy, those years, and John never seemed unhappy. But neither was he peaceful. Rather he was impatient, often irritable, and highly critical of the peace marches, the youth culture (hippies', 'flower children'), and our daughters—their rooms were never clean enough, obedience never instant enough; they loved the mini-skirts that were in style at that time, and, on their way to school, would roll up their knee-length uniform skirts.

John always heard about it (everyone in town knew him), and any infringement of any rule—including those of the Catholic school the girls attended—required punishment. But the penalties were mild: *confined to quarters for a day, no television tonight,* and, as wives were expected to do, I always backed him whether I thought the punishment reasonable or not.

Near the end of 1971, my sister Jeanne telephoned. We'd no sooner said, "Hello", when, excited, she told me, "Bill and I are giving you and John a weekend for Christmas!"

"A *weekend*?" I asked, sure I'd misunderstood.

"Yes, a Marriage Encounter weekend, it's sponsored by the Church," she added, as if to reassure me.

"Oh, no!" I said, indignant, "We're doing just fine; we don't need that!" (Jeanne knew about John's depression at the time of the Tappan-Zee episode.)

"It isn't that kind of weekend," she hastened to explain, "it's not counseling, it's nothing like that, it's..."

"Well what do you do all weekend, *Pray*?" I said sarcastically.

"*Marian,*" she said, losing patience, "*Marian*, it's *not* about religion, it's about communicating, that's all. You don't have to go if you don't *want* to! But Bill and I have never been happier than since we made the weekend."

Marriage Encounter (ME) couples spoke of *making* a weekend, of *giving* a weekend.

Before we hung up, Jeanne reminded me to talk to John, and to call her right away if we decided not to go, so she could cancel the reservation. I told her I would, in a tone of voice as dismissive as the shrug of a shoulder.

I didn't want to go on an encounter, whatever that was, and didn't think John would be interested, either. But, "Hey, let's go! What have we got to lose?" He said when I told him. So we would go.

But there was still the problem of the children. When we moved in, Nellie had said she "wasn't up for baby-sitting," having raised six of her own. John asked her anyway, and she agreed to "supervise" if Laura, now seventeen, stayed home over the weekend to help.

So on a Friday evening at the start of 1972, we were on our way to a Marriage Encounter. As Jeanne had promised, the weekend was about communication—a priest and two married couples shared personal stories demonstrating how we unknowingly confuse judgment with emotion (i.e. accusation: You *make* me feel..., instead of simply, I feel ....).

The priest spoke of a God far removed from the concept I had unthinkingly held since childhood; we are God's creations, he said, and thus always worthy, always cherished, no matter what. "God doesn't make Junk!" he exclaimed at one point. When John heard that he seemed stunned. He went to confession for the first time in years.

We laughed, we ate, we sang (the simple melody of the theme song returned to me just this minute), and we exchanged phone numbers with couples living in our area, promising to get together soon.

Schmaltz, right? Pure corn. Especially as seen from this age of ultra-extreme irony. But it was powerful. It was as if an emotional alchemy turned the base metal of us into gold. We felt golden, John and I. We rode home on a cloud, hugged Nellie like we never had before, hugged our girls as if we'd never let them go.

Keen to hold on to our renewed love (to joy!), we threw ourselves into the ME movement, working on recruitment, and writing our feelings regarding a subject of our choice (i.e. how do I feel (HDIF) about...), in composition books. The topic could focus on an ongoing conflict, or be as light as HDIF about our dog. Daily, we shared ten minutes of honest writing, and ten minutes of dialogue about what we'd written, and an emotional intimacy developed such as we had never experienced.

Soon we were close friends with many ME couples, our families gathering for barbecues, celebrations, and simply because we loved being together. We would toss ideas for discussion into the air like jugglers: HDIF about *this;* No, HDIF about *that, this, that.* Then, topic chosen, we would share the dialogue portion of our writing, munch cheese and crackers, cake and cookies, sip wine, sing songs—someone always had a guitar, I can almost hear us: *Michael rowed the Boat ashore... He's got the whole world in his hands… God didn't make little green apples, and it don't rain in Indianapolis….*

When John and I were asked if we'd like to present weekend seminars, we were ecstatic. "They asked *us* to be a team couple, us!"

But again, who would care for the children? We wouldn't ask Nellie; we couldn't leave Laura in charge. Then we learned ME couples help each other; a couple we knew would care for our youngsters, Beth, now five, and Catherine, nine, and sometimes we would care for theirs.

As for Laura and Bonnie, our two teens, "We'll be fine," they said—and we knew Nellie would see to it that they were.

Before we 'gave' a weekend, we were sent to one for training that was as rewarding as our first Marriage Encounter had been, even more so, for now we were comfortable sharing our hopes, our fears, our lives, with other couples.

Now we were an integral part of the Marriage Encounter movement. Once home, we eagerly began preparing papers we would present at our first seminar, the topics compatible with those of the priest and other couple who would be with us that weekend..

And only now do I realize that being part of a Marriage Encounter team was preparing me for a future I could never have imagined: I became a competent public speaker, became comfortable conversing with lawyers, doctors, priests, all of whom I had held not only in high esteem, but high above me (think *Downton Abbey*, think *Upstairs Downstairs),* and who, I discovered, had similar sorrows, joys, occasional feelings of inadequacy. Some became our friends, John's and mine.

It is beyond belief that I buried memories of that joyful enrichment so deep in my psyche that it's taken years, and a final solitude, for them to emerge. But then, when you walk from bright sunshine into a pitch dark room, the stark contrast is blinding for a time, and those bright Marriage Encounter years occurred on the cusp of darkness so complete that had I recalled what I'd lost, I could not have lurched, as I did, into the life that so suddenly followed.

I think the trouble began when John and I were working on new themes for an upcoming weekend near the end of the second year of our ME involvement. We had stopped writing to talk about visiting his brother Jesse, who lived in Massachusetts, and had just returned home from the hospital where he'd been treated for pneumonia. We were anxious to see Jess, and agreed that the drive north on the Merritt Parkway would be gorgeous—it was autumn, the air crisp, trees flamboyant, sky cobalt blue, I remember that clearly—but we decided to finish our papers and drive up the following Sunday.

Three days later Jesse, the brother to whom John felt closest, died while resting on his couch. We were struck dumb. *We should have gone to see him instead of writing those damn papers!* The weight of that unspoken thought was with us for days, perhaps weeks.

Nellie was diagnosed with cancer soon after, and died on Christmas Eve. ME friends extended their love and comfort. Prayers were said, Masses offered for Jesse, for Nellie, for us.

But within weeks, perhaps days, John withdrew behind an emotional barrier as thick as bullet-proof glass. Our composition books lay undisturbed, untouched.

Grief can still your hand, steal your voice. *This will pass*, I thought. And it did. With spring our spirits lifted along with the crocuses, daffodils, tulips. We began seeing our ME friends, and others, again. Nothing was the same, especially John, but I was sure he soon would be.

Then we went away for a Marriage Encounter renewal for team couples. John barely participated. "Damn you! Why did you bother coming?" I said as soon as we were alone in our room. Fighting to contain my anger, trying to stick to feelings, I calmed myself and said, "Johnny, it feels like a betrayal."

Then I went off like a Roman candle on the 4th of July, heaping abuse on him for destroying everything we'd worked for, everything we had.

"You can't *stand* to be happy, can you," I said in a bitter, accusing voice, tears spilling from my eyes. Those are the only words I remember.

What did he say? What did he do? Did he walk out of the room and away from my fear-inspired tirade? I don't know. But whether he left or stayed, he was gone.

We limped through that ME weekend but never gave, or attended, another.

I kept accepting dates with our ME friends, and, when we were with them, John laughed and joked and acted normal—at times even sharing dialogues, which frustrated and angered me, since at home there was little sharing, and no laughter.

There were, in fact, moments (sour notes, I called them), when the ice in John's voice froze me or one of our girls in place, wondering what unpleasantness was in the offing—intense anger over an offense as trivial as a child forgetting to place a napkin in her lap at dinnertime? Jokes with an edge that could slice?

And his psoriasis, "Washed away by all that love," he once joyfully said, had returned with a vengeance.

It was autumn again. John was driving us home from somewhere, just the two of us in the car, when tears began pouring down his face. "Oh, Johnny," I exclaimed, "What is it? What on earth is wrong!?"

He looked at me for a second and said, "No matter what happens, you have to believe that I love you."

"What are you talking about? What's going to happen?" I said, frightened.

He pressed his lips tightly together as if holding them closed by force, and said not another word, tears continuing to pour down his cheeks.

Jesse had died the year before, and then Nellie. Those events must have been like a fist to John's head, a sucker-punch, I thought, and he couldn't get over it, couldn't think, didn't know *what* he felt, while I kept asking him just that. *That's what's been bothering him,* I thought. He had lost weight. I hadn't noticed. How much had I overlooked while I was so happily involved with ME, and the girl's school, and our church and friends.

Incredibly, I was somewhat relieved. With help, I thought John would recover as quickly as he had from the depression he'd suffered from six years earlier. At home, I suggested he phone the psychiatrist he'd seen at that time.

"I'm not going back to that useless piece of shit!" he said, glaring.

Then I begged him to talk to Father Tony, a Marriage Encounter priest and friend, who was also a clinical psychologist. I don't know if he called him that day, but soon John was seeing Father Tony weekly, and slowly his moods lightened.

We resumed our daily dialogues; John seemed sincere, choosing topics, and sharing overwhelming emotions about his brother, his mother, his alcoholic father, and our busy life. (Together, in addition to ME work, we were teaching a confirmation class at our church).

One evening, instead of talking, he handed me his composition book, pointing a finger to indicate what I should read. He had written, *I feel as if there's a hole in me, I feel as if something is missing. It frightens me* (or words near to those). I don't remember the topic, or what I wrote, what I said, but I remember the unease I felt in the pit of my stomach when I read those words.

Yet as our third year of M.E. involvement drew to a close, we seemed close again, there was sometimes laughter again, and a semblance of peace.

By January 1975, Laura was married, Bonnie was in college, and John seemed better than he'd been in ages. We celebrated New Years Eve at a party with ME friends. I don't recall the venue, but I know I wore Laura's silver empire-waist gown, and I felt beautiful. There was a band, dancing, the usual singing, laughing, sharing. It was a new year, everything was going to be good again, I was sure of it.

In February we went to the dinner theater in Elmsford (a gift from Laura to celebrate my birthday), and enjoyed it immensely, though John was unusually nervous.

And then it was 3:30 A.M. on Wednesday, February 26th. 1975. I know the time because I glanced at the clock when I found John's side of the bed empty. Thinking he might be ill, I got up to check the bathroom. When I opened the bedroom door he was standing right outside, his eyes black, pupils so dilated they blocked all but a rim of his blue irises; his face was a mask, a malevolent mask. Shocked, I took a step back. Then, still standing there, John began babbling unintelligibly, though I understood the term 'kill', or maybe it was 'death', or 'die'.

I like to think of my shaken self bravely taking charge, getting that dangerous stranger downstairs and away from our young girls in the nearby bedroom, speaking soft words to calm him while I brewed coffee and thought of what to do.

But in fact I fell to my knees screaming, and screaming, and wondering who on earth was screaming like that.

Then John leaned over me and whispered, "Shhhh, think of the children," and I came back to myself laughing and sobbing at the bitter irony of his words. (I have asked my younger daughters, now middle-aged, about that night, and they both swear they heard nothing at all. If so, a merciful God must have deafened them.)

I don't remember how I got down to the kitchen, or who brewed the coffee, but I see myself pouring it into a cup placed in front of John, my hand trembling so violently that coffee is splattering and spilling all over the table. I see him talking non-stop, his words slower now, so that I understand what he is saying:

He hears voices. They tell him to do things, to spit out the communion wafer at Mass, to prostrate himself before the altar on Sunday, to spit at his long dead father's face that he sees in the bathroom mirror every morning when he shaves. The voices tell him he must die, and *He will not leave us behind.* He says this with determination, but softly, as if he were saying *I won't abandon you.*

I see myself lifting the receiver of the phone on the kitchen wall to telephone Father Tony, who answers so quickly his phone must be right beside his bed. His voice is fuzzed with sleep. He listens patiently to my almost incoherent words, calming my fear, asking a few questions, telling me to bring John to his office as soon as the children are in school.

When the children come downstairs for breakfast, I am standing in a daze in the middle of the kitchen. Beth puts her arms around my waist, "Come back to me, Mommy," she says. And I do, at least long enough to boil oatmeal, and to see her and Catherine off. I can't wait to close the door behind them.

The day looks like a picture Beth might have painted when she was in kindergarten—dark blue cloudless sky, bright yellow sun stuck up in a corner, pouring rays of light upon the world. It is a brilliant day. I hate it for being brilliant. It is cold. I'm colder.

On Friday, desperate to get my young girls away from both John and their perpetually crying wreck of a mother, I called Adele, a Marriage Encounter friend. "There's trouble," I told her, "Will you take the girls for the weekend?"

She agreed instantly, asking no questions. When she came to pick them up, and saw the state I was in, she reached to hold me. "No!" I said, holding my hands toward her, palms out, "If you touch me I'll shatter." I remember that we were standing in the kitchen—why the kitchen? I couldn't have offered her coffee, could I?

On Sunday evening Adele brought the girls back, again asking for no explanation. If she had asked, I couldn't have given one, couldn't bear to tell her, or any of our ME friends, what had happened to a team couple, an ideal couple, which is how we had been seen.

We were a lie, I thought with grief, fear, rage.

The following week, or maybe the next, I built a roaring fire in the fireplace in the den, and threw into the flames every notebook of our daily dialogues, every paper we had written for seminars. Still in a rage, I ran upstairs to the attic where years of my personal journals were stored, and then to our bedroom where in the bottom drawer of a dresser, a packet of letters John had sent from Korea was lovingly tied with faded blue-satin ribbon. I ran back downstairs and threw all of it in the fire, *burned my whole blasted lie of a life.*

Becoming unglued, I dropped my sack of bones into our recliner every morning as soon as the house was empty, rousing myself woodenly only to see to Catherine's and Beth's clothes, and homework, to put some kind of supper in front of them, to kiss them goodnight at bedtime.

I saw Father Tony for counseling by myself, and with John, who also saw a psychiatrist. In no time you could again set your watch by when he left for work, and when he returned. But who, I wondered every afternoon, would walk through that door?

One morning I sat on Nellie's bed, its mattress still holding her shape, and cried for hours "Oh, Nanie," I said to the empty room (I never called her Nellie to her face), "Oh, Nanie, look what's happened to us." But I was glad she wasn't there to see.

To my regret, I don't think I ever called Adele again. And only when my mind was absent did I answer the ringing telephone, wanting to avoid everyone, especially ME friends—there is no place in Marriage Encounter for broken people, or, for that matter, for half a couple. We simply dropped out of sight, John and I.

From my current vantage point, I think the shock and fear of discovering that John, whom I had known since childhood, was not only seriously ill, but dangerously so, accounts for my initial, hysterical reaction. But the depression I slipped into, the rage at John, who didn't ask to be ill, had everything to do with the abrupt end of a life I loved, and the loss of faith in a husband I would never fully trust again.

We were together for nine more difficult years. When we divorced, both of our lawyers were men who had made Marriage Encounters; that was why we chose them.

One had been in our intimate circle of friends, yet I never once thought of happy times we'd shared with him and his wife, memories of those moments having disappeared as surely as the composition books, essays, journals, and letters that went up in smoke.

Now they're back, those memories, now I recall sharing, dialogues, singing, laughing, recall the closeness—with the lawyer and his wife, with Adele and Matt, with Father Tony—and with those whose names have just returned to me: Father Ed, Father Tom, O.J. and Roger, Patty and Frank, Cathy and Howie.

I'm so thankful that the times I shared with them are again part of the story of my life. Thankful, too, to have regained that rare image of John, smiling and completely at peace.

Considering the number of years I've lived, that joyful time amounts to no more than a minute.

But what a magnificent minute!

EVERYTHING THAT HAPPENS IS INCREDIBLE

Fall seven times. Stand up eight
Japanese proverb

You could say I was a woman of extremely low ambition: I wanted a husband who loved me, children, and a home. When I was very young, I imagined a cottage with a white picket fence, roses climbing over an arched trellis on the front path. And where would you find such a home?—in the mind of a dreamer, a lover of fairytales.

I got the home, the children, even the loving husband for awhile, but the living happily-ever-after part escaped me. Still, within the limited life I'd chosen, there was a kind of freedom that I've lost, and miss, and long for: freedom to walk out the front door on a soft spring morning and dig my fingers into the rich soil just because I love the feel of it; freedom to sit on the porch with coffee or tea and a good book; freedom to visit a friend and sip a glass of chardonnay on an afternoon when our kids are in school— not that there wasn't *plenty* of work, too: no clothes dryer, no dishwasher, a big house, four daughters, a mother-in-law (a mother, too, sometimes), and John, my husband. But it never felt like work.

By the nineteen-seventies I had become a confident young woman, active in church and community, and with a strong sense of who I was, and what I could do (other than housework, that is): I loved to draw, write, paint pictures, sew, decorate. I enjoyed tending the garden, especially the fall of mountain-pink pouring down the back hill. When Laura, my oldest daughter, brought home expensive fabric, and a pattern for me to sew a prom gown for her—a prom gown! that gave me pause. But I was up to that kind of challenge. (When her boyfriend came to pick her up, I saw that the small flowers in her gown exactly matched his tie.)

The thing is, I was in my element.

Then within three months of each other, John's mother and brother died, within a year John had a serious mental breakdown, and overnight everything changed. Including me.

A few weeks after John's breakdown, my mother phoned to announce her imminent arrival. She always called to tell me she was coming for a day, a week, a month, I always said, "Fine." Sometimes I even meant it. But this time I couldn't stand the thought of her presence in my disaster-area home. I simply couldn't.

"Mom," I said, "it's not a good time for a visit, we're having some problems."

"Problems? She exclaimed, "What problems? You can tell me, you need me! I'm your mother!"

"Mom," I said in a lifeless tone, "I'm forty-one years old. If I can't solve my problems myself by now, than you haven't done a very good job."

Silence. No further questions. The call ended quickly, with Mom saying something like *Goodbye now dear* in a pleasant voice, as if I had said nothing insulting.

From that conversation, you would think my backbone had not dissolved completely, or that I wanted to save my mother from the pain of a problem that had no immediate solution. Actually, there was nothing left of the confident woman I'd been, I was saving *myself* from my mother's eyes.

It is six months after my Mother's call, and I still doubt myself, and am again as timid as when I was a child. Even an annoying look from a stranger on the bus, causes me to inwardly flinch. So how amazing is this?—I have been hired to work in an office!

For the interview I pretended I was the woman I'd like to be:

highlighted my hair, dressed in my best polyester pantsuit, and heels, held my head up; I even stopped in the ladies room to put drops of Visine in my eyes, hoping to erase the now perpetual redness.

Luckily, the director who interviewed me was a woman, I sold myself by stressing my management of household affairs— scheduling appointments, record-keeping, inventory, etc. I told her I had taught myself to make slip-covers and drapes, and was sure I could learn whatever was required. (The job was a simple one, really, clerk/receptionist. *Anyone* could do it, I thought.)

I don't know if I told the director that I had never worked in an office, and hadn't typed in twenty years, but I remember her saying the job would mainly involve meeting and greeting people, and answering the phone. *Oh, and sometime in the future*, she added, *the government will require that you pass a typing exam.* (It's a county job.)

At my desk near the entrance of the office, in this room full of other desks and people, I assume a casual stance, but I'm a wreck. Every time that black beast of a phone rings I fumble for the button; I didn't know a phone could have so many buttons, sometimes two or three light up at the same time and I have to scramble, "Hold on, please," I say breathlessly, or "Please hold, I'll be with you in one moment." There are extensions to look up, pink message slips to hand out when people in the field return to the office. I am terrified that I'll make a mistake. And then I do, not once, but for days.

They begin, those mistakes, when two men walk into the office together after lunch, and a nearby secretary comes over to introduce us. "I'd like you to meet Dr. J., and Sam Rogers," she says (they use first names here, it's hard for me to get used to). Both men are about the same age and height, are neither slim nor fat, and both have dark brown hair that reaches to their collars, and long sideburns, as is the style.

Day after day I hand Mr. Rogers the messages meant for Dr. J., and Dr. J, those for Mr. Rogers. They laugh, thank God, and finally I differentiate: the doctor's tie is always straight, his wavy hair well-styled. Sam Rogers' tie is often askew, his hair a mass of chaotic curls.

Another man here has begun calling me *the quiet one.* "and how is the quiet one today?" he'll ask. He asked about my family, too: Married? Children?

"Yes," I told him, "Married, four daughters, one already married." I want him to know I'm not as young as I look (except for highlighting, my hair is dark, I'm five feet eight inches tall and now weigh only 119 pounds. Nerves, I guess). But, really, he's a nice man just trying to put me at ease.

The thing is, I need to keep my personal life far from mind and far from this office or I'll never make it. This is a mental health department—the administrative branch, but still—and John is mentally ill.

I interviewed for an entry-level job anywhere in the County of Westchester, and here I am. What were the odds? So I resolutely avoid friendly chats, and at lunchtime hurry to a small balcony at the side of the building with my brown-bag lunch and a book, relieved to be outside and alone.

During my first three days of work, one of the secretaries, Estelle, walked around looking as if a black cloud were following her. She's black, and I'm white—and green as well when it comes to office work, so of course, being insecure, I assumed her dark looks were aimed my way. After all, there are plenty of black women with good office skills, and the department hired *me,* a white woman obviously stressed just answering the damn telephone.

One day Mrs. Goldstein, whose secretary was out ill, handed me something scribbled on yellow canary-pad sheets. "Will you type this memo for me, please?" she asked.

I had no idea what 'memo' meant—a reminder maybe? Scanning the first page I found a decipherable name for the addressee, but no address—and froze. Estelle, noticing my deer-in-the-headlights expression, came over, handed me a copy of an old memo to use as prototype, showed me which letterhead stationery to use for memos (Memoranda), and which for letters, and smiled and gabbed as if we'd known each other forever.

I had to type Mrs. Goldstein's memo twice. There was so much white-out on the first copy it was practically stiff. Even the second wasn't great, I was embarrassed to hand it to her.

So I've enrolled in a brush-up typing course at a local high school. I'm on probation here for three months, and am desperate to keep a job I never wanted.

Estelle is innately friendly. Also observant. One day she asks, with raised eyebrows, 'Do you want to go out for lunch with me for a change?"

"Sure, I'd love to," I tell her. But in truth I say "yes" only because I don't want her to think I'm prejudiced. She is a warm and funny woman about my age; at lunch we learn that we both have teenagers, and laughingly commiserate; I hear harmless tidbits about people in the office. We 'click', and begin lunching together often. One day I tell Estelle what I had thought when she ignored me with that furrowed brow the first days of my employment.

"Honey, that didn't have a *thing* to do with you," she says laughingly, "I was worried about one of my boys." Then, as if there were a connection, "I know it's none of my business, and you don't have to tell me if you don't want to, but where do you hurry off to every Thursday at lunchtime?"

I tell her the truth: "I see a psychologist. My husband and I have a problem."

"I kind of thought it was something like that," she says.

I never worry that Estelle will share that particular tidbit with someone, and she never does.

She begins calling me Funny-face. "Smile, Funny-face," I'll hear if I look too serious as she walks by my desk. I feel something akin to joy; I have a friend again. (Once, John and I had many friends. Unable and unwilling to explain his breakdown, we walked away from them.)

The psychologist I see on Thursdays is a priest, Father Tony. He also counsels John, who sees a psychiatrist as well. The psychiatrist has prescribed medicine that has stabilized John's behavior, so I am no longer afraid.

No, that's not true, I am always afraid. I can't seem to stop being afraid. John's psychotic crisis occurred in the middle of the night. He was homicidal, and though that person seems gone, the frightened person I became that night remains: I don't trust his apparent stability, I worry about our youngest girls, Catherine, thirteen, and Beth, nine, who are in his care after school (a postman, John is home by three-thirty). The girls are familiar with his problem, and I've told them to go to our next door neighbor if daddy looks angry or seems different than usual, but it's no way for us to live.

It was Father Tony who suggested I try for an entry-level position with the county. "You don't have to jump in the stew with John," he told me.

When I went to White Plains to fill out a job application at the County Personnel Office, John, sneering, said, "They'll never hire you."

He was shocked when they did. I want to leave him, but even if I had enough money, how could I pull the girls away from their school and friends when so much else has abruptly changed in their lives? And where would we go?

This job is beginning to bore me to tears now that I'm familiar with it, but every two weeks I deposit almost a third of my paycheck in a savings account, which is security of a sort, and I've passed the typing test and probationary period successfully. So at least I've accomplished that much.

The dates of upcoming exams for available county positions are posted on a bulletin- board, near the personnel office. I take every exam I'm eligible for, and in four years have advanced from Clerk/typist (Grade 3), to Senior Typist (Grade 5), to Secretary I (Grade 7).

When I began working here, I could not have imagined being this woman—I wear good wool suits now, silk blouses, stockings and heels, or knee-high boots of supple leather, and no longer feel like an imposter sitting in my own office across from G., the Director of Mental Health Services, whom I now work for.

I'm fond of her. She encourages participation in think-tank meetings, and approves my requests to attend in-house mental health seminars, and government sponsored non-credit courses at the community college. I love feeling like part of a team, Besides G., there are four professionals, and a typist, and clerical trainee, both of whom I supervise.

It is 1979 already. John and I have moved away from his childhood home, which was part of my childhood, too. I miss it. Still, I sleep a lot better now.

We're not at all close anymore, but John is whistling again, a sure sign of good cheer, and he faithfully sees his psychiatrist, as well as Father Tony, whose counsel I'm no longer in need of. I think it's amazing that, in spite of all the trouble in our home, my youngest daughters, Catherine and Beth, are doing well, and like their new school.

One November day I answer the phone to hear John, who calls me at work *all the time,* and now sounds highly agitated. He's been to the doctor for shortness of breath that we both thought was caused by allergies, "I have coronary artery disease," he tells me, "I'll have to retire. What am I going to do?" He's frantic. I try to reassure him, telling him not to worry, that he'll have some income, that I have a job, that we'll be fine.

"You don't understand," he says, "I *have* to work, I *need* to work."

For the first time, I realize that during the darkest days of his breakdown, getting out each morning to walk his route and deliver the mail, had been his slim lifeline to normalcy, and the spasm of fear I feel is not for the condition of his arteries.

But I'm worried, too, when he tells me he's going to finish his route, "Are you sure you should?" I ask.

"I don't care! I'm finishing my route!" he replies, angry, now.

Annoyed at his tone, I indifferently reply, "Well, then I guess I'll go to my class after work (it's at the community college), I'll be home around 7:30."

By 7:30, it is dark, but the sky is that deep, deep blue it sometimes is in New York. It's gorgeous, the air brisk and clear, and slightly scented by a far-away skunk when I pull into our driveway at the end of my class.

There are no lights on in the house. Instantly I'm uneasy. Beth is often at her friend's now, and Catherine's probably not home from her after-school job yet, but John should be here. Before I've closed the car door, Adele hurries onto her porch. She and her husband Nick are our next door neighbors. When John got home

69

he must have told Nick about his recent diagnosis because Adele calls out, "Marian, it's not *John*. It's Catherine, she's been hit by a car, Beth is here with me."

A fist flies into my solar plexus, I can't get my breath, and when I do, and ask what hospital Catherine is in, Adele doesn't know. Nick drove off with John so fast (I have our car), that he never stopped to tell her.

For no good reason, I'm sure Catherine's been taken to White Plains Hospital where she's been so often since becoming diabetic at the age of nine. I jump back in the car, praying "Please God, please God, please God," speeding toward White Plains, running every red light, blind to everything but my need to get to my daughter. And she's there in that emergency room, and conscious, but barely.

Wearing clothes that blended into the dark blue of that autumn evening, Catherine had been crossing Hamilton Avenue in White Plains on her way home from her after school job when a car turned the corner and hit her, tossing her twenty feet. I will forever be thankful for the man who witnessed the accident, and verified that Catherine was crossing with the light. She has a concussion, broken nose, slashed knee, and has lost four upper front teeth that just two weeks ago were released from the confines of braces. But she is *alive*!

Weeks later, I watch Catherine and her date leave for the junior prom. She's a perfect picture in her Alice-blue gown, even with temporary front teeth. Then slowly, steadily, I watch as she spirals into the abyss of clinical depression.

John is retired now, and idle, and as jittery as water sprinkled on a hot pan. His feelings regarding Catherine's depression vacillate between fear and fury, concern and blame. And day after day, in one form or another, I hear: *She just wants attention, and you always give it to her, don't you. You don't care about me anymore, do you; she's all you think about.*

"I'm so sick of this!" I yell, but it's true, Catherine's plight consumes me, there is little left for Beth, who is now thirteen, and *nothing* for John and his dreadful need for attention, I've been tired of it for ages. Now I can't stand him.

Dressing nicely and going off to work every weekday is my escape—I step into a role in which I am confident and secure, and continue to do well because I've had practice keeping work separate from my home life, but also because I work in a department where titles are dropped, demolishing distance, imparting the sense that I am among friends, easing anxiety.

Only Estelle knows about John's mental problem, but *everyone,* in every office in the department, knows what has happened to Catherine. And there are no whispers, no raised eyebrows at her ongoing struggle to regain emotional balance. She is on heavy psychotropic drugs; when she shuffles through the hall to my office at lunchtime, she is greeted with, 'Hi, Catherine, how're you doin?' "Hey, Cathy, good to see you. Here for lunch with your Mom?" "Lookin' good, Cath, lookin' good."

John finally gets a job driving a bus for Pace University students. When I learn that one of his benefits is free tuition for dependents I can hardly contain myself. Without a bachelor's degree I can only advance one grade, to Staff Assistant (Grade 8). *With* a degree I'm eligible to take exams for some of the higher positions.

Then the undermining thoughts begin: *It's a university for God's sake, it won't be like taking classes at the community college; I don't have the right background; Catherine needs me; Beth needs me; there's never enough time as it is, what am I thinking? Who do I think I am?*

Estelle and I, fast friends now, telephone each other regularly. (She's been promoted, and now works in another city.) One evening when I'm telling her all the reasons I can't possibly take classes at Pace, and how much I want to, Catherine hears my end of our conversation. When I hang up and walk back to the living room she says, "Go for it, Mom. I wish I could."

Her words twist my heart, I honestly don't know if I sign up for a course at Pace, just one, because I've thought of nothing else or because I don't want Catherine to be disappointed in me.

And so, at the beginning of a semester, I timidly slide into a seat in what I know will be an easy class: life drawing. Many of the students are older, as I am, and when I find myself comfortably interacting with them, I gather enough courage to matriculate, and find that I *love* college—my professors are excellent, my grades high (even in math, a once feared subject). And every time I walk up or down the double staircase in the main building on the White Plains campus, I feel as if I'm dreaming: *I'm a university student!*

I've never in my life been happier with myself.

When I turn around it is 1981.

I pay scant attention to the televised evening news, but get the gist of major events: the release of the Iran hostages, Ronald Reagan's landslide election to the presidency. Last year when Mt. St. Helens in Washington State erupted, I let everything go but studying, and sat with John, unable to pull myself from televised scenes of that unbelievable event.

But that was unusual. I'm always running—to work, to class, to visit Catherine when she's in the hospital—and hurrying home as soon as I can to have a bit of time with Beth, and to catch up on household chores. John helps, even having dinner ready so I can grab a bite to eat before evening classes, but he clearly resents the change in me, "I don't know you anymore," he complains.

Sometimes I don't know myself. I am one person at work and school, another—irritable, impatient—at home.

"Catherine, do something with the mess in your room!" I yell up the stairs one Saturday morning, "Beth, don't you *dare* go out with your friends before you do your chores!"

I know I'm being unreasonable, Catherine likes her room neat and would soon get to it, and Beth always does her chores before she leaves. But this day I can't seem to help myself—I want to be working on my assignments; I want to be a student without a family to worry about; I especially want John off my back, and even that thought rouses guilt, because even drained of energy, as he is from the medicine for his heart, he helps when he can.

Today I wish he wouldn't. I resent the constant praise he expects: *how good you are; how wonderful of you to do that; how pleased I am.* But most Saturdays, thank God, I'm thankful for help from any quarter at all.

These mornings I arrive at the office an hour or so before the start of the workday so I can study for exams, or type a term-paper that's due. Everyone I work for encourages me. Others arrive early, too. Sam—the man with the unruly curls, whose messages I gave to Dr. J. six years ago—works in a different unit, but he helped me solve a matrix problem one day. (Actually he helped me discover that I need eyeglasses, I was seeing the number 6, instead of 5).

Walking past my office on his way to see his friend Matt at the other end of the department, Sam sometimes stops to ask, "What are you studying now?" or, "How's Catherine doing?" or to tell me about Holly and Heather, his daughters who are close in age to my Beth.

The friendly atmosphere here makes such a difference in my life; this job, this place, is exactly right for me. The commissioner of the department even allows five days of annual leave for educational purposes. How lucky can you get!

When notice arrives from Albany (where New York State exams originate), informing me that I am required to take the typing portion of the Secretary I exam, I am stunned. In the top three of those who passed the written portion, I was appointed to my position almost a year ago, breezed through probation, and have already passed a typing test with the required words per minute for my previous position.

My job now requires little typing, since the professionals' long reports are dictated to the county's new word-processing department, and the typist takes care of short memos and letters. So for a year I've typed little, other than term papers.

The commissioner of the department calls Albany to see if anything can be done short of changing my title, which Albany will not do. No one here can believe that I will have to take the *same* typing test all over again. But I do, and I'm sick over it; I've never been a strong typist, and I have no typewriter at home for practice.

John drives me to the site of the test on a Saturday morning when the sky is a low, flat metallic gray, the air chill and damp, which suits my mood. I slept poorly last night, and my stomach is queasy. I sit before an electric typewriter in a huge room full of other women sitting before other typewriters.

This is not a difficult skill, I tell myself, and indeed for most

73

people it is not—they look at the copy, the mind disengages, and the fingers fly. And I know how to do that now.

But when I hear, "Begin!" and the instantaneous noise of a hundred or more clacking typewriters, I feel as if the sound has invaded my skull. My fingers go spastic, totally spastic, and by the end of the third sentence I know I've failed, though I gain control and struggle to stay until the end of the test.

At home, fighting tears, I tell John what happened. "I'm glad you failed," he says, "I'm afraid I'll lose you if you keep getting ahead."

He will lose me not because I got ahead, but because I was demoted, because I had to leave my office, and my job, and the building where I worked. But we don't know that when I 'bump' back to the Grade 5 position I had before, which is—bitter, bitter irony—Senior *Typist*.

There are only two Grade 5 typist positions open in White Plains, where I want to stay. One is in the health department, the other in the County Executive's office.

Armed with excellent letters of recommendation from directors I have worked for in the mental health department, and with the 4.0 grade point average I've earned at Pace noted on my resume, I'm pretty sure I'll be offered the position of appointment secretary for the County Executive, which, though only Grade 5, would be the first step on a promising ladder.

I want that job until I hear, *Of course if you're hired there will be a routine investigation of your life; it shouldn't be a problem,* or words to that effect.

I think of John's history of mental illness that has been duly recorded in hospital and doctor's records. I know about medical ethics, but in this case—consideration for employment in the office of a politician—medical ethics might not apply.

If disclosed, John's previous homicidal ideation would certainly influence them *not* to hire me. I'm fully aware that if they don't hire me it could be for a dozen other reasons, but I would always think it was because of John, and I would resent him more than I already do.

And, too, I want my privacy.

So I run from a risk that probably exists only in my mind, and grab the position in the health department.

There I will work for only two women in what is probably the smallest office in all of Westchester County. I console myself with the thought that it will be less stressful than working for the County Executive.

In honor of my six years of employment in the Westchester County Department of Community Mental Health, I'm given a farewell dinner at a fine restaurant, and am presented with a 'gold' Pulsar watch. Everyone I've worked for, and with, has come to say goodbye. "You'll be back," I'm told.

And I will be, I will take county exams and move to grades six, seven, eight.

But for now I am here, and I can hardly bear to say goodbye.

LET'S WALK

And the truth is, if you don't risk anything,
you risk even more.
Erica Jong

"Good morning," I answer the telephone at work, and hear a confused man with a strange voice and an accent I can't place:
"There ees un eppidemeek comink!"
"I'm sorry, Sir, you've reached the wrong department. I'll transfer..."
"No. No. An eppidemeek ees comink!"
"Sir, I'll transfer you to the right..."
"No, leesen, leesen, soon an eppidemeek—of tulips, daffodils, cheery cherry blossoms..." a chuckle.
Sam Rogers!" I say, laughing.
"I couldn't resist," Sam says, also laughing, "Listen, I'm sorry I missed your farewell dinner, may I take you to lunch?"
"Thank you, yes, that would be lovely," I answer.

Sam worked for alcohol and substance abuse services in the department where I had worked for mental health services the previous six years. Until he called, I hadn't realized how hungry I was for a friendly voice.

Still, a pleasant lunch with a nice man I scarcely knew might have been the end of it—certainly *would* have been the end of it—if John, my husband of twenty-nine years, had behaved differently the night I wanted to hug him.

For that matter, there wouldn't have been a beginning—Sam later told me he would never have asked me to lunch—if I had not chosen to fill an opening in a different building when I was demoted from the secretarial position I loved because I failed a typing test.

In my new office I worked for only two women, the director, and deputy director. I had expected working for these women to be less stressful, and pleasant.

Now, I see them in fussy hats with fussy veils, white-gloved fingers trailing the edge of furniture, in search of dust. I see raised eyebrows and pursed lips when my daughter Catherine comes to my desk on an afternoon that we have arranged to lunch together, as was our routine before I lost my position in the Department of Community Mental Health (DCMH).

Catherine is recovering from a nervous breakdown, and takes prescribed drugs that glaze her eyes. The women are polite when I introduce her, but I think they see her as a drug addict.

At lunch I tell Catherine to meet me outside from now on, it is early March in New York, the weather cold, but the chill inside is worse.

It is quite possible that the women were not at all as I remember them, that my perception was skewed because I so loved the job I had lost. But I know sometime during my first weeks there, they overheard my side of a conversation with Catherine's doctor, who had phoned because he was concerned that a recent test showed her blood-sugar level "out of sight" (she's diabetic).

I was more than concerned, but she was eighteen, and for the love of God I was at *work*, helpless to control what she ate, and angry that the doctor seemed to think that I could and should. Annoyed, I forcefully I said, "What can I do? I can't follow her around all day!"

The women were in the director's office right across from my cubby, discussing someone. Suddenly I heard "...*a woman who has so much trouble...*" They might have been talking about anyone, but instantly I assumed that they were referring to me.

One day a large bouquet of flowers was delivered to my home (in fact, I think the director herself brought them herself, her heart obviously in the right place, and I think I invited her in and she declined). At any rate, one way or another, the flowers arrived, and they were from the director, and I was *not* pleased—she knew nothing about Catherine, nothing about me. I suspected she hadn't even read my resume or letters of recommendation.

If I'd thought she had, I might have tried to talk to her, to tell her I was capable of handling responsibility, that I was still earning grades at Pace University that kept me on the Dean's List, that trouble at home was exactly what made me strive for excellence at school and work. But she seemed unapproachable, never asking about my classes, or my family, yet often telling me—as if it were a lesson—about her wonderful long marriage.

Looking back, I think it was not only my frustrated outburst at Catherine's doctor, but also Sam's initially innocent appearance that influenced her perception of me. The day he took me to lunch he first introduced himself to the director, and they talked a moment or so, Sam had likely explained that he was taking me to lunch because he'd missed the farewell dinner DCMH had given me, and director had thought—what?

All I know is that for the first time in my career, I was trusted only to type thirty-year-old annual reports for posterity; to type index cards; to answer the telephone. And I hated it.

And then there was Sam's friendly voice. When he asked me to lunch I'd thought it a kind gesture from a nice man, that's all. When I got home I told John, who had met Sam once when we were shopping in White Plains, about the invitation.

"You mean you're going to lunch with 'gimpy'?" he said, "Go ahead, he's no threat, he's not your type."

My type? And where did 'gimpy' come from I wondered, but I let it go.

Sam took me to an Indian restaurant with linen cloths and napkins on the tables, the air fragrant with unfamiliar spices. I had never eaten Indian food, and so ordered chicken tandoori, which sounded like a safe choice; Sam ordered a spicy curry dish that he encouraged me to taste. Both meals were delicious. We chatted lightly and easily, about the food and other ordinary things, just as we had done when Sam occasionally stopped by my office at DCMH for a minute or two. But slipped among ordinary pleasantries as if the words meant nothing much, Sam had smiled and said, "I like to watch your face when you talk," and I was inordinately pleased.

At the end of that day I walked into a home filled with the succulent scent of roasting chicken, and a hint of cinnamon from an applesauce cake. John often fixed supper when I had classes, but never a roast, or a cake. And I had no class that night.

He was worried about my lunch with Sam after all, I thought, and felt a surge of gladness as I moved through the living room to the kitchen where John was bending over the oven, checking the roast and potatoes. He was whistling. I thought of how our life had once been, and walked toward him smiling, my arms reaching to give a hug, "John, you're the only man I ever wanted to love all of my life," I said.

I didn't realize I had used the past tense: *wanted.* Maybe John did, he straightened and shoved me away so hard that I stumbled and nearly fell. (Years before, when John's psychotic episode had occurred, he had threatened violence, but he had never actually touched me in anger.)

Shocked, and again afraid of him, I turned and ran upstairs where music was playing loud enough to rattle Catherine's bedroom windows; it was how the girls liked it. Usually I yelled, "Turn it down!" But that evening, though John and I had not exchanged angry words, I was glad for the brief distraction of raucous noise.

Catherine turned the volume down anyway, as soon as she saw me, and, wanting her to feel secure, I calmed myself, talked with her a few minutes, then said I was tired and was going to lie down for awhile. Beth, my youngest, was at her friend's house.

I didn't eat with the family that night, I couldn't have swallowed. But neither did I crawl in bed and cry, as I had done so often in recent years. Later, I went downstairs—there was Beth's homework to check, there were goodnight hugs to be given, there was my façade of indifference to maintain.

The next day it was as if that explosive incident had never

happened, John and I never referred to it, ever. But it had, and when still shaken, I was resting in my room, the thought—*If Sam asks me to lunch again, I'm going*— shot through my mind as suddenly as a streak of lightening. I don't know if it was a flash of defiance at John's rejection of my love, or of longing for the company of a man who listened as if my words had value, who liked to watch the expression on my face.

But of course there was no reason that Sam would ever call me again.

A few weeks later, like John's mercurial shifts of mood, mine soared from gloom to elation in a split second when I answered the phone at work and heard Sam's voice saying, "Hi, I was just wondering how you're doing."

My delight was apparent, for the women I worked for were looking at me questioningly.

"I can't talk now, but I'm *so* glad you called," I said without thinking.

"Wait," Sam quickly said, "I miss chatting with you. How about if we grab a hotdog, and take a walk at lunch time? I need the exercise."

We agreed to meet in front of County Office Building One, where I used to work and where Sam still did, which reassured me that he had no ulterior motive. *He's a kind man, he's a psychologist, he's easing my difficult transition to this new job*, I told myself, or something similar.

We began walking around White Plains a couple of times a week, grabbing a frankfurter with sauerkraut and chili at Martin's hotdog stand, frozen yogurt at a new shop on Mamaroneck Avenue. I insisted on paying for myself, which caused Sam discomfort, in his youth, mine too for that matter, a gentleman always paid for a lady's meal. "But you hardly eat anything," he told me over and over, or, "That's only a bite, just a *bite!*" But I didn't want to feel obligated to him..

We talked about what we'd always talked about: our daughters; books I was reading; articles he'd read; courses I was taking; the latest world crises (John Hinckley had attempted to assassinate President Reagan at the end of March), but in more depth than we'd had time for before. We argued about statistics that Sam compiled for various research projects, and that I claimed, as my math professor at Pace U had demonstrated, can be biased, either unintentionally, or deliberately, to give a desired inaccurate conclusion. We enjoyed this sparring.

I learned that Sam's interests were in the field of science with its empirical methods; mine were philosophy and metaphysics. I learned that Sam was agnostic; I was Catholic, and while my concept of God had altered considerably, I had never, unless ill, missed Sunday Mass.

Sam never talked about his wife. I never talked about John.

One day, in an almost wistful tone of voice, Sam asked, "May I hold your hand?"

Feeling a little embarrassed, I said, "My life is complicated enough,"

"But we're friends now, aren't we? Friends can hold hands, can't they?" he asked.

And for a minute or so I let him take my hand. It was strange, the touch of that hand so unlike John's calloused ones, but I liked the feel of it holding mine.

Soon, so that we could hold hands, we walked farther away from the center of the city. The weather was usually warm by then; on nice days we sometimes brought brown-bag lunches, and almost ran to a small park a half mile or more away, eating, then throwing left-over crumbs to the pigeons that flocked around. We had to almost-run back to town, too, so I wouldn't be late to the office. I wonder what I looked like after those sprints—flushed, certainly. But other than holding hands, our behavior was impeccable.

When I arrived at work one day, I found a package on my desk, with a sealed note addressed to me. In the package was a book, an anthology of Japanese Haiku called A Net of Fireflies. The note said "Today I needed to hold your hand," and it was from Sam, who had been in New York City for a meeting the previous day. I was delighted that it was a book, which meant Sam had noticed how much I enjoy them. But I was disturbed by the term *needed*. For years John had told me that he needed me, and clearly resented that need.

"I don't want to be *needed*! I want someone with me because he enjoys my company, not because he *needs* me!" I told Sam when I saw him at lunchtime.

He couldn't understand my outsized reaction to the term *need*, and I couldn't explain, because the explanation involved John, whom I would not talk about. But our walks continued.

On bright days, we walked along sidewalks sun-glazed in gold; on stormy days, under skies that looked like layers of slate. When it poured rain we hurried to the yogurt shop and stayed there eating our muffins and yogurt no matter who might walk in and see us together. Our conversations were always cheerful, casual, and without a hint of romance.

Then one day when I told Sam I had recently quit smoking, he smiled and said, "I'm going to become your new habit."

And after what seemed months, but could only have been seven or eight weeks, as we strolled along hand in hand, comfortably silent, Sam said, with wonder in his voice, "I didn't know, until I walked past your empty office, that my life would feel empty without you. How could I not have known?"

That may have been the day he told me he wanted to spend more time with me—a whole afternoon, a whole day.

By then, if he was a habit it was one I couldn't imagine giving up; I needed his gentle jokes, his warm companionship; I needed what felt like love, though the word had not been spoken. So we arranged to be off from our respective offices on the same day at the end of April.

Oh, I remember that day, I can see it now:

It is an April day, the weather absolutely perfect. I leave my car in the driveway at home, and walk the mile or so to Brentano's bookstore where Sam and I have agreed to meet. I often walk to the work on nice days, and have dressed as I normally would: low heels, wool skirt, silk blouse, and my favorite glen-plaid jacket. It's so warm that I don't need an outer jacket, so warm that Sam's prediction of a coming "eppidemeek" has been fulfilled—all varieties of flowers have bloomed simultaneously: jonquils and daffodils, tulips and forsythia, cherry and plum trees, their clouds of white or pink blossoms reaching for the sky.

I feel as if I'm a woman in a romance novel—birds singing,

flowers blooming—but I'm on my way to what I'm sure will be an adulterous afternoon with a man I hardly know. I should feel terrible, I should feel guilty; I *do* feel uneasy.

But I have a feeling that this is more than an afternoon of stolen love, that God has opened a door I can choose to walk through or no, and the soft, scented morning air settles on me like a benediction.

At Brentano's, I'm browsing among books when a man wearing an old trench coat, and dark, dark sunglasses, walks in. At first I don't recognize that it's Sam; a second later I feel stark terror: *Oh God, what am I doing? What if I'm wrong? No one knows I'm going off with this man; he could be a serial killer, everyone thought Ted Bundy was a nice guy, too.*

Meanwhile, Sam has noticed me. When he walks over and tells me he's arranged for a car from Rent-A-Wreck instead of using his own, I feel a chill, and almost tell him I've changed my mind. Then his glasses—the kind that darken in sunshine though I've never noticed them *this* dark—lighten, and he's smiling, and he is, after all, Sam. "I'm *starving*," he tells me, so we grab muffins and coffee in a deli near the bookstore, then head for the Neuberger Museum at SUNY, Purchase.

As we get out of the car in Purchase, the faint drone of a bagpipe begins to weigh the mild morning air. Astonished, we walk toward the distant sound, and, reaching the top of a short hill, see below us a loan piper wearing a Scottish kilt, scarf, and cap, and standing so still on this gentle morning, in the midst of an expanse of greening grass, that he seems an illusion. There are no other people in sight; it's as if he's playing just for us.

It is mystical—which is what lovers always claim, I know, but is it not mystical to hear the sound of pipes floating toward you on an exquisite spring morning, in a place as ordinary as a college campus? I feel as if we've walked into Brigadoon.

Sam made a reservation for lunch at Stonehenge Restaurant and Inn in Connecticut. I'm impressed when I see the lovely grounds.

It is still early when we arrive, so he guides me to what seems to be a small motel-like cottage. Inside there is only one beautifully appointed room. He tells me he has never done anything like this before, and, for the first time, that he loves me.

I think he might simply be easing my nerves, calming my active Catholic conscience—he is a man, after all, and in this somewhat dark (since the drapes are drawn), but quite agreeable room, is a great big bed. I don't know what to do. But I need to do *something*. So, trembling, I strip to my bra and panties and climb in. And start crying. That is, my eyes begin to well.

"Oh, no, no, no," Sam says in a comforting tone, climbing in beside me, holding me.

Without intending to, I tell him every single thing about John's breakdown, all that happened then, and since, and even, God help me, that I still love John. I've known him since early childhood after all, and can't seem to *stop* loving him even when I want to, though now it's like loving a brother, a sick brother.

It takes a long time. When I stop, Sam says, "If you can still love John, than you won't stop loving me."

I'm not sure when a knock on the door startles us. A waiter from the nearby restaurant has arrived carrying a large silver tray holding an assortment of cheese, crackers, fruit, a bottle of wine, and two delicate crystal glasses.

Suddenly Sam and I are starving. It is the major event of that afternoon. Nothing else happens. We never make love. We never eat lunch at that fabulous restaurant famous for its excellent cuisine.

At the end of the day, Sam drops me off in a parking lot near Brentano's books, and I go to Macy's and buy a skirt so I can tell John I'm late because I went shopping after work.

When I walk back home, I don't notice if the night is clear or cloudy, but I'm freezing without my outer jacket. My feet feel as if they're not hitting the pavement—not because I am happy, but because I feel insubstantial, transparent, unreal; I don't like who I am, I have betrayed my marriage vows, and have let Sam down as well.

For a fleeting moment I wonder if he will call again, if he will still want to walk with me, if he really loves me. The thought that he might not is painful, because now I know that I am in love with him. Then I'm too exhausted to think about anything but getting home.

We had gone off together on a Thursday. Sam called Friday near lunchtime. "Let's walk," he said.

MORE ALIKE THAN EITHER OF US KNOW

It's hard to face that open space
Neil Young

Sam is waiting across the street as I hurry out among a bevy of other employees at lunchtime. I have never seen him look so serious. *What ever we had, it's over*, I think. I suspected as much when he called this morning and said, "Let's walk."

He seldom calls me at work these days, we plan ahead, but I knew "Lets walk" meant that he would be someplace nearby at about one o'clock. "Fine," I told him and quickly hung up, disturbed at his subdued tone, at the absence of the lighthearted lilt I'm used to hearing in his voice.

Since I've no real work to absorb my mind, it spent the rest of the morning spinning a web of worry: Is he breaking off this almost-affair because I'm a woman "with so much trouble," as the two women I work for once said of me? Is he mad about yesterday?

Yesterday, Sam and I went off together (sneaked off, actually), for the first time, and it was an almost perfect day: mellow April sunlight, flower-scented air, the drone of bagpipes and the mythic moment when we came upon the loan piper, in his Scottish garb, standing in the middle of a vast field as if playing his pipes solely for our pleasure. Perfect.

But then he took me to Stonehenge, an expensive inn in

Connecticut. He is married, so am I, and I've never before done such a thing. I fell apart. There were no hysterics, and I managed to stem tears that threatened, but not the flood of words—I talked and talked about things I didn't even want to think about, things that had to do with my husband John, who has a mental problem.

As if by unspoken agreement, Sam and I never complain, or even speak, about our spouses. At the end of the day, I had wondered if he'd ever call me again. And now he's waiting for me in front of a building across the street.

I hurry over. Silent, hardly even together, we walk far up Mamaroneck Avenue to where the street divides into two. There Sam stops, turns toward me, and reaches for my hand. I'm positive he's about to say, '*It's been swell, but…*', and am steeling myself not to cry in front of the many people out for lunch, or shopping, or pushing baby strollers along the sidewalk on this mild spring day, but what Sam says is, "Marry me. We'll love each other so much that everyone who steps inside our front door will feel it."

It's as if rays of light suddenly descended from the sky, and we're standing at the center of them. "Yes, I'll marry you," I tell Sam, my voice muffled because my face is pressed to his shoulder as I hug him right in the middle of White Plains (if relatively far from our offices).

We talk, then, about how hard it will be to tell our families, about our concern for our children; about the things we'll do, the places we'll go, the friends who will be utterly shocked.

I've known Sam for about six years, but we've only been actually getting to know each other—walking *miles* on our lunch hours (except for yesterday, which he planned beautifully, and I ruined)—for about two months. And now he's asked me to marry him.

Three of our daughters are in their early teens, my older teen is ill, and there is my husband John's heart condition, the shock might kill him—I want to be free, but I don't want him dead.

Sam and I need more time, I know this, but the moral code of the era in which we came of age was stringent and is carved in our bones, we are 'goody-two-shoes' and 'Mr. straight arrow', and the term 'affair' with its nasty connotation is guilt-provoking. So Sam will call the following weeks "courtship." But it is an affair, and it is almost all we ever have.

Each morning, we meet at Richard's luncheonette before work. Sam gets there before I do. When I walk in I see him watching the door, a steaming cup of coffee on the table in front of him, another waiting for me.

We plan our time: what days will Sam be out of town? When will I skip our walk to study, or prepare an end-term paper? Something else? A medical appointment maybe?

Twice we meet at Victoria Station restaurant after work, once for dinner, once for a glass or two of wine—I am particularly affectionate when I've had wine and have eaten no dinner, and that night, before we say goodbye, we cuddle & kiss in the front seat of Sam's car which is parked as far from the entrance as possible, "Good lord, all you have to do is smell the cork," Sam says, laughing.

The two evenings that we go to Victoria Station, I tell John I'm meeting with my study group at Pace University where I'm working toward my undergraduate degree (Sam and I both work 8 A.M to 4 P.M.). I hate deceit, but I tell myself, *this is different, Sam is going to marry me,* and the thought makes the bald-faced lie seem acceptable.

Sometimes, chillingly, I have the eerie feeling that John knows exactly where I am, and who I'm with, because for several years he's had the unsettling habit of following our daughters and me around just to see what we're up to, which, until now, has been nothing of note.

Still, some Saturdays I leave the groceries I've shopped for in the car, and meet Sam at Saxon Woods Park for a picnic. We sit on a blanket, munching on fruit and cheese and crackers. We don't make love, or not completely—our affair might be the coolest hot affair that ever was—but Sam whispers poetry in my ear in a voice that makes me melt. When I ask him if he knows Browning's "*My Last Dutches,*"(a long poem in which the duke implies that he murdered the dutchess), he immediately begins reciting it. I don't know why I like that poem, it makes me think of John, but I don't tell Sam that.

One Monday, after a Saturday picnic when we had lain beneath lacy leaves watching an indecisive caterpillar, Sam hands me a long poem. It's simply called, "The Caterpillar," and when I am old and read the following few lines from it, I will think Sam, without knowing it, was psychic.

> One crystal summer's day we sat
> And hand in hand watched a tiny caterpillar...
> It spun down a hundred caterpillar miles of thread
> Then hung there undecided for yet awhile...
> And inched its way back up towards its friendly leaf
> And we, with nothing else to do,
> Watched, mildly amused by its dilemma...
> Ah, little friend, we are more alike
> Than either of us know...

I'm smiling as I finish reading it. Then Sam says, "Tonight I'm going to tell my wife I want a divorce."

"Wait, wait, not yet!" I exclaim, "I *do* want to marry you, but I need time."

My older daughters, Laura and Bonnie, who live in Arizona and are alienated from their father, know I'm seeing someone. (When I told Laura she said, "Oh my God, Mom, be careful, *please* be careful, you have no experience with these things!)

But my two youngest, Catherine and Beth, know nothing, and it is Catherine, almost nineteen, that I am most worried about. She suffered a nervous breakdown a couple of years ago after being hit by a car, and is now doing well. I'm afraid new turmoil in our already troubled family will undo her progress.

She's heard Sam's name, knows he works where I used to work, might have seen him once or twice when she came there to meet me for lunch, but that's all. (Beth, fourteen, escapes our erratic home to be with her friends as often as possible, and seems fine.)

Of course Sam knows about Catherine's difficulty, as does everyone where I used to work, and his background is psychology. But what guarantee is that? Will he like her? Will she like him?

And how will she and her sister feel about me leaving their father? They are often upset by his unpredictable moods, but as far as I can tell they haven't given up on him, as I did long ago.

Sam understands my concern. At Richard's one morning he tells me, "We just have to bring this to her gradually," and we arrange a "spontaneous" meeting: he will go to the open-eating area at the White Plains Galleria at lunchtime, I will meet Catherine there for lunch, and as we stroll past Sam's table he will act surprised to see someone who used to work in his department (me), and will ask us to join him.

Then—well, then we'll see. Maybe Sam will tell his wife about me, and maybe I'll tell John about him. (That I want a divorce will be old news to John, but that I want one so that I can marry Sam, devastating.)

At the Galleria, the prearranged meeting goes beautifully: Sam is completely relaxed with Catherine. I've told him she loves to read and do needlepoint, and he talks to her about books and hobbies, with warmth and that sweet quirky humor that quickly puts her at ease. As we walk away from him at the end of lunch, she's happy and smiling. "He's nice," she tells me, "I like him." I glance back at Sam, then, and nod 'yes'—*Yes, you can tell your wife about us; yes, I will tell John.*

Sam phones me around three o'clock that afternoon, "I *have* to talk to you," he says, sounding harried. We decide we'll meet at Richard's for coffee after work.

We never get there because it seems Sam can't hold what he has to say for another second—as we near Richard's entrance he blurts, "I can't do it, I can't ask my wife for a divorce, I just can't."

I am stunned, and at first can't speak. He *just* met my fragile daughter and *then* decided he couldn't marry me?

Over and over Sam assures me that his decision has nothing to do with Catherine, but I don't care whether it does or not, I could kill him. I feel like a fool, a gullible fool. Of all the women on God's green earth, I'm one who should have known better than to trust a man.

"Give me back everything I've given you!" I tell him (poems, letters, pictures), "and don't call me again, EVER!" I add, then hurry away.

Do I walk? Drive? I have no idea how I've arrived at my front door, and only when I walk through it do I begin to cry—and cry and cry. And where is John, I wonder? Where are my girls? They must be out, and I'm so glad, so glad, because I can't stop crying, and I don't want them to see me like this.

Later, when they return, I appear calm but am actually numb.

The girls glance at my horribly swollen eyes, but say nothing. Beth hugs me as we sit down to dinner; Catherine asks if she should stay home instead of going bowling with her friends. They must think my eyes have something to do with their father. "No, everything's fine, you go ahead," I tell Catherine, thankful that she's seeing her friends again, thankful that she's going out, as Beth is. I just want to be alone.

The next morning Sam strides to my desk, hands me a manila envelope containing letters, poems, etc. that I've given him, and dashes away without a word. (Which surely gives the two women I work for something new to whisper about.)

For weeks I am angry, and unwilling to acknowledge that I miss Sam. But I do miss him, and dreadfully. Without him my world is flattened, faded, dismal.

I'm thankful I've told no one, not even my close friend Estelle, about our short affair. It saves me the embarrassment of awkward explanations, it lets me pretend I've had a near escape and am relieved that Sam, with his empty promise, is gone, and that I'm glad it's all behind me.

And then it *is* behind me, the anger, the dullness, the effort to keep Sam out of my thoughts, and, once again as I leave for work in the early morning, my heart lifts of its own accord at the ordinary sight of dew dazzling the grass.

About two months later, I'm hurrying toward Macy's on my lunch hour when I see Sam standing on the corner of Martine Avenue, in front of the luncheonette that was once a Mayflower Doughnut shop. He doesn't see me, and, as if he can't decide what to do, he doesn't move. I watch him while I wait for the light to change. Older than I, he hasn't a gray hair on his head, and is usually youthful and vigorous. Now he looks drawn, and deeply unhappy. When the light changes, I cross the street and, almost without volition, walk up to him saying, "Sam, we can still be friends."

Without a word, he grabs my hand. "Come with me, *please,*" he implores, leading me around the corner and down the short avenue to Main Street where there is a lone bench at the edge of dug-up land that once held the old stone court house. "Please sit, just for a minute," he says.

He seems agitated. I sit, and he sits next to me, reaching into the inner pocket of his jacket and withdrawing a small box. I'm too confused to think it might hold a ring, to confused to think at all. Sam opens the box, saying, "Look," and I see a silver charm of the god Pan.

"I had a jeweler pour it for you because you made me hear the pipes again," he tells me, adding, "Listen, listen, I *know* you don't trust me, and I won't talk of marriage—*I'll* hold that dream for us—but please, *please* keep seeing me; we can at least have pockets of happiness."

It's so sudden that I'm dizzy. But I take the Pan charm from him, and hesitantly agree that we can resume out lunchtime walks. And soon, it seems, we begin what will unequivocally be a long love affair.

On a late summer day, when the sky is a vibrant blue with a few cumulous clouds in the distance, when the sun is sharp on the skin, and almost blinding—a day totally unlike the soft, spring morning that we went to Stonehenge—Sam takes me to the Bird and Bottle Inn. This time we eat. "Are you sure?" Sam asks when we finish our lunch. I am.

We go upstairs to a room that is just like a charming bedroom in an ordinary home, chintz throw pillows, a quilt, light airy curtains at the windows, it is perfect, and we are perfect in it as we finally consummate our love.

But at the end of the afternoon I have a pounding, punishing headache. *I'm not going to be able to do this,* I think.

Sam drops me off in White Plains. I don't want to go home, so I get my car, and drive to my friend Estelle's. She knows and likes Sam, and John, too. When I tell her about my affair with Sam, she is shocked, and worried, but not disapproving. As we gab over strong cups of coffee my headache disappears, and I realize I've had no coffee since early morning—I was not being punished, as my active conscience dictated, but simply suffering from caffeine withdrawal.

Other than our time at the Bird and Bottle, Sam and I share only hours now and then, experiencing moments that may seem ordinary to others, but to us are extraordinary—one afternoon as we enter Rockefeller State Park, a deer with a full rack of antlers sails over the hood of our car as if he has wings, like Pegasus; at Saxon Woods, a red fox peers at us from beneath a canopy of ferns, he knows we see him, but stays, giving us the gift of his company; a few times we escape to Manhattan where Sam takes me to the Museum of Modern Art, the Frick, the Guggenheim, and delights in my delight. I feel as if he's spreading beauty at my feet.

But for the most part, we continue meeting at Richard's before work, walking around the city at lunchtime, living the lives we committed ourselves to long ago.

Sometime early in the following year, or the next, or the next, John and I are saying goodbye to friends with whom we sing at Sunday Mass. Catherine and Beth are with us, all of us in high spirits. "Who wants to go to the diner for breakfast?" John asks as we get in the car, and with a chorus of, "I do, I do," we're on our way to the North Castle Diner. Once we're seated at a table, the girls discuss whether to order pancakes, or Belgian waffles. John looks at me, smiles, and with exceptional warmth says, "Order anything you want, anything at all."

Then, instantly, his face expressionless, his eyes shards of ice aimed first at Catherine, then at Beth, he says, "Not *you!*" and "Not *you*! You can have either a muffin or a roll."

His emphatic voice is as cold as his eyes, and devastating. Our young daughters' faces express shock, dismay, confusion. They don't know what has happened, and nor do I, because, unlike John's usual shifting moods, this seems deliberate, and sadistic. I am sick to my stomach—*how can Catherine continue to get well, how will Beth maintain her steady course, in such a toxic atmosphere?* This day I hope John's clogged arteries *will* make his heart stop beating. And soon.

(In the future I will see myself leaving John there while I take the car and drive the girls home, but I will never be sure if it's what I actually did, or what I wish I had done, and my grown daughters now have but the vaguest memory of that episode.)

A week, two, three pass, and the evil wind that blew that Sunday brings the unbelievable: John, who has been apologetic, and sorry to the point of tears over the diner incident, tells me, "I'm no good for any of you," and leaves. He has arranged a house-share with a few other divorcing, and divorced men. Our girls are not troubled, as I feared they would be if we separated, in fact they hardly seem to notice that anything has changed.

I'm overjoyed, as is Sam when I tell him John has left. But when John calls a month later, tearful and begging to come home, all I hear is the boy I once loved—the boy, the young husband— not the man I've been living with for too many years. "Of course you can come home," I tell him.

Then, on Saturday afternoon I tell Sam not only what I've done, but that I won't see him anymore, that I can't keep living two lives.

"Don't do this," Sam says, "Don't give up on us; we have so much to lose."

"I don't know, I just don't know," I tell him, "I can't *stand* this."

My resolve to return to my former life lasts until Monday morning when I hurry into Richard's. I am almost weak with relief to see Sam at our usual table near the back of the luncheonette. There is no cup of coffee waiting for me. As I sit down across from him, he looks up, closes his eyes, and sighs as if he's been holding his breath.

Since John returned home he is more agreeable than he's been in years. When I tell him about Sam—which I know I must finally do—he ignores my attempt to be honest, ignores everything, as I suspect he's been doing for a long time. It's as if my words were never spoken, as if Sam doesn't exist.

But now, at least in *my* mind, John knows the score: Sam is part of my life, and someday soon I'm going to marry him.

And now, of all times, *now,* my mother—who has been living with either of my sisters, Jeanne, or Dorothy—telephones beseeching me to let her come and live with me once more, "before she dies."

"Mom, you'll be ninety in a few years, " I tell her, "You're unable to go up stairs, and we have no bedroom downstairs, no tub or shower either, only a powder room. There's no way that you can manage here."

"Yes I can," she says, "We managed without a lot of things when I was young."

My mother hasn't stayed with me since John fell apart more

than seven years ago. At that time she phoned to announce her upcoming visit, as she always did, and for the first time in my life I told her, *No.*

What else could I do? I couldn't say, *See Mom, John isn't himself, he thinks he needs to die; that is, he thinks he's being told he must die, Yes, I know it doesn't make sense, but there you have it. Oh and he thinks it's a good idea if we all go along with him wherever he's going, to hell probably, so please don't come right now.* She would have insisted on coming, she would have gotten hysterical; she might have had a heart attack.

(There was never a diagnosis for John's mental illness, or rather there were several: clinical depression with psychosis, borderline personality, etc., etc. Different doctors, different diagnoses.)

But now our home is astonishingly stable in spite of my affair with Sam (or perhaps because of it, who knows?). So John and I give away our heavy dining room furniture, have a closet built on one wall for Mom's clothes and small treasures, bring down from the attic a bed, dresser, chair, and small table for a desk—then I hang an opaque curtain over the French door at the dining room's entrance, and Mom moves in. She brings with her a small television, and a Windex bottle full of water.

I have dreaded her arrival. I am in college, and working, and have children who need attention, and *my God I'm having an affair!*

I worry that Mom will find out about Sam, worry about how she will manage without a tub or shower, worry that she will be unable to avoid asthma from our cat, and I won't get rid of the cat. I worry about her nerves, and mine, especially mine—she is possessive, my mother, my sisters and I are expected to put her first, then our husbands, then our children, then everything else, like college—*Oh God, I'll never be able to do this!*

When Mom has been with us a week or so, I begin to breathe more easily. She doesn't question my coming and going, and is surprisingly uncomplaining, calmly taking care of most of her needs. I think she bathes in the kitchen when we're all out, for she's always sweet-scented and clean. With the Windex bottle of water, she sprays our cat away from her, and so far has had no severe asthma attack.

Week follows week, and this new changed mother remains. Occasionally I wash her hair in the kitchen sink, sometimes I rub lotion on her feet—she asks for so little. The only hard thing is when I wake at two or three in the morning to the sound of her puttering in the kitchen, "Mom, be careful!" I call from the top of the stairs, worried that her bathrobe might catch on fire.

"I'm fine, go back to bed," she tells me.

"Mom, I can't sleep when I'm worried about you!"

"I'm just pouring my tea, I'll be back in my room in a minute, she says.

She is the only one in my family, now, who doesn't know that Sam and I are integral to each other's happiness, and he has told his family, as well.

One day Sam brings his daughters, Holly and Heather, to meet me at the small Neiman Marcus café where he and I sometimes have coffee and frozen yogurt. It is an awkward meeting for all, but the girls, who are in their late teens, greet me with grace and acceptance. When I am old, and have learned how families take sides, and fight, and fall apart in similar situations, I will know what a miracle this is, and how incredibly special Holly and Heather are.

Beth is comfortable with the idea of Sam in my life, but still spends her time with her friends.

However, Catherine, who is much better now, enjoys Sam's company. Late one afternoon, she and I meet him at Mamaroneck Harbor, where we sit on a bench, under his spell, as he regales us with an extraordinary story about a man who swam from the harbor all the way to France. Sam is serious, and we are listening raptly, gullibly, until he bursts out laughing, and we realize it's a tall tale and laugh with him.

The last Christmas Eve before John leaves, Catherine and I meet Sam at a diner in White Plains to exchange gifts. He gives her a Gund stuffed bear, and a poem he wrote about a hairy bear that lost its hair, and so was bare.

Years earlier, I opened a beautifully wrapped and beribboned gift from Sam to find a large bottle of vitamins. I'd been nonplussed, "Well I wanted to give you the gift of good health," Sam told me then.

I love the way his mind works: a gift of good health, light, funny poems, tall tales, "pockets" of happiness.

On a cool, damp early autumn day in 1984, red and gold leaves bright against a grim, gray sky, Catherine, Beth, and I help John move into an apartment, lugging boxes of clothes, linens, kitchenware, a few pieces of furniture. I give him a treasured afghan that Mom crocheted for me, because he asks for it (he will later it give back).

We have seen lawyers, so this is separation prior to divorce, a sad occasion, yet the girls and I are relieved, and maybe John is, too. I like to believe that he finally wants to see me happy, wants our daughters to have the peaceful home I've begged for. (It is curious that I will not be able to recall why John finally decided to leave. I will remember only this day, when the girls and I helped him to move out.)

With trepidation, I tell my mother that I am divorcing John, and am going to marry a man I met at work a long time ago. I hold my breath, waiting for the explosion that is sure to come: *Her* daughter? Her *Catholic* daughter, getting *divorced*!?

"I never did like John," she says mildly, "he made me nervous."

It's not true! She loved John, who was devoted to both our mothers. And there is *nothing* wrong with her memory.

But I am her youngest, she will not be with me much longer (in fact she will die at the age of ninety, in 1985), maybe my sisters told her about John's mental problem, and she wants me to be safe, or maybe she simply wants me to be happy. I don't ask, I just accept: John is out, divorce is in, and Sam, who has moved into his own apartment but spends evenings with us is "That very nice gentleman you're seeing."

With all indecision behind us, Sam and I finally marry on March 22, 1986, exactly five years and six days after the first time he asked me to lunch. Among those sharing our joy are our daughters, sisters, brothers-in-law, close friends, and several colleagues from the Westchester County Department of Community Mental Health, where I was first introduced to Sam eleven years ago, and could not remember his name.

We exchange our wedding vows before a Unitarian minister, a

woman, with our daughters standing to each side of us. "Blessed art thou among women," I laughingly tell Sam when the ceremony is over. But I am the most blessed.

The Feel of Our Hands

We lunched
among a medley
of talking laughing people deaf
to strident horn, screaming siren
you murmured, "Your hand
is the perfect size for mine."

We followed a path
that wound like narrow ribbon
through summer-tangled woods
climbed over fallen trees to a lake
walked around its shining
surface hand in hand

and that
evening of lavender sky
and wine, and wine when you drew
a blueprint of our future, you reached
across the table for my hand
then, too—

Now your mind
holds memories like hands hold
mist, and still you reach for mine
you smile; I reach back
and hold tight

BUT THERE WERE DAFFODILS

Take your life in your own hands and what happens?
A terrible thing: no one to blame
Erica Jong

It's obvious, to me at least, that second marriages will be different from first marriages, aside from the fact that one was unhappy in that first marriage. In a second union, things you took for granted during those years with your first spouse float in your unconscious like twigs along a clear or muddied stream, or like logs, creating a logjam, you could say, of unmet expectations.

The grass had grown an inch, then two inches, three. It was higher every time I looked out of the front window. Soon it would sprout seeds. Neighbors looked askance when they walked past our yard. I looked askance at Sam, who was trying to finish his *Times* crossword puzzle.

"Sam, the grass is getting high," I said.
"I'll get around to it."
"Sam, the grass really needs cutting."
"Mmmmhmmm,"
"Sam! *When* are you going to mow the lawn?"
"What do you want, a house boy? He asked mildly, continuing to work on his puzzle.

"A *house boy?*" I yelled, "And what does that make me? Your chief cook and bottle-washer? Your maid? Your laundress?"

I stomped upstairs, rummaged through the hamper, pulled out Sam's dirty shorts, shirts, socks, marched back downstairs, threw them at his feet, and screamed, "Do your own damn laundry!"

Sam got up and walked out. It was what he always did if I was really angry, he went for a walk. When we were both working in White Plains we walked all over the city on our lunch hours. Now I worked at the medical center in Valhalla, Sam in White Plains, but when we were home, we still walked all over—in *opposite* directions.

It was 1986, full summer: lots of rain, lots of sun, lots and lots of grass.

Sam and I had married on a warm March afternoon, leaving for a honeymoon in Williamsburg, Virginia several hours after the wedding reception. At Newark Airport our flight was delayed. Exhausted, and finding no place to sit while we waited, I perched precariously on our suitcase while Sam paced nearby. By the time we reached Williamsburg, dead on our feet, we crawled into bed as quickly as we could, and instantly fell asleep.

The next morning I woke, stretched luxuriously, realized Sam's side of the bed was empty, and smiled, waiting for him to walk through the door with a hot cup of coffee for me. It's what my first husband, John, had done whenever we were away from home and staying in a hotel or motel.

About fifteen minutes later Sam walked in. "What a breakfast!" he said, and proceeded to tell me what it was like to eat his morning meal at the famous Williamsburg Inn: the exquisitely set table, the fresh flowers, the fresh blueberries, the best pancakes he'd ever eaten in his life, the best orange juice, and eggs, and bacon, and, and, and…. He was exuberant.

"You went *without* me? How *could* you!" I said.

I sat there stunned, disbelieving, confounded. He had abandoned me on the first morning that I was finally his wife, I didn't know whether to cry or run—where was the Sam who had wanted to start every work-day over a cup of coffee at Richard's luncheonette with me sitting across from him? The Sam who wanted to go *everywhere* with me, even grocery shopping, even to the dentist or the eye doctor? "I want to share the nitty-gritty, too," he'd once said.

Now crestfallen, he tried to explain: "But Marian, you were so tired, I wanted to let you get some sleep."

In a way, that was typical of Sam. It was like the time he wrapped a box of vitamins in fancy paper and ribbon, wanting to give me the gift of good health, an endearing characteristic. But this was not at all the same, and he didn't seem to understand why; it worried me—is this what our life is going to be like, each of us going our own way with no thought to the other? Was it me? Was I just used to John's sometimes hovering attention?

No. No, this was different, this was the *first morning* of our life together, and Sam had gone to a fancy restaurant, and eaten a fancy meal, without me.

It was a bad beginning, and I would refer to it directly or obliquely every time we argued in the first months, the first *year* of our marriage. Or rather, every time *I* argued. Sam never would. He was "perfectly happy, he said.

"How can you be perfectly happy when someone you say you love is *un*happy?" I asked, exasperated, "You were clueless on our honeymoon, and you're clueless now!"

I would use that term often: he was "Clueless!" when he cluttered the house, "Clueless!" when the grass grew too long, "Clueless!" when he walked away from a discussion. Sometimes, if I were only mildly upset, I would look at him, shake my head sadly, and softly say, "Clueless," with a sigh like surrender.

That first year most of my complaints were over things that bothered me out of all proportion. Used to John's neatness, I was appalled when Sam dropped his socks on the floor at bedtime, strewed sections of the *Times* from one end of the living room to the other, and flatly refused to mow the lawn.

The more I complained, the more he dug in his heels, acting deaf to my nagging pleas. Not one thing that bothered me was up for discussion, *ever*. If Sam was angry, which he sometimes obviously was, he walked out—just left without a word—which upset me more than anything else.

Compared to what I had sometimes experienced with John (who

nevertheless liked a ship-shape home and did his share to keep it that way), this was ordinary misery. But ordinary misery is still misery.

Oh God what have we done, I said to myself, remembering the lovely times Sam and I had had during our five-year affair. Sometimes I was sorry we'd married.

"Sam, what's happened to us? What's happened to our romance?" I asked one day.

"Romance?" he said, "That was leading you down the garden path, that was courtship." (He said this in a quiet, reasonable tone of voice, as if it were a fact that any idiot would have understood.)

"And now what!" I retorted, "Now I'm supposed to hand you your pipe and slippers?"

He was reclining in the recliner with his ever-present *Times* crossword puzzle—I hated those puzzles the first year that we were married. The argument continued:

"You're lazy!" I accused.

"No, I'm not, I'm relaxed," Sam calmly said, "It's just that you're compulsive."

"No, I'm not, I'm meticulous!" I answered hotly, "and for all your knowledge of crossword puzzles, you wouldn't know what *that* word means."

"Tell me, do you still love me?" I asked.

"Well I'm here, aren't I?" he answered.

Near the end of that first year I thought there wouldn't be a second.

But there were children, you see, there were six daughters to consider. My four had been living in an already broken home when Sam and I began seeing each other, but as far as I know Sam's two hadn't, and yet all six stood with us at our wedding, blessing us with their love and acceptance. And now we would throw up our hands and walk away over almost nothing? '*Sorry Charlie, big mistake*'? No. Impossible. Besides, Sam and I were both too stubborn to admit defeat.

So, since it was also impossible for me to talk to him, I wrote a note that turned into a long, sorrowful, raging letter listing grievance after grievance, the most serious being that he walked away from every weighty discussion. "I spent enough of this lifetime banging on doors that wouldn't give," I wrote, "Either I misread you, or you *misled* me! What is bigger than an elephant? Whatever it is, it's sitting in the middle of our living room!"

Sam said not one word in response to my missive, but he began dropping his socks in the hamper, putting dishes into the dishwasher, piling sections of the *Times* together on the coffee table or next to his chair; and his chair was often empty as he looked for things to do:

He built a spice cabinet out of a kitchen cubby that once held a small drop-down ironing board; put a shelf up beside the cellar stairs so we'd have more storage space; bought and hung new Venetian blinds throughout the house. He removed all the brass escutcheons from our home's ancient doors, soaked them in turpentine for days to loosen decades of paint, scraped the paint off, and polished them to a soft brilliance.

It was clear that Sam still loved me, and I had never stopped loving him, I'd just wondered how we could ever manage to live together for the rest of our lives.

Now, with Sam's obvious efforts to please me, I relaxed. And as I relaxed it dawned on me that the house didn't need to be 'just so' every minute of every day, as it had had to be when John was my husband.

Still, I did like a neat-looking lawn, and mowing ours was not among Sam's new activities. The healthy green growth in our front and back yards was cut by Catherine, who—amused at this particular obstinacy on the part of the stepfather she had come to love—assumed the chore for his sake (and mine), coming home every other weekend for, as she insisted, "the exercise."

I tried to hire Tony, who took care of our neighbor's yard, but the day that he began mowing ours, Sam rushed outside saying, "No, no, I'll do that." And he did, for the first and only time in my memory.

It wasn't a matter of money, we could afford to hire Tony. It had something to do with Sam's strange fixation on cutting grass, a fixation that never left him, that he never explained, and that I gave up trying to understand.

Unlike John, in the years after that first difficult one, Sam seldom spoke of his love for me, but he showed it in a thousand different ways. Mowing the lawn was never one of them.

As for me, I would weed, rake leaves, shovel snow, wallpaper, paint, scrub, I would do almost anything—but I'd never had to mow a lawn and wasn't about to start. So, unless Catherine came to "exercise" on weekends, our freshly painted house, with the new front door and new shutters, was surrounded by shaggy, unkempt grass.

But every spring, in each of the nine years that we lived in that house, our front and back yards glowed with colorful satiny tulips, and the sunny radiance of dozens of daffodils reaching for the sky.

In the autumn of that first challenging year of our life together, when I thought I'd married the laziest man on earth, Sam had quietly planted a hundred bulbs.

GRANNY GLASSES

The little things? The little moments?
They aren't little.
Jon Kabat-Zinn

There were only twenty minutes left until the beginning of the work-day, and I needed to complete an assignment for my math survey course which was that evening. Each time I completed a particular matrix problem I got the same answer—the wrong one. I tried again, my third try. Again, wrong. "Damn it!" I said, flinging my pencil across the room just as Sam Rogers walked past my office. Sam stopped and stuck his head in the door,

"Is something wrong? Can I help? He asked.

"No. No, it's just homework, I replied, clearly frustrated, "I'm positive I'm doing the problem right but I get the same answer every time, and it's the wrong one."

(The correct answers were in back of the book so we could check our work, and I'd checked.)

Sam walked in, picked up the paper with the problem I'd been working on, looked it over, checked it against the one printed in the book and said, "You're doing it right but you've written a wrong number on your paper. See here?" he said, pointing to a number in the book, "it's a 5, not a 6, see?"

I looked at the number, it still looked like a six. I squinted and, yes, it was a five.

"Oh Lord, thanks Sam," I mumbled, embarrassed, "time for eyeglasses, I guess."

"It's nothing, glad to help," he said, and was quickly on his way to the other end of the building where he walked almost every morning.

A few days later I went to an optometrist near the office and got myself a pair of half-glasses with a rose-colored metal frame. They were called 'granny glasses' at that time, and probably still are since they look like the kind a grandmotherly Mrs. Santa wears in pictures on current Christmas cards.

My office, directly across from the office of the director of mental health services, for whom I worked, was in the middle of a relatively long hall. At each end of the hall was a large room for clerical workers, and off of these rooms, offices for professionals in various sections of the department. Sam's section was substance abuse services; his office was on the left, while his friend Matt's was on the right. When Sam walked past my office, he was heading for Matt, so I never wondered about him stopping at my door with a "Good morning," or, if I was studying, a "How are you doing?"

And he was friendly with everyone, it was not the least unusual for him to stop to ask what I was studying, or how my daughters were, or to tell me about something special that was happening in his daughters' lives: a prom, a birthday.

But then, if he had been particularly interested I wouldn't have noticed anyway, immersed as I was in my tumultuous life—school, work, two daughters still teenagers, and a husband, John, who had been central to my life since he was a blue-eyed boy with flaxen hair that turned brown, then gray, then pure silky white.

John was in his forties now, and still central to my life, if painfully so; in spite of our troubled marriage my mind, whether I wanted it to or not, leaned toward him (or perhaps toward a younger version of him). And Sam, with his bright brown eyes, dark curls, and smiling countenance, was just a really nice man who worked in another branch of the department, a professional who took the time to chat, even with support staff, like me.

Less than a year after the morning that led to granny-glasses, I moved from my position in mental health to another in a different county building, and Sam, who was sorry he'd missed my farewell dinner, invited me to lunch. A few weeks later—sedentary office workers at that time becoming aware of the importance of exercise—we began walking together during our lunch hours. I'd often seen Sam walk with women at lunchtime (though they were professionals whom he worked with).

But the day that he took me to lunch, I had told him how much I missed my position in the mental health department, so he knew I wasn't happy in my new job, and he was a psychologist, and not the type of man who told dirty jokes, eyed the women in the office, made inappropriate passes, I'd thought, *he probably wants to cheer me up*, and so it seemed, for weeks.

Then one day when we were walking around the city Sam handed me a folded sheet of paper. "Read it when you get back to your office," he said. It was a poem he had written about my eyesight:

To Marian
(Or 20/20 Don't Necessarily Cut It)

Some men fall for soulful eyes
Or golden curls or husky sighs.
Others go for nubile lasses –
I love a girl in granny glasses.

When wearing them she looks so prim
But ah, the fires which burn within!
She has a certain hocus pocus –
(Because her lovely eyes don't focus.)

So all you lads of middle age,
When teenage girls are all the rage,
When skin-tight jeans a la Brook Shields,
Are advertising's hottest deals;

Still slightly damp behind the ears,
Will they still bewitch in twenty years?
Leer if you must at the teenage lasses,
But make you're move on granny glasses!

The poem was unsigned, and I loved it, though I wasn't sure if it was complementary, I mean *"make your move on?"*

But there was more: "Some men fall for..." and "I love," words that had never been spoken, and that I would not hear, or read in another poem, for many more weeks.

As I read the poem, I *felt* like one of those "hottest deals," and it felt wonderful.

I don't know exactly when Sam began to love me, or when I first felt I couldn't live without him, but at some point our light friendship became something more, and suddenly (for so it seemed to me), we were in love. Once, while we walked, Sam told me he didn't know life would feel empty without me until he walked past my empty office in the department where he worked, and I no longer did, as if it were that sudden.

But though I was in my forties then, I could still turn a head or two, my hair a wavy brown with reddish highlights; eyes more green than hazel; a body tall and slim yet far from skinny, so I wonder, when Sam passed by my office on his way to see Matt, did he sometimes fantasize? Did he imagine what it might be like to know me better, to know me even in the biblical sense?

I don't think so, I really don't, he was such a straight arrow. But I do wonder.

I found the 'granny glasses' poem when I was going through keepsakes a few days ago. It was tucked among other papers, along with the original version written in Sam's hand on a sheet of yellow canary paper, which was titled "Advice to Middle-Age Men," but otherwise was about the same as the one that he gave me.

I wish I had found them when Sam was here, when he was alive, when he still had his memory.

When did you write this poem? I would have asked him. When did you begin to love me?

Did it creep up and take you by surprise, as it did me in that long-ago time when we walked all over White Plains?

Could it really have been as sudden as a glance at my empty office?

When did you begin to love me? I would have asked, was it—could it *possibly* have been—the granny glasses that did it?

LOVE, HAPPINESS, GHOSTS

To view your life as blessed does not require
you to deny your pain. It simply demands a more
complicated vision ...
Nancy Mairs

When the kitchen telephone rang, Sam answered it and called upstairs, where I was busy with something or other, "Pick up the phone, its Peg, John's sister."

Peg lived in California. I hadn't talked to her since my separation from John, hadn't even told her that I'd wanted to divorce John for years. As soon as we greeted each other she said, "I have just one question for you." I steeled myself for what was sure to come: *how could you divorce my brother after all these years?* Instead, with genuine concern she asked, "Are you happy Perk?"

Her question, spoken in the deep husky voice I was so familiar with, raised tears of gratitude and a host of other complex emotions; I hesitated a moment then said, "Yes, I'm happy, but never as happy as when I was happy with John." It was true, but my words carried memories of time when our four daughters were young and I could imagine nothing but fairytale endings in their futures or ours, time before John became mentally unstable, and home a place the girls preferred to avoid.

When Sam and I married, I was fifty-two, Sam fifty-nine, both of us set in our ways. The day Peg called we'd been married less than a year, and the atmosphere in our home was chilly. But in spite of unexpected dissention while learning to live under the same roof, Sam and I had created a home where any of our six daughters (my four, Sam's two), could walk through the front door and not feel their toes curl, their shoulders tense, their stomachs churn, while they scanned the atmosphere for trouble. I did not, even for a second, wish to return to my old life.

And now I learned that Peg, and her sister Helen, both of whom I had known and loved for years, still returned my love, still wanted to remain connected to me in this new life of mine, an astonishing joy that I had not expected.

But was I happy, really?

Sam was not neat—alright, he was *sloppy*—newspapers strewn about the house, cold cuts left on the counter until he finished eating his sandwich, the lawn un-mown week after week. I had loved that he was easy-going, but now he seemed simply oblivious, especially regarding me and *my* concerns. John was excessively neat, he worried about one thing or another *all the time,* and that's what I was used to.

"You're clueless!" I spit out at Sam every time we argued— which could not *possibly* have been as often as I remember during that first year of marriage, because Sam usually just walked out. I suspect that's what had caused a chill in the air of our apparently peaceful home on the day Peg telephoned: small issues, unresolved. Sam and I loved each other, we were great together, but *living* together? Not so much. Sometimes, wondering if we'd made a mistake, I thought of leaving him.

Peg's call had arrived with flawless timing. Her question made me think of the reasons I fell in love with Sam: his relaxed attitude, his equanimity, his acceptance of things that most men would run from—when he asked me to marry him I had an ill daughter and an elderly mother at home, both of whom would have come with me if we had married at that time; when, worried about what he might expect of a working wife, I'd said, "You know, I don't do breakfast or lunch," he had laughed and answered, "As long as dinner isn't at McDonalds."

I had even told him that I still loved John, not as a husband, not for years, but as someone I'd known since early childhood who had *wanted* to be a good husband, that I would sometimes want to share a cup of coffee at the diner with him, that I would visit him when he was in the hospital. Sam understood my love for him was in no way compromised by my continuing concern for John, and he married me, and all that came with me.

That was Sam. Leave him? No. No for many reasons, but mostly because now that I seriously thought about it, life without him was inconceivable.

At the beginning of our second year of marriage I needed eye-surgery at the New York Eye and Ear infirmary in Manhattan. Sam stayed home one of the days that I was there so that John could visit me, knowing how important it was to him, and, on my account, sensitive to his feelings.

When John's illness became serious, and his hospital stays frequent, we took care of his dog Rags; knowing that I had never been an animal person, John worried about his dog until I told him Sam loved animals and took Rags for long walks, rain or shine.

One evening I arrived home from the hospital with a message; "Tell *that man* thank you for me," John said as I was leaving. (*That man* was how Churchill referred to Hitler during World War II; John read a lot and may have come across that fact, for Sam was only ever *that man*, to him. The memory makes me smile.)

By then I had forgotten I'd ever thought Sam clueless. In fact, by then the rough patches of our first difficult year of marriage, as if planed and sanded into new shapes, had smoothly merged into the daily rhythms of life, often in the form of inside jokes: One day, on our way to Newark Airport to pick up my daughter Beth, Sam was about to miss a turn—"Go straight around that curve, Sam," I quickly told him. He did, and then, chuckling, said, "Those were *meticulous* directions."

It took me a second to realize that you can't go straight around a curve, and to remember a fierce argument we'd had:

"It's just that you're so compulsive!" Sam had calmly accused.
"No I'm not, I'm meticulous!" I had retorted furiously.
In the car on the way to the airport, I laughed, we both did, but I

wish I'd thought of the ideal riposte: *perfect* directions for a *clueless* man.

Sam and I were married almost six years when John died. That night, with three of our daughters, I stood by his side watching as he struggled for breath, then as he was intubated, and silent, and leaving. When I returned from the hospital mourning for the deeply troubled and troubling man, the too-young husband, the laughing, teasing boy of my childhood, memories of those playful days flooding my mind, tears streaming from my eyes—Sam held me.

I had thought of John's love for me as painful love; it was painful *joy* to be in sorrow for John, and to be loved and comforted by Sam.

"Are you happy Perk?" Peg had asked when she called. She wanted to know, of course, if I was happy being married to Sam. Now I could have answered unequivocally, "Yes, oh yes."

Little more than a year after John's death, I was again in the New York Eye and Ear Infirmary for my last trabeculectomy (there would not be space in my eye for another.) The problem is Iridocorneal Endothelial Syndrome (ICE), which thankfully always occurs in only one eye. The version I have affects the cornea, whose endothelial cells multiply beyond the number required to maintain health, blocking the eye's normal drainage system and causing secondary glaucoma.

A Tabeculectomy creates a means of drainage, eliminating the glaucoma, and eventual blindness. The trouble is, there's no known cause or cure, so endothelial cells continue to over-multiply, sometimes blocking the newly created draining process.

So the year was 1992, and I was in the New York Eye and Ear Infirmary for my third surgery since 1986 when Sam and I had married.

As usual, Sam took the train to Manhattan to visit me every day that I was in the hospital. On the day of my discharge, dressed and eager to go home, I lay on the bed expecting him any minute. When I heard his steps coming down the hall—I was positive they were Sam's—I smiled, looking at the door.

And in walked John. When he died, I had closed that chapter of my life and hadn't thought of him since, nor had I remembered his visits the last two times that I was a patient in the infirmary.

Now here he was, looking as solid as the floor, and wearing a denim shirt and jeans that for some reason instantly impressed me with the idea of the sea and ships that, as a navy man, John had loved. I gasped and began breathing in a way that sounds like sobbing, but isn't, while babbling away. (I've no idea what I babbled about.) John was silent but looked radiantly happy. If he had spoken, his words might have been something like: *It's all good.*

When he disappeared, I had a deep, deep sense of peace. (And it is of note, I believe, that the trabeculectomy I had at that time lasted for *seventeen* years.)

A few minutes later Sam, who believed in nothing after this life, arrived looking, not radiant, but certainly happy. I didn't tell him about John's appearance, worried that it would trouble him, that he would think, *Oh God, what's happened to my wife?* I don't think I told him about John's visitation in all our years together, mainly because the living quickly and rightfully claimed my attention.

I would have told him, though, if I had remembered an exceptionally happy time some twenty years earlier, when John and I had promised that whichever one of us died first would try to contact the other. If I had remembered that, I would have tried to exact the same promise from Sam.

That discussion on death and dying, John's and mine, had been suggested by a priest, but our promise was inspired by an event that had occurred several years earlier when we returned to New York from a failed attempt to relocate to Florida.

That year—with four daughters (Beth a recent arrival), *and* my mother (who, incomprehensively had left her Florida home to permanently dwell with *us)*—we were living in four rooms on the forth floor of an apartment building from which I had recently banished my mother, insisting that she move to my sister Jeanne's large home (filled with her large family), in Long Island.

The husband of our downstairs neighbors had insomnia. Our girls' room was the big master bedroom right over theirs. One night, when Mom was still with us, and John and I were sleeping on the Castro Convertible couch in the living room, his wife phoned complaining about the baby crying and me walking around in the middle of the night to pick her up for her feedings.

I didn't *want* to walk around in the middle of the night, half of the time I wanted to go to sleep and never wake up. Exhausted, discouraged, enraged over a complaint I could do nothing about, I put on my high heels and stomped around the apartment while feeding Beth at 2 or 3 A.M.

The couple moved to the top floor. I cringed every time I saw them in the elevator.

I felt mean, I *was* mean: to the poor insomniac, to my mother who had left in tears while I rejoiced, glad that she was gone and guilty for being glad. And I was perpetually angry that the downstairs apartment of the two-family house a block away (that John and I had fixed up, and lived in, and loved before our Florida misadventure), was now unavailable to us. I was a pure mess.

Early one morning—it was dark, everyone asleep—I woke to the sight of my father standing at the bottom of the bed. He had died while John and I were living in Florida, and we had made that fiasco of a move because of his and my mother's encouragement. That morning, appearing deeply distressed, Dad said, "Sorry, Perk," and quickly disappeared through our closed bedroom door.

I shook John awake telling him what I'd seen, and then flew out of the room looking for my father.

Never having heard of such a thing, I was shocked, and not the least bit happy to have seen this beloved person looking healthy again, wearing his gardening clothes (gardening had been his passion), and, even after death, concerned about my happiness, or rather my unhappiness. I was terrified. I thought I was losing my mind.

A few weeks later a woman I barely knew handed me a book by Thomas Sugrue titled, There Is a River, "You're always reading," she said, "I think you'll like this." It was (is) a biography of Edgar Cayce, a psychic who in trance gave accurate information about people's health or behavior (he spoke of "entities" gaining, or losing in a lifetime). Having been firmly raised in the Catholic tradition, I found it interesting, but of course unbelievable.

Yet a year later I saw a paperback copy of the book, and

impulsively, unthinkingly, bought it. A second reading instilled in me a belief that we are on earth to learn to love a little more perfectly. I didn't believe it was possible, though, to *learn* to love—it's just an emotion, isn't it? Love?

But for awhile that was my prayer: "Please help me to love, please help me..." because John had become deeply depressed that year, and even when we moved out of the four-room apartment, and were living in my mother-in-law's large house, which delighted me, I was not happy with my life in a hundred different ways, and was irritable, impatient, definitely *un*loving.

For awhile I read every metaphysical book I could get my hands on. Some made me laugh. Some made me think. Many offered anecdotal confirmation of my experience the morning my dead father appeared.

I don't try to explain that appearance, nor John's apparition years later—you can call it hallucination, call it imagination, call it a dream; but as Ludwig Wittgenstein said, "Call it a dream, it does not change anything."

I changed, though. That visit from my father opened my mind, or at least began to, and I still find it extraordinary that the Cayce book landed in my hands so soon afterwards.

A decade later, well after John had had a serious mental breakdown; after my daughter Catherine had become so ill that I was dizzy at the prospect of pain life might hold for her, she came home from a book store she had walked to one day between hospital stays, saying, "Here, Mom, I think you'll like this," and handing me a paperback book with an evil-looking, garish, purple cover—a book I *never* would have bought. And there were those words again: *I think you'll like this.*

I tore the cover off, replacing it with one I made from a plain file folder so I could carry it around inconspicuously, and read it, and read it again.

The book was (is) <u>The Nature of Personal Reality</u>, one of many by Jane Roberts, who in trance received a prodigious amount of philosophical information from a discarnate personality called Seth. And yes, I *know* how this sounds to those of conventional beliefs, But believe me when I tell you that had I *not* read that book I would never have been open to loving Sam, I would probably not have continued to love John, and I surely would not think, as I do, of my challenging life as a rich education.

In fact, I would likely be a bitter old woman with not a glimmer of a laugh line among the myriad wrinkles.

Make no mistake, I'd like to have had more of a formal education, I'd like to excel at *something*—painting, singing, cooking; I'd like to speak several languages fluently, as some of my friends do; and I will *always* wish the frightful twist in John's brain had not happened—the sudden release of some unknown chemical, the triggered gene, the thing that controlled him more than love.

Yet I could never wish that Sam had not entered my life. What irony that his brain too would become damaged, its tissue slowly becoming a gray macramé with holes where once was memory, with knots of delusion. God knows I was not happy when that began. But then, when that began I couldn't know that at the end of hard years, what would be left of Sam, and what he would give to me almost every minute of every day, was his essence which was the purist form of love.

"Are you happy, Perk?" Peg asked me almost thirty years ago. Now I ask myself that question, and I have to say that I don't feel happy at all when I hear that yet another person who shared a portion of my life is now a 'ghost'. I don't feel happy when a child, a stepchild, a grandchild has trouble, or even when I ache in these late years.

But when I think of becoming Sam's North Star near the end of his life; of being John's childhood sweetheart near the beginning of ours; when I think of daughters, to whom I am close, and loving stepdaughters, sons-in-law, grandchildren, a great-grandson— when I am *aware* of the abundance of love I've been given on this long journey of mine, and the guidance: the 'ghostly' experiences, the books handed to me when they were most needed, and other seemingly minor events that occurred at exactly the right moment—well what could my answer be but, "Yes," at my core I am a deeply contented woman.

And that is happiness.

BEAUTIFUL COUNTRY

That's the way things come clear.
All of a sudden. And then you realize
how obvious they've been all along.
Madeleine L'Engle

Life was full: noontime chamber music at Grace Church on Wednesdays; workshops and Sunday concerts at Wainwright House in nearby Rye, New York; long walks to the book store or around the Rockefeller Estate with friends.

In fact, I was out with two of my friends on the day that changed everything; we'd gone to Mario's on Arthur Street in the Bronx for lunch, and then to the bakery for cappuccinos and cookies. It was an afternoon of closeness and laughter. When I got home that day, I walked in the front door cheerily calling, "Hi, I brought us some homemade ravioli for dinner."

I could smell coffee brewing as I went through the living room to the kitchen, where Sam sat chatting with a man I didn't know. "Hi," I said again, smiling as I laid the package of ravioli on the counter and turned toward the men. Sam looked up, grinning as if he'd just won a million dollar lottery. "I put the house on the market!" he said gleefully.

"You what?!" I replied, shocked.

"Well, we talked about it," he said, looking uncertain now.

"Well yes, but..."

The man sitting with Sam was a realtor who looked more anxious by the minute. The conversation Sam referred to had occurred *years* before. At that time we agreed that we were happy right where we were. I didn't want to embarrass Sam (or maybe I didn't want to embarrass myself), by admitting to this realtor that we had never discussed putting the house on the market. He'd probably think: *What kind of a marriage do these guys have*, you know?

I should have said, *Bye now, we have to discuss this a bit more, we'll be in touch. Don't call us, we'll call you.* But I calmly poured myself a cup of coffee and sat down at the table listening to Sam expound upon his dream of living in the beautiful country (a dream I'd never heard about), my mind careening from one thing to another. I felt a flash of intense anger that without my knowledge, and while I was out, Sam had put *our* house on the market; then amazement, and, of all things, a kind of pleasure—that is, I was pleased that Sam had taken initiative, pleased to see him so animated, so enthused—I hadn't seen him like that in ages.

Then I heard, "Well, okay then."—and it was *my* voice.

I can't explain why I said "okay" without a moment's hesitation, why I never once thought *Hey this is crazy, Sam would never do something like this without talking it over, something's way off here.*

Maybe it was because I'm from an era when husbands made all major decisions, or because I'm an inveterate 'pleaser' and didn't want to stick a pin in Sam's bubble of newfound enthusiasm. More likely it was because I'd been studying the concept of nonattachment, and thought I could be that kind of person—spiritually enlightened, happy wherever I landed. If so, I had blinded myself to the fact that every move from a home I loved had left me feeling as lost as a child abandoned on a stranger's doorstep.

I'd said "Okay" to a major move as if I were agreeing to walk across the street to borrow an egg from a neighbor. It's incomprehensible.

But I think I know, now, why Sam called that realtor, why he was excited about moving to 'beautiful country', even gleeful, as if certain that I would be delighted by what he'd done:

We had been married ten years by then. I'd taken early retirement so Sam and I could travel, and we'd made dozens of road trips. Then we flew to Italy. I arranged for the trip with Cross-Culture tours, which specialized in small groups and visits to off-beat sites like Paestum—a once Greek city where massive Doric temples sat in the middle of a large grassy field, poppies and weeds sticking up here and there like cowlicks. Sam and I climbed on the temples, calling to each other from their open areas that were as high as the second floors of buildings.

There were no people there, other than our small group, no guards, no guides, no signs warning of danger, and I'd felt as free as when I was a child speeding my bicycle over uneven sidewalks, long hair streaming behind like a banner.

From our hotel window we could see Vesuvius looming against the sky across the bay of Naples. It was like being inside one of the books I'd read; like being in a dream—the days more golden, the air softer, the sunsets more beautiful.

At the end of every vacation, I'd looked forward to getting back home. At the end of two weeks in Italy, I wanted to stay. While packing, I talked about the freedom Id felt in Paestum; about centuries falling away like dominos when I walked in the steps of Caesar, Cicero, Claudius; about the cascades of flowers pouring over some balconies in Rome, laundry drying on others—I loved that. 'A story, a dream, and yet, "Life feels more real here," I told Sam, "I wish we could stay."

"We'll come back soon," Sam he said..

On the flight home, we discussed whether our next trip should be to Florence, with its works of art, or Venice, with its canals and gondolas. Once home, the discussion continued, becoming almost a form of amusement as we imagined ourselves in one city or the other. Then we fell into the peaceful rhythm of our daily life, and forgot about Italy altogether.

Three years later, on a calm Sunday afternoon, Sam and I were each enjoying a section of the *Times* when I read something about Italy (I can't remember what), and was instantly irritated.

"Well which is it going to be,, Florence or Venice?" I asked out of the blue, adding, in a voice sharp enough to cut through his intense concentration on his crossword puzzle, "I'm not the only one who can pick up a phone, you know!"

Sam didn't answer immediately, likely wondering what got in to me, and why I was suddenly upset over a trip to Italy; maybe he didn't even recall our long ago discussion, our indecision.

But then, "Either one," he responded mildly.

Engrossed in his puzzle, ignoring my irritation, he seemed to withdrew behind a wall of silence guaranteed to fuel the flames (my flames, that is, Sam remained cool)—I was in a nagging huff the rest of the afternoon, complaining that he made me feel invisible; that he just sat back and let me do everything; that he never took initiative anymore, and if he didn't, then we would *never* get back to Italy because *I* wasn't going to do all the planning!

That afternoon I had talked about the beauty of Italy as if beauty existed no other place on earth.

It's easy to see, now, that my ill will had nothing at all to do with procrastination over a trip to Italy, and everything to do with the fact that it had been months since I'd heard Sam say, "Hey, let's go..." *anywhere.* I had become the one suggesting a walk, a movie, lunch or dinner with friends. Sam was absent in a way that I couldn't put my finger on, and when I tried to discuss my concern he'd say, "Just tell me what you want and I'll do it!"

I wanted *him* to want. I wanted to hear him say, as he once would have: *Call that travel agent you like Honey, and get the ball rolling. We're not getting any younger.*

Less than two weeks after that spoiled Sunday afternoon I walked in our front door calling, "Hi, I'm home, I brought us some homemade ravioli for dinner," and found Sam chatting with a realtor about his dream of beautiful places, beautiful country.

And our house was on the market. And I had said "okay" like a mindless puppet.

Now I would leave another home I treasured, one built in 1929 that Sam and I had refurbished: new water-pipe from the street to the house, so the flow from faucets was a torrent instead of a trickle; new bathroom and kitchen; refinished oak floors; oak bookcases custom made to fit each side of the large double windows in the small den; an attractive deck added to the back. (Sam had even hired an architect so the design of the deck would complement the style of our small stucco home.) Our house sold in three short months, and we still had no idea where we wanted to settle. Just, "Someplace beautiful," Sam said.

Two of our daughters lived in Dutchess County with our three latest grandchildren, all infants. I knew I'd like being near them, and so decided we'd move someplace nearby. There are lovely Catskill Mountain views there, and real estate is far less expensive there than in Westchester, so we would buy our dream house, we agreed (with no idea what kind of house that was).

A few days a week, we drove north on the Taconic Parkway looking at homes in Pleasant Valley, Salt Point, Lagrangeville, and other small towns. Every house we looked at was too big, too small, the wrong layout—it was always something, and I was always relieved when we returned.

Once, as I walked through the front door of our Westchester home after a fruitless day of house hunting I said, "This is a *wonderful* house to come home to, isn't it?" I don't remember if Sam answered.

The date of the closing on our home was drawing near when, one cold, gray November day of house-hunting, we stopped for coffee with our Dutchess County realtor. That afternoon we had looked at house after house, none suitable as far as I was concerned. Suddenly the realtor looked at me, and with a hint of impatience said, "I don't think you *want* to move," or words to that effect.

Of course it was true—while filling carton after carton with pots, pans, china, and linens, incongruous, and unwelcome thoughts suggested the true state of affairs: *if I changed my mind we would have to unpack everything; if I changed my mind that young couple would be so disappointed.*

Yet I would not admit, even to myself, that I did not want to move, and the realtor's comment had greatly disturbed me. When we finished our coffee he said there was one more house he could show us, if we wanted to bother. "Well we might as well have a look," Sam said. I agreed. I just wanted the whole thing over.

It was past twilight when we stepped out of the realtor's car into air pleasantly scented with wood-smoke from someone's fireplace. The house was on a rise, with a long curved driveway bordered by low brick walls. Inside, lamplight reflected softly off of gold-tinted walls, three ceiling lights focused on a large raised fireplace where wood was set for a fire but unlit. There was little furniture as I recall, so the rooms looked spacious, as well as warm and inviting, and I was pleased.

But since I was easily intimidated, I've no doubt that the realtor's earlier comment, perceived by me as criticism, influenced my decision when I quickly said, "This is it."

Sam asked no questions, nor did he turn on water faucets, or flush toilets, or examine the oil-burner—all things he would normally do. I took no note of that, nor did I check anything in the house myself.

By then it was too dark to walk around outside, and, though I can't imagine not doing so, we didn't return the next morning to view the house and grounds in daylight. We made an offer on the spot, and it was accepted.

In December we moved into the nine room house that sat on an acre of gorgeous wooded land with a sparkling brook running through it,

I admired the long, nicely landscaped front lawn, but was dismayed when I saw the back yard, where several layers of frozen leaves covered uneven ground that sloped toward woods only four yards or so from the screened-in porch. I didn't like them being so close to the house, and come spring that small yard would look like it had had a bad haircut.

But I liked the large family room on the lower level, and the two rooms next to it, one for my desk, sewing table, bookcases, and our computer, the other still to be fitted with tools for Sam's home-improvement projects. (In our old home he had remodeled the bathroom, calling in a plumber only to certify that pipes were installed according to city code. When he discovered the new tub was inches short of the old one, he created a shelf to fit the empty space. I'd begged him to hire a tile-setter, but he'd refused, and even that work had been done perfectly.)

For this new workroom, Sam had purchased a dremel, a tool he called his "toy" with which he planned to carve small wooden chessmen. The box it came in was never opened. The tools we'd brought with us were never unpacked. The workroom never materialized.

Of course, as with any major move, there were a dizzying number of things to do: cords of wood were needed for our fireplace, food to stock the refrigerator and freezer, and we had to shop for a Christmas tree and unearth cartons containing decorations, and gifts we'd purchased in advance of the move, because with *impeccable* planning, the sale of both homes had closed on December 18th.

It seemed that the rooms on the main level of our large home were smaller than we remembered. Over and over we rearranged furniture the movers had placed exactly where I told them to. Finally Sam said he'd go crazy if I changed another thing; by then I wouldn't have cared if he chopped every stick of it for firewood. It was just one hectic day after another, and no time for personal interests, not even for reading. Flattened by fatigue, we fell asleep each night with the newspaper or book in our hands.

We were not happy to discover there was no town or village center in this new place. I quickly found my way to grocery stores, and shops strung along the nearby arterial, then learned how to get to the mall in Poughkeepsie.

But Sam had trouble. In Westchester, he had driven highways and byways the way geese fly south each winter, mindlessly, instinctively. If he took a wrong exit, as he was inclined to do (his sense of direction always slightly awry), he knew where he was and how to get where he wanted to be. Dutchess was another story: "It took me *two hours* to find my way back!" he exclaimed after his first lone trip to the supermarket ten minutes away (we had gone there constantly when we first moved in). His every excursion seemed to end with a version of *I thought I'd never find....*

At first, aware of Sam's weak sense of direction, I wasn't concerned. When he continued getting lost, sometimes for hours, and came home wrapped in a silence that screamed, *don't ask,* and when he stopped attempting to drive to the Poughkeepsie mall where things that fascinated him could be found: tools, gadgets, and especially computers, I began to worry—when we lived in Westchester, where Sam belonged to a computer club, he had browsed computer stores for hours, asking savvy young men questions, arriving home at the end of an afternoon happy and excited about all he'd learned.

Even more disturbing were Sam's lapses in judgment: trying to reheat a piece of pizza directly on the burner of the glass-top stove; insisting on going down the ice-covered slope in the back yard to get wood for the fireplace when there was plenty stacked in our attached garage. Once he slipped and fell on the ice, and hit his head, and suffered a headache that lasted the whole night long.

The following weeks I held my breath while he ventured over the ice for wood again and again. He wouldn't listen to reason. I was so angry I told him if he fell again and couldn't get up, I'd let him lie there until he froze.

Sometimes I wondered if his headstrong behavior was fueled by Alzheimer's, which his father had had. Sam might have been worried about that, too, and been afraid and fighting the only way he knew. I don't know. Neither of us would mention the disease, as if the very act of speaking its name would cast an evil spell.

The only thing I was certain of was that the big house we'd bought was far too much for us.

And it was strange, that house—there were mosquitoes inside in December and January (Sam hunted for their source in vain). Grasshoppers the size of hummingbirds appeared in the tub in the master bathroom (we couldn't figure out how they got in). Then one night in October when my daughter Catherine and I were sitting at the kitchen table visiting, she stopped mid-sentence and said with alarming urgency, "Don't move fast, Mom, there's a *huge* spider behind you!"

Until the spider moved, Catherine thought it was a rubber toy one of the grandchildren had left behind. With its legs out, it was almost the size of a saucer.

Forget *don't move fast!* When I saw it I got up and *ran,* Catherine with me, both of us colliding in the door to the hallway while yelling for Sam, who stumbled out of our bedroom sleep-fogged and surely expecting mayhem; he was probably relieved, at first—*Oh these hysterical women, it's only a spider.* But when he saw the spider, even he, who had a high regard for spiders and would never kill one, was leery of its size, its unfamiliar markings.

Was it poisonous? Were there more?

Sam quickly grabbed a Tupperware bowl, placed it upside down over the monster, and slid the cover underneath, nicely capturing it. But when he placed the bowl on the kitchen table and was trying to punch holes in the lid so the spider could breathe, the bowl flew out of his hands, careening through the air.

We must have looked like frenzied characters in a Charlie Chaplin film, running in every direction, Sam's arms reaching to catch the flying bowl (which he managed to do with the cover intact, thank God), and Catherine and I screaming our way out of the room.

"Brandy!" Sam said when the creature was finally secured.

As the adrenalin rush eased, we relaxed into laughter and jokes about "Freddy"—the name of a murderous character in a horror film, hence the name with which Catherine christened the creepy arachnid. "You could call this place Jurassic House," she added, referring to the winter mosquitoes, the oversized grasshoppers, and now, Freddy.

The next morning she drove Sam to a conservation center where Freddy was identified as a nursery web spider, a nonpoisonous species that lives near shallow water—*like the brook in our backyard*, I thought—and feeds on small fish. *Fish!*

Catherine and I still laugh when we talk about Freddy's appearance. But that night of horror and hilarity the anxiety I'd begun to experience as soon as we moved in, strengthened and never let go.

I didn't like mosquitoes mysteriously appearing in January, or giant grasshoppers in our bathtub, and the mere *thought* of spiders the size of saucers invading our kitchen chilled me to the bone. I watched for them constantly.

And it was a lonely place. I was used to neighbors who stopped in, who invited us for a cup of coffee, a glass of wine, even—on one cold snow-shoveling day—for a bowl of hot homemade soup.

It wasn't as if there were no other homes in our new

neighborhood, one autumn day Sam and I had walked down our long driveway to introduce ourselves to a young couple who were raking leaves in their front yard. They were courteous, but never asked *How are you doing? How do you like it here? Where were you living before?* Feeling awkward, Sam and I quickly left.

In all the months we lived there, not one person ever greeted us by name, not even our surname.

Increasingly, I longed for our old house in our old neighborhood where elderly Louise, who lived across the street, stopped in with her special "heavy-on-the-rum" rum balls, and Mary, next door, baked sugarless muffins for Catherine who's diabetic, and where I could walk a mile and be in a city full of people and stores and the big library I loved.

And I knew, I *knew,* that if I had just been honest with myself, and then told Sam that I didn't want to move, he would have accepted it and been his usual serene self. In fact, I'm quite sure that he would have forgotten all about his dream of living in beautiful country.

Instead, I had moved into that dream—the seed of it planted, I believe, on a Sunday afternoon when I talked incessantly about the beauty of Italy, and complained incessantly about Sam's lack of initiative. A dream born of a slip of his mind, a slight confusion, a desire to please, to give me the beauty I'd raved about.

And suddenly, I could hardly move at all, couldn't get out of bed without help, or bend to put socks and sneakers on, or lift my arms to shampoo my hair. When I had to walk, I walked with a painful, shuffling gait, like that of an ancient woman. Polymyalgia rheumatica (PMR) was diagnosed, and prednisone prescribed.

Within forty-eight hours I could move normally, and, with *fierce* intent, decided I had to get myself out of a place where, in spite being near loving family, and in spite of my desire to be a spiritually enlightened, unattached soul—I was homesick almost to death.

Sam was not happy, but agreed to put our new home on the market. It was a lovely place, really, and sold quickly.

Meanwhile, in Westchester the price of homes had skyrocketed, becoming unaffordable for us. But in a *Pennysaver* newsletter, I found a town house listed for sale in Pawling, New York, which is on the southeastern edge of Dutchess County near interstate 684. From there I could get to White Plains in about half an hour.

I took Catherine with me to look at it, made an offer to the owner, who accepted it, and then went home and told Sam, who reluctantly returned to view the house with the understanding that we would purchase it.

"I'll feel like I'm living in a birdcage," he said when he first laid eyes on the town house complex.

But he didn't object to the move; sadly, it was the first time I wouldn't have listened even if he had raised objections, for I was fairly sure Alzheimer's had begun its stealthy claim on Sam's brain.

Yet, in Pawling he would seem fine, we would walk around the village holding hands; we would make lifetime friends; we would watch the sun sink behind the far off mountains, in a sky so red you'd think it couldn't be real.

It is beautiful country, Pawling.

THE GROUND BENEATH MY FEET

Who has not sat before his own heart's curtain?
It lifts: and the scenery is falling apart.
Rainer Maria Rilke

As we turned into the cul-de-sac where our new town home in Pawling, New York, sat empty, waiting, I could understand why Sam, dreading this move, had said, "I'll feel like I'm living in a bird cage." At the time, puzzled by his comment, I'd ignored it. But now straight ahead was a row of five connected homes, on each side a row of five more, and I recalled Sam once telling me about colonies of Purple Martins, birds who prefer to nest in apartment-like dwellings. *That's the bird cage he was thinking of,* I realized, but I said nothing.

Better not to remind him, since I was the one who had insisted we sell the big house on an acre of land, that we had lived in for only fifteen months. Sam was still morose. But our new town home was a large end-unit, with windows on three sides, I hoped he'd soon feel as if he were still living in a private, unattached house.

It was a sunny day, exceptionally warm for March; we were dropping off cartons of books, a coffee machine, a small lamp, and linens and clothes enough for a few days. That evening, our sons-in-law, David and Michael, would bring our bed-frame, box spring, and mattress, and Sam and I would camp in our unit until the moving company we'd hired brought the rest of our belongings. (I can't remember the reason for that interim, nor do I remember closing on either property).

We looked terrible, both of us wearing dirty worn-out jeans, and sweatshirts that looked as if we'd slept in them. Sam was unshaven, his wild, iron-gray curls springing every which way, his eyes baggy and bloodshot. My hair, beginning to gray, was equally unkempt, my eyes surely as red; we were as worn out as the clothes on our backs; we must have looked like aging vagrants to the young man who appeared from one of the homes on the side row.

He introduced himself as Mike, chatted with us a minute or two, probably to confirm that we were there legitimately, and then proceeded to help us carry in the odd assortment of boxes we'd brought. When his wife, pregnant with her second child, joined us, he introduced us to her, too. They were Mike and Lisa, two friendly young people who told us they were glad we were going to be their neighbors.

"See Sam? It's going to be wonderful here," I said as soon as we were alone.

Sam, though genial by nature and obviously pleased at the warm welcome we had received, didn't respond. It was his way when he was angry or upset: a rock wall of silence.

"For Pete's sake! You could at least give this place a chance!" I yelled (but quietly, because we had opened all the windows. I can actually yell in a whisper, though it's far less satisfying.)

Sam was pouting, but I was joyful, I'd been starved for warm and friendly neighbors. Walking around the spacious town home I liked everything I saw—the huge master bedroom and bath on the main level; the upstairs bedroom and bath where my daughter Catherine, plagued by complications of diabetes, and staying with us, could have her own space; the good size basement we would later finish; and the light—in that season every room was flooded with light.

When we woke up the next morning, Sam seemed flooded with light, too, his usual good nature magically restored. He sang in the shower, hugged me good morning, told me to hurry up and get dressed so we could look around.

In the village, we parked in front of a small bakery and went in for coffee and muffins. The bakery is part of a fine restaurant called McKinney and Doyle. For the three days that we were alone (Catherine staying with Laura and Dave until we were properly moved in), we went to bed early, rose early, headed for the bakery for breakfast, and then explored the small village, enthralled.

It was as if we'd fallen fifty years back in time: there was a small library in a house, a small post office, small shops, including The Book Cove which we browsed (and where we would later join a writer's group and develop life-long friendship with four of the writers). There was no stop-light, not even a STOP sign, but there was a railroad station where every two hours a train arrived on one track; Sam called it "The Toonerville Trolley."

It's like being on vacation," I said as Sam and I strolled around holding hands like we had years ago.

Those first mornings, when we went to the bakery, there was always the same man sitting on a bench outside of the shop, sipping from a tall cup of coffee. We would see him many more times, until the morning we saw only a full cup of coffee sitting in the middle of the bench. The man had died, and the coffee had been placed there in his memory. Pawling was that kind of place.

When we'd moved there, I was sure that Sam had Alzheimer's. Now, as often happened, I was unsure again, maybe in that big house he had felt as lost and depressed as I had; depression can wreak havoc with memory. Sam never spoke about his emotional state, so I wouldn't have known.

Our new neighbors certainly noticed nothing amiss; Dennis, who lived in our cul-de-sac, and was Sam's age, invited him to join the Pawling Rotary Club.

"Oh Sam, that's great!" I said, "You'll meet people, we'll make friends!"

"No, I'm not joining the Rotary, I can't, I won't fit in." he replied.

He told Dennis he was a psychologist, not a business man, confessing that he was afraid he'd have nothing to talk about with other Rotary members; that sounds insulting if you think about it, but Sam didn't mean it that way, and Dennis didn't take it that way, persisting until Sam agreed to go to just *one* meeting.

He joined that day, and soon was telling me about the interesting people he met, the presentations he heard.

When Tom, another neighbor and Rotary member, who was also editor of *The Cedar Valley Newsletter*, learned that Sam was a writer, ,Sam began writing articles and stories for the newsletter.

Then a woman I met at the Cedar Valley sewing group invited us to join the renowned Shakespeare Club that actor James Earl Jones belonged to (maybe still does). Sam, who loved anything Shakespearian, jumped at the invitation, but I declined—and for the silliest of reasons: the members were *old* (as if age were contagious).

The memories of a lovely luncheon with Shakespeare Club members, of a fine evening when we met a gracious James Earl Jones at a special event the club sponsored, are mine. All the hours Sam and I could have enjoyed together at regular meetings are lost to what was my hollow idea of youthfulness.

In Pawling we made friends more quickly than I ever have in my life, going with them to dinners, and parties, and trips to the summer theater in Connecticut. There were philosophy discussions at The Book Cove; our writer's group; my sewing group, and friendly neighbors all around us.

With Catherine's ongoing health crises, life was not worry-free, but she was happy, I was happy, and, unbelievably—considering how he had hated the thought of this move—Sam was happy and loving the town home he'd once seen as a confining cage.

'May you live in interesting times.

In Pawling, life was the interesting in the best sense of those words. But behind the curtain of our light, bright days, a problem hovered that I refused to think about, except when I was almost asleep when it rose to consciousness and claimed me. It was a problem that would make times interesting in the evil sense of that Chinese curse—'May you live in interesting times'.

The phone would ring and calamity would present itself. The calls were from my daughter Bonnie, and for years had been coming when she was in one kind of trouble or another. Now they were coming regularly.

Yet it was Catherine who I was most worried about that summer. She had developed so many complications from the diabetes she'd had since childhood that writing them all would look like a grocery list. Among them were gastroparesis, giant abscesses, a hand frozen into a claw (requiring several surgeries), and kidneys that had begun to show signs of damage. Her endocrinologist at the Westchester County Medical Center had placed her name on the list for a pancreas transplant.

Bonnie, well worrying about Bonnie had been constant—and a constant irritant—for so long that anxiety for her well-being was old hat, background noise, life as usual. Her illness was alcoholism, and her tears, anxiety, anger, and despair traveled through the ether at any hour of the day or night from wherever she was: at home, or in bars, psych wards, rehabs.

Once when she called and was drunk, I'd yelled, "No one can help you when you won't help yourself!" and slammed the receiver down. But of course she called back. Usually I just listened. Or pleaded.

In October, Bonnie called to tell us she was in the hospital again, and this time had been diagnosed with bipolar illness. *Of course*, I thought, *those mood swings*! For years there had been mood swings. Oh my God, with the right medicine…!

For the first time in a long time, I had hope. Sam, Catherine, and I drove to Pennsylvania to see her, and for the first time she was hopeful, too.

Near the end of November, Bonnie spent a long weekend with us in Pawling. Laura and Dave had moved into a town home on our cul-de-sac. When Bonnie, wearing only her plaid flannel pajamas, walked back and forth between their home and ours with Sean, Laura's new baby son, I was embarrassed for about two seconds, then laughed—she could have walked around the whole town house community, the whole village, in her pajamas, and I wouldn't have cared—she was with us, and sober, and happy. She sang lullabies to Sean. I have that: the sight of her cradling Sean, the sound of her voice singing to him, her laughter.

Sometime after the new year, maybe during the New Year's

Eve celebrations, Bonnie stopped taking her medicine. It made her feel flat, she said, made her hands tremble so that she couldn't crochet—a hobby that filled hours that seemed empty to her. (Kent, her ex-husband, of course had custody of the children.) She began drinking again. Again there were DUI's (Driving Under the Influence), there were delusions—a cop was out to get her; an assassin had her on his hit list.

Visits with her children were reduced to a couple of hours a week with supervision. Phone calls became frequent, and frantic, and finally arrived from a Pennsylvania jail where Bonnie had been arrested for public drunkenness and lewd behavior. We wouldn't pay bail. At least in jail she was sober, and safe.

Bonnie had met many of our friends when she visited us the previous November, so when I put together a small package for her (a book, candy, little things), I drove to a post office in another town to mail it, wanting no one in our new community to learn that she was in jail.

The package was returned. Our mailman left it on our doorstep while we were out, the name of the jail stamped on its front in bright red ink with, 'No Packages Aloud' [sic]. We laughed, Bonnie, too, when I told her. What else can you do?

One night the Westchester hospital called with news that they had a pancreas that was a match for Catherine. Neither she, nor Sam, nor I had eyes for night driving, so around 2 A.M. Beth, my youngest, sped us down the Saw Mill River Parkway where dozens of deer were grazing on the grass verge of each lane. In no time we realized Beth's night-vision was as bad as ours.

"Oh God," Catherine joked, "Slow down, Beth, I'm supposed to be a recipient, not a goner, I mean doner." Again we laughed (a superb defense, that).

The hospital-run was a false alarm, the pancreas not usable after all, but it primed us to want to stay near home, so we didn't go to Bonnie's trial when it came up. Instead I wrote to the judge telling him that she suffered from severe mental illness, as well as alcoholism; that normally she would not behave in such a manner, that she would never deliberately hurt a soul. All of which was true: sober, she was considerate and caring.

The judge must have been a compassionate man because instead of prison, Bonnie was sent to Charter Cove, on New Beginner's Road, in Williamsburg, Pennsylvania, where there were programs designed to instill confidence and increase self-esteem.

Packages were allowed. Catherine and I went to Ames and bought deodorant, soap, washcloths, shampoo, a blue denim shirt with ruffles down the front that we knew Bonnie would love, shorts, tee-shirts, undies; we added a couple of our paperbacks and sent the small carton off.

While she was at Charter Cove, Bonnie called me every week. I can still hear her happy, excited voice:

"Mom, I walked five miles today!"

"Mom, I jumped off a cliff into a net the other guys were holding. I did it, Mom!"

"I love it here, Mom, I feel like a kid at summer camp."

And an occasional, "Oh mercy me, what a pity-party I had today."

She was beginning to trust herself, she told me, and of course she attended AA (Alcoholics Anonymous) meetings, which were mandatory.

Released at the end of June, she returned to the apartment she had lived in prior to her arrest.

On July 3rd Kent, my kind ex-son-in-law, brought my grandchildren to Pawling for a visit.

Bonnie was on probation and couldn't have left Pennsylvania even if she and Kent had not divorced, but she called that afternoon. "I'm so glad Kent brought the kids to see you," she said, sounding wonderful. She told me she was doing great, taking her medicine, and had joined an AA group in her area. We had already said goodbye when she added—with such depth of feeling that her words brought tears to my eyes, "And Mom? I *love you,* Mom."

It had been more than a month since the Medical Center called with a pancreas for Catherine, but on July 8th the phone finally rang at 6:30 A.M. Sam was already up and making coffee. We had no cell phones then, just one tethered to the wall in the kitchen, another by our bed where I still was. I grabbed the receiver, eager to hear, "We've got a match, bring her in."

But it wasn't a doctor or nurse on the line, it was a pastor. He was calling from a hospital in Lehigh Valley, Pennsylvania. For a moment I was utterly confused, then he asked, "Is someone with you?"

And I knew Bonnie was gone; he didn't have to say another word.

Sam was by my side as soon as I cried, "No!" and held me a long time, it seems to me now, until I'd calmed. Catherine heard me and came downstairs crying. I guess she called Laura, for suddenly Laura was there, too. When I got hold of myself, I called Beth—or maybe Laura or Catherine did—I don't know who did what, really, though probably Sam called Holly and Heather, my stepdaughters.

Bonnie was kept on life-support until her sisters and I got to Pennsylvania to say our goodbyes. Sam offered to stay home and take care of the dog, and I was glad. Truthfully, I wanted to be at Bonnie's side with only her sisters, who had known her all their lives, as Sam had not. But I was glad when Kent came to the hospital; he was as sorrowful as we were.

Later I would grow resentful that Sam had not insisted on coming with me, or at least argued the point, as I would have done if it had been either of my stepdaughters, but not then, not at all.

I donated those of Bonnie's organs that were useable, had her ashes sent home, arranged a one day wake, and a Mass for her in the local church the next morning. (Though a Mass of the Resurrection was not permitted for my soul-sick child, the Catholic Church being less forgiving than God.)

Family flew or drove in from all over the country: my two sisters and brother-in-law, Sam's sister, many of Bonnie's cousins. And even though we had lived in Pawling only sixteen months, friends and neighbors filled the funeral home, and church.

At home, when refreshments were on the table for everybody to help themselves, I stepped outside for a moment with my brother-in-law Charles, who had gone for a breath of air and was sitting on the front steps.

Suddenly, we saw a slice of rainbow—just a slice, as if it had been cleanly cut from the whole arc. It was so bright it looked as if it were crayoned against the vivid blue by a child's hand. Astonished, I caught my breath. Bonnie loved rainbows, and I'd never heard of one appearing in a perfectly clear sky.

"It's a sky-bow," Charles, who was a scientist, explained,

"Sometimes ice-crystals form way up in the atmosphere and the sun catches them." He looked at me then and said, "That doesn't make it any less a miracle."

Two weeks later the Medical Center called for Catherine, and another family began grieving for another child, a son only seventeen years old, whose pancreas became Catherine's, her surgery successful.

Sam was delighted for her, but was otherwise imperturbable during the aftermath of Bonnie's death and Catherine's transplant. When home, he seemed couched in the comfort of his *Times*, or science-magazine articles, or the televised news.

Possibly he felt helpless and therefore withdrew from my grief and anxiety, but maybe, (and I wondered about this even then), maybe his dispassion was caused by Alzheimer's. I didn't care. Increasingly resentful I behaved normally while ice formed on every word I spoke. Sam didn't notice. Sometimes I felt achingly alone.

It is terrible to be the mother of a child who commits suicide; you feel responsible, you feel you have failed, you feel like a pariah who doesn't belong with all those normal mothers (at least that's how I felt).

But right before Catherine's transplant, I forced myself to walk over to the club house sewing group where a kind woman, whom I hardly knew, leaned toward me and whispered, "We had the same thing happen in my family."

Another neighbor came often with cookies, and still another stopped in every week to sit with us at the kitchen table, sip coffee, chat, and to tell me that after Mass on Sunday he'd lit a candle for Bonnie's soul, and for Catherine's recovery.

When I was numb, undone, exposed, adrift, these people, whom I had known scarcely more than a year, were the ground beneath my feet.

It was that kind of place, Pawling.

YOUR SON, MY DAUGHTER

At Days end
all our footsteps are added up
to see how near
W. S. Merwin, "Lost People"

I'll call him David, your son. He may have been Michael or Jack, Lamont, or Zoran, Ahmed or Aaron, but I like the name David, so that's what I'll call him. I hope you don't mind. If I write "your son" over and over, it puts him at a remove that I do not feel.

You must have waited for hours that Saturday in 1999, just as my husband and I waited, to hear *All is well, the surgery is over, and was accomplished without incident, and all is well.* As it was for my daughter Catherine..

When her doctor told us about David, that he was only seventeen and had died during an elective surgical procedure, I cringed, imagining the stunning shock you surely felt when you learned he would never again come home. My daughter's surgery was elective, too, and I never once considered that possible outcome.

I am in awe that in your stricken state you were able to consider donating David's vital organs, his heart, lungs, liver, kidneys, corneas, and pancreas. Catherine received the priceless gift of his pancreas that day, July 24th, her thirty-seventh birthday.

The transplant of Davis's pancreas (sans liver or kidney), was the first of that kind ever done at the Westchester County Medical Center in Valhalla, New York, and was therefore a noteworthy event widely covered by local media. Doctor L., who performed the surgery, told us David had died in a New York hospital, so perhaps you read some of the articles.

At the time I asked for your name and address so I could extend our gratitude for your incomparable gift, and condolence for your terrible loss, but of course that information was confidential. Dr. L. told me to write my letter, and he'd see that you received it, but I never did. I so regret that.

But now I would like to tell you about Catherine—why she needed the gift of David's pancreas, and what has happened since she received it.

On another July day, thirty years before, I was reading at a lakeside beach one morning when I looked up and was suddenly aware that Catherine was all bones. I remember hollering at her for drinking most of the Kool-Aid before her three sisters had had a sip, and I knew diabetes causes excessive thirst, but it was her skeletal body that grabbed my attention, how could she be so thin when she ate *all the time*?

My heart seized for a second, then I reclaimed the peace of that tranquil day—the lake had the sheen of polished glass, except near shore where the children played. I watched Catherine laughing, splashing water at her sisters, swimming away when they splashed her back, and told myself she was fine.

We were vacationing in a rustic cottage on Lake Ninevah in Vermont, no television, no telephone, but a great stone fireplace for roaring fires on chill nights; a private lakeside beach and dock; a canoe, a row boat, and games, cards, and a ton of books we'd lugged from home, along with the linens.

Catherine's ninth birthday arrived that week. We had brought with us her presents, a cake-mix, candles, cupcake papers, and more M&Ms then needed to fill the paper cup I placed by each plate. I baked the cake while our older girls, Laura and Bonnie, kept an eye on Catherine and little Beth at the lake.

I remember putting black-eyed Susans in a butter-yellow teapot to add cheer to the table, and calling the girls in, remember Catherine's father walking in, as I was about to put the cake out, with two pints of half-melted ice cream from the country store, that we had to gobble immediately because the freezer compartment in the refrigerator held only a tray of ice cubes. Because it was a day of celebration, our girls were allowed to nibble the extra candy all afternoon.

The next morning, when Catherine got out of bed her legs folded under her like a puppet whose strings came loose.

With no telephone, no knowledge of where the closest hospital was, and no one to ask, we threw everything into suitcases and boxes and bags, and headed for home—a six hour drive with Catherine curled in the back of our station wagon wanting only to sleep. "Wake her up! Wake her up!" I kept yelling at her sisters, afraid that she was dying.

We made the trip in record time, dropped Beth and the older girls at the house, and took off for the hospital emergency room. For some reason I thought that Catherine had leukemia, so it was with relief that I heard her diagnosis: Type 1 diabetes.

It's only diabetes, I thought. *Insulin! Life!* But why, I wondered, did the doctor seem so sad when he gave us that news?

I didn't know that only about 5% of all diabetics are Type 1, and that for many of these it is extremely difficult to control the disease. I didn't know that.

But I remember feeling sorrow when I stuck her thin arm with the needle full of insulin every morning; I remember thinking diabetes was like a thousand cuts no Band-aid could cover—the daily needle, the "No you can't eat this," "No you can't have that," "Yes, you can have some, but only a little."

In those days, Catherine was good about the strict dietary restrictions, likely fearing that her legs would again refuse to carry her if she wasn't. And yet every morning her urine test, the only kind available at that time, flared to a violent orange, indicating high sugar in her blood, *very* high.

The other extreme, too *low* blood-sugar (an insulin reaction), can lead to death. On too many occasions Catherine was rushed to the emergency room because, while climbing the hill behind the house, or running around the neighborhood, she hadn't felt an incipient insulin reaction. "She's a 'brittle diabetic' her doctor told us, and gave her permission to carry small sugar cubes, with the admonition that she try to be aware of how her body felt when her blood-sugar was falling.

It didn't always help. There was still the early morning when she collapsed and lay unconscious on the kitchen floor while reaching in the refrigerator for orange juice—a quick glucose-fix, but too late for that severe insulin reaction. An ambulance that day. A race to the hospital. Panic. She was ten when that happened.

When she was sixteen, I found empty Scooter-Pie boxes under her bed. That year, and probably when she was fifteen, and surely when she was seventeen, and eighteen, dietary caution was discarded like a dress that no longer fit and furthermore was out of style. Consequences be damned, she would be like her buddies, congenially sharing pizza and beer, defiantly eating forbidden foods like those Scooter-Pies.

Then it was 1982, and your David was born. That year Catherine celebrated her twentieth birthday. By then she no longer ate with total disregard for her health, but already complications of her disease had begun, and for the next seventeen years she would ride an *un*-merry-go-round of hospital and doctors' visits:

An abscess on her head became a cyst the size of a baseball, requiring surgery and three days of hospitalization; ulcerations required debridement; retinopathy required eye-laser therapy; neuropathy caused painful tingling and burning in her feet; and gastroparesis interfered with digestion, making it even more difficult to control the diabetes. By the time of the transplant, her kidneys were beginning to fail. Too ill to work, she was living with her stepfather and me.

And then David became part of her life, and, little more than a week after Catherine received the gift of his pancreas, she was sitting before another birthday cake that she could eat without a twinge of guilt. My God, how I blessed you that day, not because she could eat cake, but because she could look forward to working again, to living on her own, and maybe completing the second half of college.

For me that day was uncanny, our whole family jubilantly singing Happy Birthday—and of course we were happy, we were thrilled for Catherine—but for moments, still smiling, I spun into a vortex of grief so intense I thought it would not let me go. You see, as much as Catherine now fought for life, her sister Bonnie, who suffered from bipolar disorder and alcoholism, courted death, succeeding in her dark quest just two weeks before Catherine's transplant.

If I had written that letter to you sixteen years ago, I would not have told you about Bonnie. The shock and grief I felt at her death may have been similar to what you experienced when David died, but I was also deeply ashamed—those thoughts: *I'm her mother, I should have been able to. . . .Why didn't I. . .*—You know?

When reporters asked about our family for articles they were writing about the transplant, I told them I had *three* daughters and two stepdaughters. "How could you leave Bonnie out?" Beth cried.

But I had also been afraid reporters would find out how Bonnie died (which was in Pennsylvania newspapers, and that I can still scarcely stand to think of), and I didn't want that grim story juxtaposed with those about your peerless gift, and the superb goal of the transplant team: a cure for diabetes.

Bonnie was kept on life-support at Lehigh Valley Medical Center in Pennsylvania until we arrived to say goodbye. As we stood next to her, Catherine, distraught, said, "Mom, I have this stark image in my mind of someone else going through this horror so that I can have a new pancreas. It's surreal."

While doctors discussed with us the harvesting of Bonnie's still usable organs—for of course we agreed to donate them—Catherine murmured "Surreal, surreal," over and over.

Two weeks later, Bonnie was a part of others whom we will never know, and David was a part of Catherine.

The dedicated transplant team at Westchester County Medical Center closely monitored Catherine's recovery, and for more than a year she was better than ever.

Sometimes I heard her singing to herself, as she had when she was a small, happy child.

Then her white blood cell count plummeted from the anti-rejection drugs, she became deathly ill, and was hospitalized with viral meningitis. Ten days later she was home, a line inserted into her neck (or somewhere near her neck; I remember worrying about it), so she could continue receiving intravenous therapy, a nurse checking in weekly.

It is amazing to me that throughout that ordeal Catherine remained cheerful—drawing cartoons of a stick figure moving the IV pole around, of her dog, of Sam lost in a crossword puzzle, of me knitting frantically.

Though she still had your son's good pancreas, soon after that infection,, gastroparesis (dormant since the transplant), reappeared with a vengeance, her digestive tract now causing unremitting bouts of vomiting.

There were medicines that helped; there was also an episode so unyielding that even water remained in her stomach less than a minute. Fearing dehydration, I called 911 that midnight, and held a pot near Catherine's head while the EMS team rushed her to the hospital almost an hour away from where we lived, for an IV sedative.

During that harrowing time I feared for Catherine's emotional stability, which had been exceedingly fragile during her teen years. Yet she remained essentially cheerful, joining a group of fellow-sufferers on the Internet who called themselves "Bellybusters," and reveling in their black humor.

One day, Catherine shut down the computer and told me about one of her Bellybuster friends who had died.

"Mom, I want to handle this with grace," she said.

"And just how does one do that while vomiting?" I asked in a lilting, joking tone.

"Why as quietly as possible, of course," she replied as quick as a wink and with an impish grin.

We laughed, and the subject was dropped.

Catherine had wanted to discuss how she hoped to die (we have talked about this since), and I had turned that important conversation away, refusing to consider that I might lose another daughter (though at night, always at night when I was in bed, that fear rose and all but strangled me).

By then, plastic baggies had become Catherine's ever-present accessory, and brown bags so the plastic ones would not be visible after she vomited into them. Somehow she kept going, urging me to do the same when I drove her anywhere and she couldn't stop retching.

The day of the massive 'The World Says No to War" peace march in New York City (a frigid February day in 2003), Catherine was determined to participate. On the hour and a half train ride from Pawling to Manhattan, one of her remarkable friends held her ski-jacket up in front of Catherine to give her a modicum of privacy, and not gross-out other passengers while she vomited (which was inevitable in a moving conveyance).

Weak, nibbling only plain bread, and taking small sips of water, Catherine managed to complete the peace march with us. I was never more proud of her.

Sometime after that, a gastric pacemaker was implanted in her abdomen, and mercifully the vomiting all but disappeared. Again she embarked on a reasonably active social life: concerts, trips to Manhattan to meet Bellybuster friends she had met on the web. But near the end of that happy year her body began to reject David's pancreas. Rejections can be prevented if caught early, but her transplant team had moved to medical centers in other states, somehow she fell through the cracks, and was soon diabetic again.

But—and this is so important, this is what I wish I could tell you—*merely four and a half years* with you're your son's working pancreas relieved my daughter of some of her most dreaded physical problems: her kidneys are no more compromised now then they were at the time of the transplant sixteen years ago; the ugly ulcerations and abscesses have never returned; hospitalization for thyroid removal, and out-patient surgery for cataract removals occurred without complications—and this is because of your astonishingly painful, priceless gift.

During the four and a half years that Catherine was recovering from the transplant—then recovered, and then ill again—she lived with her stepfather and me.

Soon after her body rejected David's pancreas, diabetic again, and with the threat of complications from the disease worsening—

with that same fierce determination that kept her going on the New York peace march—she impulsively rented a tiny apartment in an old house in Poughkeepsie, before she even had a job. We thought she was losing it, her step-dad and I, but she wanted to "have a life," as she put it. And by the grace of God, within a week she was hired for an office job right near her new home.

Several months later, finding it physically impossible to manage full-time work, she quickly found another job working part-time per diem, as a 'watcher' of elderly or emotionally compromised patients, walking a mile each way to Poughkeepsie's St. Francis Hospital.

Catherine lived in Poughkeepsie for five years, managing with minimal help (Christmas gifts, birthday gifts), and now lives in a Westchester apartment with her friend, and works part-time at an A & P store—again within walking distance—where she stands several hours a day, a few days a week, on ever more painful feet. "Fighting to stay in the world," she calls this.

Doctors are not as much a part of her life as they should be, because she is not eligible for Medic*aid,* and cannot afford insurance to supplement Medic*are*, which alone covers only 80 percent of doctors' bills (hardly enough for someone disabled by a chronic, progressive illness, complications from that illness, and an income only marginally above the poverty level).

Still, she perseveres through the many bumps and gullies in her path: the neuropathy and retinopathy, the exhaustion, the confusion when her blood sugar drops suddenly, as it still sometimes does.

"How do you keep going?" I asked her recently.

"I don't know, Mom," she said, and then, as if thinking aloud,

"You know, when Bonnie died I realized what it meant—what it *really meant*—that someone else had to die to give me a chance at life. And then it turned out to be such a *young* boy, you know?" She stopped a few seconds then added,

"I guess I want to honor him by living every minute I can as well as I'm able to."

And she does. And I believe it is your son's spirit that helps my daughter keep going, that sparks that determination of hers.

So David is always near, you see, and I thank you every day of my life for allowing him to become part of Catherine's. I wish I could tell you that.

But maybe—though I can't speak to you, and I can't write to you—maybe, *for just a second or so*, your heart will inexplicably lift as these words of mine travel into the Universe that connects us all, and maybe in that second you will sense the love I send to you, whom I have never met.

Yes. I would like that.

SECOND DAUGHTER

She sleeps still with her shoes under her pillow
Her feet—and often her spirit—itch to move on
To some promised land,
To milk and honey.
Gail Burlakoff,
"You Are Where You Are for a Reason"

The woman always loved trains, but that was only natural, her father was a railroad man who worked for the great New York Central Railroad. When she was four years old he guided her through the dark tunnels beneath Grand Central Terminal, a bright beam from the light attached to the brim of his cap, gilding their path. She thought he owned the railroad.

Years flew, as years do, and in no time the woman was mother to her own children and taking them for walks to the village railroad station to watch for the huge engine that would arrive pulling a dozen cars behind. Her daughter loved trains as much as she did. "Can we go to the trains today?" she'd beg, "Please mommy, please!"

This was the woman's second daughter, born of an unwanted pregnancy at the end of nine months of painful toothaches, treated with ice-packs, and oil of cloves, and no dentist because the stress might cause a threatened miscarriage to occur. The woman had taken hormone pills prescribed by her obstetrician to prevent this. In the beginning, she had lain in bed, the foot of it raised, while her mother cared for the small family. She had done everything she could to stay pregnant, afraid that God would damn her to hell if she didn't try to save the child she hadn't wanted.

During that pregnancy the woman's first daughter, a year and a half old, developed trachea-bronchitis, with croup so severe that with every breath she took her chest appeared to touch her backbone. Upon hearing a strange sound, her father had looked in on her to see her turning blue. He grabbed her from the crib, wrapped her in a blanket, handed her to the woman, and rushed to the hospital emergency room, the woman holding her sick baby to her breast all the way, and begging God over and over to take the unborn child she was carrying, and not this little one whom she already knew and loved.

The first daughter survived.

The second arrived four months later.

When the nurse handed the pink-swaddled infant with purple skin and a mass of black hair to the woman, she said, "There's been a mistake, that's *not* my baby, my babies are fair!"

The nurse insisted, so the woman accepted the child, counting tiny toes that looked like peas in a pod as she would do with each of her four babies, but falling in love later—much later—with this one.

They named her Bonnie. And the child was indeed a bonny lass, her black hair fell out within weeks, replaced with reddish fuzz, her purple hue faded to skin so fair it burned at the glance of a sunbeam, her eyes turned green and were graced with long lashes.

Bonnie would never know that the woman, her mother, had denied her, of course, but who can say what develops along with tiny toes, what inchoate knowledge might cause a child to feel less wanted, less special, less loved than her sisters, might haunt her with a feeling of being less-than-is-required, that lasts a lifetime.

You have to wonder.

It couldn't have helped that the woman was at odds with this second daughter throughout her childhood. The child was active, assertive, spontaneous, the woman thought her wild, bold, impulsive—bad qualities, she thought, for a girl.

This was the daughter who loved trains as much as the woman did—at first in the way that she loved the one in her favorite book, The Little Engine That Could. Then, as she grew older, for their excitement, their delicious, dangerous, power.

One summer day Bonnie, now thirteen, took her two little sisters for a walk. She returned flushed and exuberant, telling the woman they had gone to the village railroad station and stood just a foot from the edge of the platform while a train roared in.

You did what?" the woman shouted, "Don't you know how dangerous that is? You could have been killed, your sisters, too!"

"No, Mom, no," Bonnie said, "I held their hands tight, they laughed. It wasn't dangerous, it was exciting!"

Walks to the railroad station were forbidden after that, and the trains perhaps forgotten for awhile as Bonnie grew into her beauty, and dated, and danced, and scorched her lovely skin lying on sandy beaches with her boyfriend.

But for this child, the ups and downs of teenage years were mountain peaks and bottomless crevasses, Bonnie was either ecstatic or desolate, either spinning like a Sufi, or curled in bed, quilt to chin, refusing comfort. Worried, the woman took her to a doctor who determined that the child's extreme mood swings were caused by hypoglycemia. A specific diet would fix the problem.

Bonnie abandoned the diet, and her erratic moods continued, but now there was an explanation.

It was such a relief.

Soon Bonnie was in college, and then out of college and married to the boy she loved. She liked her job, liked being married, liked decorating her little apartment. She baked cakes when her mother visited.

The woman thought all was well until she heard of drinks and drugs and raucous scenes to which police were summoned. The marriage, of course, self-destructed.

There was a second marriage, and two infants that Bonnie presented to the woman like the holy gifts they are.

And there were years—many, many years—of rehabs and relapses, of psychiatric hospitalizations, and conflicting medical opinions, and, finally, the dual diagnoses of bipolar illness and alcoholism.

During those years Bonnie phoned the woman at work or at home at any hour of the day or night, her speech clear and sorrowful, or slurred, angry, delusional.

Increasingly, as if they had worn a track in her brain, she spoke of trains that sped through a crossing near her home—their beauty, their strength, their power—and her desire to board one and be carried far from the fear and failure her life had become.

And during those years of intoxication, Bonnie began playing games of chicken—lying on the railroad tracks at the crossing and jumping up at the last possible moment as the engine of a huge train bore down.

The woman's heart felt struck each time her daughter, in a high mood, gleefully told of winning against a train.

Her child was past forty before the woman dared to have a hope that was more than a faint glimmer. The last rehab—a special wilderness-training camp that a judge sentenced Bonnie to after she had been arrested for public drunkenness—was the best ever, Bonnie said.

When she telephoned her mother a few weeks later, she was still sober. "This is it," she said, "I'm taking my medicine, I've joined AA; I'm going to be fine."

They talked for a long time. They had already said goodbye to each other when, with deep feeling, Bonnie said, "And Mom? I *love you,* Mom."

Five days later, on a sultry summer morning, the phone rang at six-thirty. It was a pastor calling from the Lehigh Valley Medical Center in Pennsylvania. The woman's second daughter—now so beloved, so beloved—had lost her last bet with a train. The distraught engineer thought there was a pile of rags on the railroad tracks, until he saw them move.

They called it suicide.

You have to wonder.

HONEY AND THORNS

My grandfather always said that living
is like licking honey off a thorn
Louis Adamic

When I think of living in Cedar Valley in the small town of Pawling, New York, I think of light. The valley was wide, the Catskill Mountains, behind which the sun often descended in blazing glory, were far to the west, the Berkshires far to the east, our town home in the valley bright and sunny, except in winter when the sun, low in the sky, was early hidden from us by the town home across the way.

It is strange that in spite of losing my daughter Bonnie, in spite of her sister Catherine becoming deathly ill a year after having a pancreas transplant, in spite of Sam's Alzheimer's symptoms increasing—all of which happened during the eight years we lived in Pawling, I see myself, at least until sometime near the end of those years, surrounded by light—my husband still fully engaged in favored activities; good friends; our daughters and sons-in-law, grandchildren and parents-in-law, gathering together to celebrate birthdays or holidays.

For days at a time I would forget that Bonnie had died. When the memory surfaced it hit like a bucket of ice-water thrown in my face, I couldn't breathe, couldn't move at all for a second or so, then the brief paralysis would ease and I would get busy, always y, always needed, and glad for the need, for the distraction.

After Catherine's transplant, and after the gastroparesis (a complication of diabetes), reoccurred and became severe, I drove her back and forth to Westchester County Medical Center in Valhalla, New York so often it felt like a second home.

At first I brought books, then, knitting; that first Christmas, or the next, or the next, everyone—family, friends, even Rags, our dog—got scarves or hats or a wrap, simple items I had learned to knit at the Cedar Valley sewing group.

Catherine drew stick-figure cartoons to amuse herself; one shows me sitting on the edge of a chair, tongue out, eyes wild, frantically knitting. She titled it *Madame LaMom,* after Madame LaFarge in Dicken's *A Tale of Two Cities*, who knitted while heads fell. It felt a bit close to the bone, but made me laugh then, and makes me smile now

One morning, running late for Catherine's medical appointment and flying by the kitchen on our way to the front door, we saw Sam slicing a banana into his coffee.

"Sam! We exclaimed simultaneously.

Sam looked up, looked down at his coffee, looked up grinning at us, and said, "I thought I'd try something new."

I don't know if he was simply preoccupied with the hustle and bustle going on around him, or if it was an Alzheimer's moment; he was a marvelous confabulator, and joked about his illness until the time came when he was no longer aware that he was ill.

Catherine lightened the days, too. Walking down the long hospital corridor one time when she had dressed with special care—brand new jeans and a patterned shirt with a tee-shirt underneath that matched perfectly—I noticed that she was dead white. "You don't look so good," I said, quickly adding, "But it's only your face." She cracked up. (It's become one our "in" jokes: *It's only your face.*)

These foot-in-mouth comments of mine she calls "Momisms," like when I gave a sweater to her sister who had gained a little weight, and said, "Don't worry it will fit you, I got extra-large."

When Catherine's sight began weakening, she joked about walking into a pole in the supermarket, about tripping on an edge of sidewalk and falling flat on her face, about the time she kept trying to get into a locked car that had stopped, thinking it was her friend picking her up. (Imagine the poor woman-driver's panic!)

The sweet relief of humor—Sam's, Catherine's my inadvertent faux pas—eased days of unremitting stress, especially as the gastroparesis Catherine suffered began to cause daily, sometimes intense, vomiting.

When I drove her (sick all the way), to the Poughkeepsie Mall about an hour away from Pawling, we'd head for the food court where she could rest, and sip water and nibble saltines until she garnered strength enough to shop for clothes that fit her shrinking shape. I could not imagine how she kept going, though usually, once at our destination, the plastic bags she carried remained in her pocketbook for a time. She joked about those bags, too. Taking her there wasn't a chore; it was a day out, it was fun.

"I'm home; did you miss me?" I cheerfully called to Sam one day when Catherine and I arrived home from the mall.

"No, not at all," he replied, continuing to work on his crossword puzzle.

I was expecting to hear *I always miss you, Honey,* or something like that, and hardly spoke to him the rest of the evening.

He either ignored my suddenly glum mood, or didn't notice it. (Quite possibly, knowing Sam, it was his way of giving me freedom to devote as much time to Catherine as I needed to. But I'd wanted him to miss me, and wanted to hear him say it.)

When I contracted Lyme's disease (undiagnosed for almost a year), and was too ill to drive anyone anywhere, Medicaid, which Catherine was eligible for at that time, arranged for a driver to take her to and from her Westchester appointments.

Finally on medication, and feeling better, but still uneasy about driving (extreme vertigo having been one of Lyme's nasty symptoms), I decided to fulfill a social obligation; I would have a dinner party for our Pawling friends, twenty-one in all.

I've often had twenty-one for dinner, half adults, half children—daughters and stepdaughters bringing their specialties, the smallest grandchildren perched on chairs raised with a phone book, or cushions, the dining room table, with both leaves added, plus my sewing table and a bridge table, extending the seating from the dining area through the living room—almost twenty-five feet.

That was how I arranged seating for the formal dinner I planned. Instead of a few wash-and-wear tablecloths, or a plastic party-cloth, there was white damask spread from one end to the other; silverware polished to a lustrous glow; crystal water glasses and wine tumblers; good china serving dishes; flowers from the florist in the village. I am not good at formal dinners, not even small ones, so I was nervous, but confident by the day of the party, that everything was under control: the house immaculate, table ready, cakes baked.

I was preparing chicken cacciatore when the phone rang late in the afternoon. "Honey," Sam called, "Catherine needs you."

Medicaid had sent a new driver to take her to the medical center that day, one who became unhinged when she begged him *not* to stop driving as she gagged into her plastic bags. She had eaten no breakfast, other than the usual saltines and water (a bottle of which she carried with her to rinse her mouth). But whether she ate or not, constant retching was a given for Catherine, in any moving vehicle, and the driver refused to transport her home.

Since Sam was no longer a reliable driver, I dropped everything, drove to Westchester, got Catherine, and arrived back a frazzled wreck, with little more than an hour to finish cooking, and shower, and dress. In my haste I forgot to add garlic to my chicken dish, or added too little or something, it was the most tasteless meal I have ever served.

But Catherine was safely home, and my cheesecake was superb—and the chocolate cake, the wine, the marvelous restorative warm laughter with good friends.

In February of 2003, Catherine, as ill as she was, and her friend Laura and I went to Manhattan by train to join a march in protest of the threatened war against Iraq. Sam, who could no longer walk easily, stayed home. Hordes poured from various trains, carrying their fantastic hand-made signs, or picking up an already printed one from a group in the main terminal.

There were almost 500,000 jovial marchers (of course televised newscasts focused on police in riot gear herding *fifty* who had argued with them when not allowed to join the march late in the afternoon). But kindness and cheer prevailed among the policemen we met along the way, as well as among the large crowd: when we stopped for coffee at a standing-room-only Starbucks, someone insisted I take his seat; marchers sang songs and hymns, or danced, beat drums, blew horns. Spirits were high, this was happening all over the world—*millions* of people marching for peace. We were sure it would make a difference.

When in April the war against Iraq began with appalling "shock and awe," Sam, Catherine and I walked around in a haze of disbelief, stunned at America's crass act, stunned that while millions knew what was happening, other millions believed the mendacious propaganda in newspapers, on radios, on televisions.

Frightened people chatted while waiting on line in the supermarket. In a nearby town the glass window of a small 7-11 type store owned by a Muslim, shattered under a rain of rocks. It seemed there was no sweetness anywhere. Laughter died. Even in Pawling the light seemed to fade.

Then something wonderful happened for Catherine (and so for me, and for Sam's and our fast approaching future). Later that year, or perhaps at the beginning of 2004, a gastric pacemaker was implanted in her abdomen and the violent episodes of vomiting all but disappeared. Eager to work again, but unable to drive because retinopathy had affected her vision, she came with me one day when I drove down to Mt. Kisco (which is on the Metro-North railway line from Pawling), for my routine visit to a rheumatologist, so that she could submit applications for a job in the village.

I had noticed construction on top of the hill across from my doctor's office and assumed more medical offices were going up—Northern Westchester Hospital being only a block away—never bothering to read the very large sign at the bottom of the hill, which Catherine did as we drove past it.

"Mom, that's going to be affordable housing for seniors!" she told me, excited.

"Oh!" I said, feeling eager for a second, then, in a resigned tone: "It's probably only for Westchester residents."

"Well you could at least call and find out," Catherine retorted, annoyed at my instant negative response, "Here, I wrote down the number," she added, handing me a scrap of paper.

"Just put it in my pocketbook, will you?" I told her impatiently.

I was happy living in Pawling, but for a long time, especially after Catherine's transplant, when we so often drove to the medical center there, I'd sometimes *longed* to live in Westchester again. Catherine knew that.

Back home I forgot about affordable housing in Mt. Kisco, until a few days later when, figuring I had nothing to lose, I rummaged in my pocketbook for the scrap of paper Catherine had scribbled the phone number on, found it, called for information and learned that three, three-storey buildings were under construction—a condominium complex for seniors aged fifty-five or older.

As I recall, the conversation went something like this:

"Oh yes, a few units were indeed set aside for non-Westchester residents, unfortunately they're gone. But we're starting a waiting list, and you and your husband would be first on it, if you like."

"Yes!" I quickly said, "Please put our names down."

Mt. Kisco was familiar territory; I'd worked there for a year in 1981 when Sam was courting me. I liked the shops, the restaurants, the diner, the park.

When the saleswoman called back three days later I could hardly believe it. Buyers had changed their minds; they didn't want to live in a patio (basement), apartment. "Are you still interested?" she asked.

"Definitely!" I answered, and we scheduled an appointment to view the architect's plan at which time, if we wanted the apartment, we would leave a small deposit. If we changed our minds within two weeks, it would be refunded, if not it would be applied to the rest of the down payment and we'd sign the contract.

I said "Fine," to everything.

Then I had to tell Sam, who was not happy. In fact he was seething, which was unlike him.

"It's a crazy idea," he said. "Buy an apartment you've never seen? No way! It's crazy. Why do you want to move again, anyway? Aren't you sick of moving? Well I'm *not* going to move, I don't *want* to move, I like it here, I thought you did, too!"

"I do, oh I do," I said, "But...."

But to be near everything again—the medical center, a local hospital, White Plains—I wanted that.

Sam agreed to at least drive down to look at the apartment design with me. Unbelievably, he said nothing when I wrote a check for the deposit. Then we drove to the village, and strolled around looking in shops, stopping at Borders to buy a couple of books and grab a snack at the café before we left for home.

I asked Sam if he remembered driving from White Plains to Mt. Kisco in 1981 so that we could spend our lunch hours together, he said he did. And maybe it was true, or maybe he had forgotten all about his objections to the move, for that afternoon he agreed to use our savings for the rest of the down payment on the condominium. I was thrilled. And anxious, *extremely* anxious—I had talked Sam into buying, sight-unseen, a *basement* apartment that we both might hate.

Now we had to quickly sell our town home, or pay a large penalty to the condominium builders if we were not ready to move in by the deadline they gave. As soon as I signed the contract (Sam being ill that day), I put our place on the market.

Our Mt. Kisco condominium was not ready for occupancy for more than a year. During that time Catherine's body rejected the transplanted pancreas, and our frequent visits to the medical center in Westchester ended. To Sam's and my amazement, though diabetic again, she found a tiny apartment in Poughkeepsie, and a job. I was glad for her—what mother wouldn't be?

But suddenly our home felt empty. I missed Catherine; I missed Bonnie as if she had died yesterday, and not five years earlier, grieved her death for what might have been the first time, given that it had occurred so close to Catherine's transplant and ensuing medical problems.

Sam noticed, "Let's walk," he said uncharacteristically (his arthritic legs bothering him these days), "Come on, you'll feel better, let's walk to the village and get a bite to eat at McKinney's."

I walked with him that day, and others, but I couldn't seem to snap out of it. In the dark hours after midnight, I sat like carved ice, not writing, not reading, acutely aware that I was losing Sam, too, that Alzheimer's meant an insidious, unrelenting series of goodbyes.

Everyone was leaving: Bonnie, Catherine, Sam, even my

daughter Laura, and Dave, and the children, had moved away.

I looked at pictures on our living room wall—watercolors of birds, and one of a coyote that reminded Sam and me of a fox who had once graced us with his presence while we ate a picnic lunch, and thought, *they look ready to leave, too, to fly, to run.*

Sometimes I felt as if I were walking in a heavy fog, at the edge of a cliff; I began to panic about the move to Mt. Kisco.

"Sam, we have to talk about things, we have to plan while you can, while you're able to," I said one day. He ignored me.

"Sam!" I implored, *"Please talk to me,* this is not something that will go away, I need to know what you want me to do about this move, I need to know if you want your name on the contract. It isn't on it, you know, I signed it when you were sick that day. Talk to me!"

"It's *my* problem, not yours," he responded," speaking of the Alzheimer's.

"It's going to be *my* problem too," I said, "don't you care about *me?*"

"Of course I care, but what can I do about it? Just forget it, will you?" Sam said, aggravated, frustrated, and probably more afraid than I was, though he'd never show it.

I left the apartment in my name, but kept begging Sam to help me plan our future, especially as his losses increased, as Tom (whose newsletter Sam wrote for), asked, "What's up with Sam?" as Sam came home once, then again, with the mirror hanging off of the car and no idea how that had happened.

I took his car keys away then, and the credit card he kept leaving behind (kind store clerks calling to say they would hold it for him), and he let me take them—the keys, the credit card— sullen for a day or so, then fine again, perhaps somewhat relieved, or maybe just forgetting about them, I don't know.

The business with the car mirrors happened some time near the end of our years in Pawling, after I had taken Sam to the Burke Rehabilitation Hospital in White Plains for memory evaluation.

At Burke He'd had three hours of tests, both physical and written, the diagnosis, as I fully expected: dementia, probable Alzheimer's. On a scale of 1-30—1 being best, 30 worst—Sam was already down to 20. I'd hoped that with that definite diagnosis, he would at last talk to me about his fears, about mine, about our coming move to Mt. Kisco, about *anything* that directly affected us. But he continued to act as if nothing out of the ordinary were happening.

The doctor at Burke prescribed Namenda, a drug helpful for many suffering from Alzheimer's, which Sam took in addition to the Aricept our family doctor had prescribed years earlier.

Sam began saying,

"It's not a good day today."

"This is a bad day, this is a bad, bad, day."

"This is a dangerous, bad day."

His *Times* went untouched. He began walking in circles.

"I can't go to Rotary anymore! I can't go to Rotary!" he repeated over and over one particular day while walking back and forth the length of our apartment.

"It's alright, you don't have to go to Rotary if you don't want to," I said, trying to sooth him.

"What do you mean I can't go to Rotary? Why don't you want me to go to Rotary?" he suddenly screamed.

When he quieted some, I put my arms around him to try to comfort him. Still agitated, and incredibly distraught, he said,

"I'm sorry, I'm sorry, I just want to find a hole and sit in it; I want to just sit in a hole and stay there." (These are direct quotes from a journal I kept at the time.)

At first I thought, *this is how the rest of our life will be.* Then I thought of how completely unlike Sam this behavior was, and realized it had begun a few weeks after Namenda was added to his drug regimen. *It's the Namenda! It has to be*, I thought, and called the doctor at Burke Hospital, who first cut the dose in half, then discontinued it.

In no time Sam was his sweet, contented self, trying to complete crossword puzzles, reading the *Times,* and going to the Rotary Club, a friend now driving him. (I dread to think what happens to Alzheimer's residents having bad reactions to a drug in some nursing homes. No one would notice, least of all the patient.)

That Sam was himself again was a tremendous relief, since prospective buyers were regularly arriving to view our town home.

To save money (this was our third move in nine years), I was selling it with helpful advice from our attorney, but without a realtor. The market was booming, and it sold quickly, but the first sale fell through, and the closing on the second was delayed and delayed yet again as the purchaser tried to close on his other property.

Sam and I ate out, and, when home, sat in the living room, surrounded by boxes packed and ready to go, while my stomach tied itself in knots. I could hardly eat when we finally got to Mt. Kisco, the stress having caused a mild gastritis.

We moved on a November day in 2005 when the sky was leaden and dropping wet flakes of snow. Our new apartment, half the size of our Pawling home, was dark.

But in spring we would sit on our patio in front of a well-kept grassy lawn. And one year there would be dozens of daisies among the weeds on the small hill beyond the manicured grass.

Sam and I would make new friends. When Sam was able, we would walk to the nearby park, or drive to the village and stroll around holding hands just as we had those many years ago. I began to relax, less afraid now that we were near doctors, a hospital, help if help were needed.

Catherine was on her own, now, and reasonably well and happy. My grief for Bonnie eased. All of our children visited, as they always have, and though Sam was not pleased at living in an apartment, I was sure he'd settle in.

As for me, at last I was back in Westchester, not actually *home*—in my mind 'home' is always the White Plains house Sam and I lived in years ago—but close, very close. And that was sweet.

And In The Morning

Heron rising out of lake
like spirit dancing out of body

peregrine wings widespread
to lift, catch a high thermal, coast

osprey hovering over branch, fish
in claw against camouflage sky
                    and that
sly coyote, head down, eyes sharp,
left foot stealing forward in a stalk

poised for a breath, a heartbeat

Tonight I might wake to the
            purl of water
                falling from feathers
            whoosh of wings
                in displaced air
            scurry of paws
                across carpet and floor
and in the morning, wood frames
on wall before me, empty

ASTONISHMENTS

Alice laughed. "There's no use trying, she said.
One can't believe impossible things."
"I dare say you haven't had much practice,"
said the queen.
Lewis Carroll, *Through the Looking Glass*

This warm, sunny day in White Plains, we are sitting on a bench in front of Starbucks on Main Street, sipping coffee and watching fountains of water lift and curve from one to another of three rectangular, shallow ponds, as if dancing to music flowing from speakers mounted on the building.

Twenty-five years ago this block of land was empty, the earth lumpy and strewn with bits of debris from a demolished building, an old scarred bench at its edge so construction workers could take a break. We'd sat on that bench, Sam and I, while he begged me to keep seeing him even if marriage was out of the question. "We can have pockets of happiness," he'd said.

"Do you remember?" I ask him now, and am immediately sorry. In this pleasant moment I've no wish to remind Sam of the Alzheimer's whittling away at his memories.

"Of course I remember," he answers.

160

And maybe he does. It doesn't matter, really, today life seems normal, and it is enough to be sitting on this new bench, mesmerized and delighted by dancing fountains that were but a dream in someone's mind, when I was a dream in Sam's.

That summer we drove to White Plains again and again, old roots pulling me to the city where I had lived much of my life, and where I fell in love with Sam. It was only a twenty minute drive from the new Woodcrest Village condominium community we had moved to the previous autumn, and it was the place where I felt most at peace.

At home Sam was restless, incessantly complaining about living in an apartment: *apartments always run down; no one takes care of places like this; in ten years this place will be an eyesore.* The thoughts had lodged in his brain and would loop round and round, over and over, as sometimes happened since the Alzheimer's had progressed. It drove me crazy because it was I who had single-mindedly insisted on moving to this apartment.

Rescue arrived at the beginning of September when Woodcrest developers gave a buffet at the clubhouse to welcome residents, most of whom had moved to this new Mt. Kisco community from homes in town where they had lived lifetimes. The décor was pleasing, the food delicious. Sam and I helped ourselves, then walked over and sat across from a couple we'd not yet met and began chatting.

In this new community of ninety families, most, as I've said, from Mt. Kisco, the couple we'd spontaneously sat with were the only ones, a doctor and his wife, who had moved here from—of all places—Poughkeepsie, the city where Sam had grown up and gone to high school. (Tell me, what were the odds?). Sam's long-term memories were still largely available to him, so conversation was lively and the evening particularly enjoyable.

As we walked back to our apartment, Sam (whose father had been a doctor), said, "Well, this place is okay after all. Doctors have good judgment, you know."

"You mean I don't?" I retorted with light-hearted humor.

I never heard another complaint about having moved here.

It was also in September that I began taking Sam to a

philosophy discussion group we had enjoyed in Pawling, where we'd lived before moving here. Chronically ill with autoimmune problems, the trip to Pawling by train (since I no longer drove at night), was exhausting for me, but worth it—I say, "I took Sam," and of course it was good for him, but I needed that stimulating conversation even more than he did.

One night, realizing I had responded to a subject of special interest to me a bit too long, I said something like, *Oh, I'm sorry; I don't want to dominate the discussion.*

"Well then why don't you stop?" the leader, a professor whom I had admired and considered a friend, said. It felt like a slap.

"Okay, I will," I answered, and said not another word, fighting not to cry, not to alarm Sam, not to make a spectacle of myself.

It was so unlike this professor. What had I done? What had I said?

We would not return to the discussion group, and Sam, who had enjoyed those evenings as much as I had, would not remember to miss them.

With the taxing move to Mt. Kisco well behind us, I had thought myself emotionally strong. But when we got home that night I went into a tailspin way out of proportion to the professor's mild rebuke. For days I cried whenever I thought of it, hiding in the bathroom so Sam, who was now easily upset, would not see me.

Until then I hadn't minded taking Sam anyplace at all (or possibly I had, and had denied it), but now I noticed couples in our building going out to visit friends, to the mall, to dinner in the evening, the wives gracefully stepping into cars their husbands had driven to the front steps, and I wanted *my* husband to pick me up and take *me* someplace! It wasn't Sam's fault that he couldn't do that anymore, but neither was it mine, and a simmering resentment at all that had happened, and *was* happening, lodged in my heart like a low-grade fever.

In 2007, Sam's neurological muscular weakness increased: He fell walking home from the corner grocery and broke his arm; he fell on the front steps, hit his head, got a shiner and cheerfully said, "I look like I've been in a barroom brawl; he fell, but was unhurt, while walking across a field with my stepdaughter Holly and Zoran and the grandchildren; and he fell while stepping up a curb outside of Borders' book store as we were returning from dinner in town with Pawling friends.

He was badly bruised that time, and I, landing under him, sprained my right wrist, broke my right leg, and learned, to my dismay, that Sam's short-term memory was now short indeed, every morning, seeing me in a wheelchair (my balance too poor for crutches), he asked, "What *happened* to you?!"

Usually I said " Oh, I fell and broke my leg." Sometimes I reassured him, "Don't worry, I'll be better soon." "Don't worry, it doesn't hurt."

But once, feeling deprived when Sam was unable to get the wheelchair over the metal strips of the patio doors so I could sit outside on a gorgeous warm day, I told him in a flat voice, through clenched teeth: "You –fell–on–me!!!"

"Oh, say not so!" Sam said then, like one of his beloved Shakespearian characters might have done, downcast, and sorrowful.

Two minutes later he had forgotten and was in the kitchen getting cereal and making coffee, still able to do these things, able to make sandwiches for us, too, though the ham or cheese or mayonnaise or mustard, might disappear until I found it in a cabinet, a drawer, or sometimes in the freezer, where coffee filters were almost always found, and once, in winter, his hat.

One day, guilty and sorry over some mean thing I'd said (I don't remember what), and wanting to erase the sadness I'd drawn on Sam's face, I quickly said,

"Don't mind me, Sam. When I don't feel well I'm mean as a striped (pronounced stripe-ed), snake."

"I never saw a mean snake," he said, laughing out loud.

Another day I complained about something done or not done in the kitchen and he yelled: "It's my home, too!"

I was glad; it was such a normal response.

During that difficult time neighbors who were now friends, brought meals and drove me to the orthopedist; Laura, Catherine, and Beth came to bathe me; Holly took Sam on Saturday or Sunday so I'd have a day of peace, all of which was not easy for daughters to do in this age of liberated women who have responsible positions outside of the home.

My resentment at Sam (or at his Alzheimer's), had dissipated, but I welcomed the solitude of being completely alone when Holly took him for the day, feeling lonelier when he was with me.

Strangely, Sam had become exceedingly, unnaturally polite, and was annoyed with me if I wasn't. I was supposed to say, "Would you mind putting the light out, please?" Not, "Get that light, would you, Honey?" Of course when he corrected me he was unfailingly kind. But love?

One morning Sam came out of the bedroom and into the kitchen where, fully functional again, I was getting our breakfast:

"Good morning, Love," I said.

"Who told you to call me that?" Sam asked.

"Call you what?"

"Who told you to call me 'Love'?"

"Sam, I'm your *wife*, we've been married more than twenty years."

He paused, looked at me questioningly—probably wondering why this stranger, which I obviously was to him, was standing at the stove in her pajamas. Then he shrugged his shoulders and said,

"Well, I must love you then."

It was said in such a matter-of-fact way, as if he'd said: *Well, the sun is shining. Well, the newspaper is at the door*, that even though I was shocked, I burst out laughing.

I started keeping a journal again, needing to talk about my diminished life, and unwilling to burden our daughters, or my sisters (both much older than I and devastatingly ill), even though we were close.

And some time that year I joined a meditation group at the local hospital to help nourish my starved soul. I would set Sam's breakfast place, and leave cereal on the kitchen counter with a sticky note on which I had drawn a smiley-face with wings: "At meditation. Home soon, Love, M," it said. When I got home he would have eaten, and would be sitting in his favorite chair in the living room reading the *Times*. Until he wasn't.

Journal excerpts, 2007
- He may have trouble finding the measuring scoop or filters,

164

but Sam still makes good coffee! He brought me some. I am pleased, and he is pleased that I am pleased. How simple life seems at times. How simple and pleasant it is in this moment.

- I am ill, ill, ill, ill. Makes me sick.
- If I could be alone, no one to take care of …would I get better?
- I long for someone who can remember that I'm ill.
- At least Sam doesn't wander off (yesterday I wished he would!)
- Stopped for groceries after mediation today. Didn't get home 'til 3. Sam still in bed.

It seemed sudden, Sam's need to be gotten up, to be told to shower, shave, what to wear, when to eat. Arthritic legs kept him from wandering, so I could safely leave him for a few hours while I went for groceries, and if I had to go someplace for a whole day, say the eye doctor in New York, Holly came from work on her lunch hour to get Sam up and fed and settled in his chair.

Now I woke him around 10 or 11 A.M. He slept better mornings, likely exhausted from nocturnal roaming. At night I'd listen with trepidation when I heard him up, afraid he would go into the kitchen and turn on the stove.

Once, hearing him there, I hurriedly got up and asked, "Are you hungry, Sam?" (He was looking for the bathroom). Once I faked sleep while he stood at my bedroom door for God knows how long, at God knows what hour, until I finally asked, "Are you alright, Honey?" Then he said "Yes", and went back to bed. (I had moved into the guest room when my small book-light for reading in bed began to bother him, leaving both our bedroom doors open so I could hear).

And then, one day Sam didn't want to get up no matter how late in the morning it was.

So for both our sakes, I tried to set our days in place with a bit of cheer: "Rise and shine," I'd say, bright and smiling no matter how I felt, and he would answer, "No shine today," then I'd say, "Glow? Gleam? Twinkle? Shimmer?" And he'd play along, laughing.

It became a wake-up game he seemed to love. Sometimes he belted out a song he had probably sung with buddies when he was in the army, to the tune of *'Oh how I hate to get up in the morning':*

"Some day I'm going to murder the bugler,
someday they're going to find him dead,
I'll amputate his Revielle
and stomp upon him heavily,
then I'll spend the rest of my days in bed."

And one rare morning in 2008 he looked at me and said, "You are a pure joy," and I felt all the love he'd once had, I felt like he'd come home to me. But still:

Journal excerpts, 2008
- No inner resources left...what to get up for? (Snapped myself out of that!)
- I may not love Sam, but I care about him. I could not leave him and be happy... Oh I do love Sam, just so tired I can't feel anything.
- Today is our twenty-second anniversary. I didn't remind him. No cake.
- This morning when I woke Sam he said, "Oh, I didn't know where I was, and then I saw you." I melted.
- He's so locked up. How am I ever going to do this if he won't let me love him?

But a mind is a strange and unpredictable thing, or rather a brain, even a brain leaking memories like eyes leak tears. When I had fully accepted that to expect anything from Sam was an exercise in futility (it was around the time I was sick with a stomach virus and asked Sam for a glass of water, he filled the glass, and drank the water). And when, far less willingly, I had accepted that the Sam I loved was gone, and the love I longed for from him impossible, something amazing happened.

I don't know what, or why, or how, but I suspect some part of his brain, the self-protecting part that had so thoroughly guarded his inner self, his deepest thoughts and fears, was annihilated by the Alzheimer's he refused to acknowledge, even as his symptoms worsened.

I had once told Sam, "I love the way your mind works."

166

He couldn't possibly have remembered that, yet one summer evening he touched my arm as we were walking into the living room, and, looking worried, asked:

"How will you love me now?"

"I will love you *gladly*," I instinctively answered (wondering if I could).

He seemed relieved; it was as if the walls of Jericho had fallen, and his vulnerability and fear were fully exposed, and it was okay after all.

Then the corners of his mouth lifted, his eyes sparkled with merriment, and he said, "And I will love you *madly*."

It was a rhyme and a joke that became a nightly ritual, and it was Sam who began it, saying with a grin as I left to go to my own room at bedtime:

"I love you *madly*."

"And I love you *gladly*," I laughingly responded.

I refer to it as a nightly ritual, like our morning wake-up game. But it was far more than that; it was an affirmation of love said every single night for the two years we had left to us.

Affirmations are powerful when repeated daily for weeks, months, years—which might be why on Thanksgiving the following November, we fell into a day of romance as if we were still those middle-aged lovers who sat on that scarred bench in White Plains long before the fountains danced.

I had declined invitations from our daughters, telling them that we wanted to stay home and relax, and would have turkey at the diner. On Thanksgiving day I didn't even want to go to the diner, so I threw on jeans and a sweater and rummaged in the kitchen to see what I could scavenge for a meal.

There was a small chicken in the freezer, which I dropped into a pot of warm water to quickly thaw it; salad greens; Stovetop dressing; potatoes; a can of cranberry sauce (though I usually made fresh), and even left-over pumpkin pie I had bought a few days earlier when I stopped at a bakery on the way home from a medical apointment. Perfect. And easy.

While the chicken and potatoes baked, I put on CDs: *The Fantastics, Camelot*.

Then, in a holiday spirit, I set the table with china and candles and cloth napkins. Music filled the apartment. Our neighbor Dominick heard it and invited us over to spend the afternoon with him and his family, but our dinner was already cooking, so he left and returned with more CDs of songs from when I was a young child, and Sam a teenager. I don't remember the titles, but those words—*...Pistol packin' Mama, lay that pistol down..., Mares-eat-oats and does-eat-oats and little lambs-eat-ivy, a kid'll-eat-ivy, too, wouldn't you?*—erased the years, and Sam remembered most of the words and sang them with gusto.

Later I played some Sinatra, some Peggy Lee. Sam reached for me, and folded me in his arms, and we danced around the living room—awkwardly, two stiff old folks—but lovers again. That evening we listened to television: Chris Bott playing his trumpet as sweet as the angel Gabriel; Andre Boccelli singing "Like the stars in the sky, we are meant to shine." It was a day lifted clear out of ordinary time.

In sharp contrast, hours, and days were lifted out of ordinary time for others, too, lifted into a time of nightmare and heartbreak:

There had been a massacre in Mumbai, which used to be Bombay, and in my imagination was the mystical land of snake charmers, gurus, and other marvelous things. Terrorists had attacked seven hotels, more than a hundred had been killed; hostages had been taken.

And yet what I wrote in my journal that evening was: "What an absolutely perfect day."

Because that was my reality: a day when Sam and I danced, and held hands, and listened to exquisite music, a day I'd thought could never happen for us again.

In bed that night, I thought about the suffering souls in Mumbai, prayed for them, and prayed that some of the joyful energy vibrations of our exceptional day, Sam's and mine, had entered the energy of this sad and needful world.

There would still be times when I would scream to my journal, call myself stupid for choosing this crazy life of mine, stupid for dropping out of college to marry Sam. There would be times when

I'd want to tear my hair out.

But as impossible as it sounds, there would also be this—the most astonishing of all the light and dark astonishments in my life—during the coming dreaded years, I would fall in love with Sam all over again.

And Sam, even as Alzheimer's took more and more of his memories, would never forget to love me back.

THE BLUEST BIRD

The day was counting up its birds
And never got the answer wrong
Jules Supervielle

I had a Canary once, a bright yellow little bird that sang every morning as soon as I lifted the cover off of his cage. Mom didn't like it but at least she wasn't allergic to birds as she was to dogs and cats, so Dad, knowing I wanted a pet, brought it home for me. He enjoyed it as much as I did, laughing when a waltz played on the phonograph and Petey, as I called the bird, sang his heart out along with the music.

My father had shared his love of birds with me well before he brought Petey home, identifying and naming the robins on our lawn, the rose-breasted grosbeaks and red-winged blackbirds that flew over the wetlands across from our house, orioles and cardinals, sparrows and wrens, blue jays that made a nest in the eve of our porch and scolded us whenever we approached, until their eggs hatched. His pleasure in birds was contagious, so I began watching for various birds, and telling Dad, with growing pride, the names of those I had seen and identified while I was outside playing.

When I was eleven years old, my sister Dorothy and brother-in-law Charles gave me a *Birds of America* book for Christmas. It was great in both size and content: about 11x9x4 inches thick, beautifully bound, and with exquisite color plates of birds throughout. Probably Charles, a scientist and natural born teacher, thought of that gift; he would have wanted to encourage my interest in birds, and did. I intended to keep that book all my life, but after sixty years it disappeared in the chaos of moving to this apartment. (I hope I inadvertently donated it to the library at that time, along with many of my other books. I like to think of it on a shelf in that good place.)

In addition to that marvelous book, knowing of the pleasure I took in watching our winged companions Dorothy now and again gifted me with their likenesses—a lovely little porcelain bird sent when I was living in Florida and dreadfully homesick; a paper-mache duckling, old and battered now, and as dear as that worn Velveteen Rabbit that Margery Williams wrote about; a dove ornament for my Christmas tree. The last Christmas gift she sent was a large ornament without a bird but with the word JOY. She would give me that, too, if she could.

One long-ago year when I was seriously unhappy, two clear-blue-glass birds arrived in the mail, one tiny, one large. "They're Bluebirds of Happiness," Dorothy told me on the phone when I called her. "I want that for you." I keep them on a shelf with other mementos. Each time I see them my spirit lifts, as it's inclined to do when you remember that you're loved.

The Christmas Eve before her death, Dorothy's heart was so weak she had little breath, yet she asked her aide to place a telephone call to me. Worried about her, I'd tried to cut our conversation short but Dorothy wanted to talk, she wanted me to know she was looking forward to seeing our mom and dad, and Bill and Hank, her oldest sons who died many years ago. Near the end of our talk my sister—who was ten years old and the baby of the family until I arrived—gave me the best gift of all: "I'm so glad our parents had you," she said.

"I'm glad, too," I'd laughed, my throat tight with unshed tears. I had felt a happy kind of sorrow (is that possible?)—glad for the gift of her loving words, sad that she'd soon leave us, glad she would be free of that worn and bothersome body; I wished that for my older sister Jeanne, who had Parkinson's; I wished it for my husband Sam, who had Alzheimer's. I knew that their love would not die with them..

A month and a half later, Dorothy told her son John, "I don't want to die on Marian's birthday."

So she waited, and died the next day.

Charles, who was a brother to me, had died two years earlier. Because I'd been ill, I had missed his farewell, and because I'd been busy taking care of Sam, I hadn't visited Dorothy while she was ill. But when she died my daughters rallied around, Beth leaving work and coming immediately to organize travel plans to Illinois where Dorothy had lived her life, Catherine arranging to come to the funeral with me, Holly, with our littlest granddaughter Maya, taking care of Sam, and Laura taking over when Holly and her family had to leave for a prearranged trip.

Dorothy's funeral was wonderful—does that sound insane? But it was, because for all the tears shed, it was a celebration of her generous loving spirit, and—not least for me—because I found I could talk for hours and hours with my now middle-aged nephews and nieces whom I hadn't seen in years, I fell in love with all of them.

Then too, I was suddenly free. I was so used to being always with Sam and alert to his needs that I never even thought about it, and now this sudden heady freedom. So it was with a buoyant spirit that I left Illinois, bringing with me the warmth of renewed relationships with my sister's family, arriving home to the warmth of my own.

Two weeks later I woke feeling as if a sea of sorrow had engulfed me while I slept. The sense of closeness to far flung nephews and nieces that I'd had since the funeral was gone. (Would I ever see them again?) And Dorothy was gone, and I left behind like when I was little girl. Suddenly I was intensely aware of the fact that Sam, with Alzheimer's, and my sister Jeanne, immobilized by end-stage Parkinson's were in many ways already gone from me, too.

Desolate, full of tears, I hurried to the kitchen to set coffee to brew and try to get a hold of myself before I woke Sam.

I usually don't answer the phone early in the morning, but that day, moving around in a cloud of grief, when the phone rang I absentmindedly picked up the receiver, and then only half-listened to my chatty neighbor as I walked into the living room and opened the drapes in front of the patio doors.

No sun that morning, just gray sky, bare trees, dry weeds, brown grass. No blue jays or sparrows, no woodpecker hammering on the side of the oak tree on the hill, even the raucous crows were absent.

The barren world looked as drained of life as I felt.

Then a bird landed on the patio, stayed two or three seconds, and flew off.

"Oh!" I gasped.

"What's wrong? my neighbor on the telephone, who had been in the middle of a sentence, cried.

"Nothing, nothing," I told her, "It's just that this *beautiful* bird landed on my patio. It's gone already."

"My God, I thought you'd had a heart attack!" she exclaimed.

I tried to explain my outsized reaction to the common occurrence of a bird on the patio, but couldn't.

This bird was different. It was not a blue jay or an eastern bluebird—smaller than either, and bluer than both, it looked like a jewel, a dark blue sapphire. I had never seen one like it before, nor have I since, nor was I able to find a picture of it in my pocket-size *National Audubon Society Field Guide to North American Birds.*

Imagine—just two weeks after Dorothy's death, on a bleak and bitter February day when my spirit was darker than the wintry weather, and suddenly on my patio for a split second of time was the bluest bird I have *ever* seen.

What could it have been but a message from the sister who knew I loved birds and who had once, at a most difficult time of my life, sent me Bluebirds of Happiness.

You are loved, she was reminding me. *Be happy.*

173

TRIALS

From the palm of one hand now the rain falls.
From the other the grass grows. What can I tell you?
Vasko Popa

"I feel like I'm in prison," I'd told Sam's sister when I returned
from Illinois after my sister Dorothy died, "a comfortable prison,
but prison."

Yet life was really not that limited, I could leave Sam alone for
a couple of hours to grocery shop, or to go to my meditation group;
we got together with friends, enjoyed eating out, loved Borders
book store, where Sam would sit in the café, contentedly sipping
coffee, and munching on a bagel while reading a current issue of
the *Times* that I'd bought for him (a week old copy would have
been new to him). I would go upstairs, then, and browse through
books. They were still quite pleasant days.

A funny thing happened there one afternoon when he needed to
use the Men's Room and found it too late. Having had a slight
accident, he came up to me where I waited on line to pay for a
book and said, "Here," holding out his damp plaid under-shorts for
me to take care of.

"Put them in your pocket! Put them in your pocket!" I
whispered frantically, which he did, looking utterly bewildered.

On the way home I commented that the other customers on line must have gotten an unexpected thrill, and we laughed over it.

Sam laughed easily and often, even as his Alzheimer's losses increased, even when I was barely present to him for months, a state that began in May of that year, 2009, when I had a cataract removed from my left eye which is affected by Iridocorneal Endothelial Syndrome (ICE).

The disease had been under control for seventeen years, and I knew removal of the cataract might cause it to reoccur but took the risk, though not without trepidation. In fact, a few days before the operation I was suddenly enveloped in a black cloud of doom at the thought of it.—It was so sudden, so intense, that sense of doom, that I felt as if it were a warning, and almost cancelled the procedure, but instead told myself *you're just afraid, that's all; stop being irrational.*

The surgery went perfectly but the ICE reoccurred, the cornea becoming acutely painful as eye-pressure increased. Train trips to a specialist in Manhattan were constant, Catherine coming with me for support, Holly coming on her lunch hour to get Sam up, fed, and settled in his chair. When Catherine and I got home around 3 P.M. Sam would be dozing, sometimes holding the note I had pinned to the lampshade by his chair: "At the doctor's, home soon, Love, M."

I have no memory of our large family gathering at Christmas that year, though I know we had one. I only remember the pain in my eye reaching such a pitch while I was wrapping Christmas gifts that I had to stop and curl up on the couch, unable to look at the bright television screen, or read a book, or move my head. I remember asking my doctor (since there is no cure), to take the eye out. Oh my God, how I wanted it *gone!*

I remember dozens of eye drops a day, and a medication containing sulfa, which I am allergic to. It lowered eye-pressure (easing the pain), but made me so ill that I had to stop taking it on a Saturday in order to be well enough to drive Sam to White Plains for Wednesday or Thursday appointments at Burke Hospital Memory and Treatment Center in White Plains, where he was participating in a clinical drug trial for the treatment of Alzheimer's.

Sam occasionally looked at me sadly and said, "That eye is giving you grief, isn't it." But most of the time he sat in his chair unaware and contented. A blessing.

How did I manage to get Sam to Burke to be tested, and registered for the clinical trial at the end of 2009? How did I manage to do anything at all?

I have absolutely no idea. Without the help of our daughters, Beth and Laura, as well as Holly and Catherine, I think I'd have fallen apart completely.

The clinical trial at Burke began in January of 2010. I believe Sam was in the control group that received the actual drug, because we soon agreed (me, our family, our friends), that there was a subtle improvement in his condition: he seemed brighter, more alert.

But one chill, gray day—perhaps in February, perhaps March— I showered, slipped into jeans and a heavy sweater, put the coffee on, went to wake Sam, and stepped into time that soon resembled the stuff of nightmares:

"Rise and Shine, Honey," I said as usual that morning when I opened the blinds.

Instead of joining our morning game with "No shine today," Sam lay in bed staring at the ceiling.

"Come on, Honey, time to get up," I told him cheerfully, reaching into the closet for his bathrobe, and holding it out as I did every morning so he could easily slide his arthritic arms into the sleeves.

Without a word he got up, started slipping into his robe, then suddenly shrugged it off, and me with it, screaming, "Stop helping me! I want *Self* determination! *Self* determination!" banging his fist into the wall next to my head with each exclamation.

"You can have self determination, you can have whatever you want; what do you want for breakfast? Do you want poached eggs?" I said in a rush, quickly moving away from him.

The offer of what was once his favorite morning meal did not distract him, as I had expected it to. He followed me down the short hallway to the kitchen, hammering the wall all the way, and shouting "Self determination!" with such force and anger that I expected a neighbor to knock on our door, or even the police. I couldn't calm him, and he couldn't seem to calm himself; when we reached the kitchen he tried to, I think, gripping the edge of the counter and quietly mumbling "Self determination" through clenched teeth. But then he lifted a hand and began pounding the countertop.

Quickly, I telephoned Holly, sure that she could free Sam from his sudden fixation. When there was no answer, I called Catherine (they are the two daughters he saw most often), to my relief, she was at home. Walking away from Sam, I briefed her on what was happening, then called out in as merry voice as I could manage, "Sam, Cathy wants to say "Hi.""

He took the phone from me and began talking to her in his normal, warm manner, even chuckling once. And I relaxed. Until then I hadn't realized that I was shaking. Sam said goodbye to Catherine, hung up the phone, and, to my stunned amazement started banging the counter all over again, glaring at me, clearly enraged.

I got my coat and hurried out. I didn't care what happened to Sam, didn't care if he wandered outside into the middle of heavy traffic. All I wanted was to get away, and not only away from Sam, but from *everyone*: neighbors who must have heard the commotion, friends I often met in the village, everyone.

Disheveled, red-eyed, I ran out, drove to the nearby Target department store, and sat far back in the Starbucks section nursing a large cup of coffee, still shocked beyond thought except about what I might find when I got back home; which I finally did a couple of hours later, so afraid that I tip-toed through our unlocked front door.

In the kitchen, the coffee I had made earlier was untouched. In the living room, Sam huddled in his leather chair, the hood of his bathrobe pulled half over his face, no newspaper in his lap, the television silent. Not sure what he might do when he saw me, I walked in slowly and sat on the far end of the couch, saying nothing.

With no memory of how the day had begun, Sam knew *something* had happened, and could tell that I was still upset. He didn't ask where I'd been, didn't say a word, but smiled at me tentatively.

Once I was sure he was the Sam I knew, I told him about the bedlam of our morning.

"My God!" he said, "If I ever do anything like that again, put me away."

It is possible, though by no means certain, that the trial Alzheimer's drug occasioned in Sam a sudden consciousness of needing help that he didn't want to need, and his awareness—if it was that —was inarticulate but for those few raging words: I want *Self* determination!

That happened on a Sunday (of course). On Monday I called the doctor at Burke who was monitoring Sam's health during the drug trial, and explained the frightening episode to him. He added a low dose of Seroquel, a sedative, to Sam's daily drug regimen, informing me of the maximum amount that I could safely administer if Sam became violent again. (He never did).

The doctor's kindness, and belief in my ability to manage caring for Sam, steadied my shredded self-confidence, and Sam was not dropped from the clinical drug trial, which I had feared would happen.

In early March, when I could barely breathe from the minimal amount of sulfa I was still getting from the medicine that kept my eye-pain barely tolerable, my New York doctor performed a surgical procedure called Cyclocryo Therapy. It eliminated the bit of sight I had left in that eye, but also the pain, and the need for a multitude of eye drops and the dreaded medicine—a tremendous relief. After that my eye was (and is) little more than a bother.

I think that procedure must have been done before Sam's violent outburst because I don't recall being in pain, or worrying about missed eye drops after I walked out that day.

In any case, to be relieved of debilitating pain at that particular time was providential, because two months later when life was again filled with the small pleasantries of our daily routine, Sam fell.

The night before, he had been so weak he needed to lean on me all the way down the hall to his room. But I didn't think he was ill, only that he sat too much and didn't get enough exercise, so his legs were stiff, and he was weak.

I remember our pleasing night-time rhyming ritual, remember

pulling the comforter up to Sam's chin, which he loved me to do, giving him a goodnight kiss as I once had done for my children when they were young, then heading to my room for an hour or two of reading, feeling content with this new version of love in one of its many manifestations.

Those days when I slept, I slept attuned to the slightest irregular sound, like a mother with a new infant, the doors of our bedrooms wide open. Yet I heard nothing the next morning—a beautiful May morning—when wide-awake much earlier than usual, I suddenly got up, looked in on Sam, and saw him lying on the bedroom floor, a pillow under his head, the comforter pulled half off the bed, to cover him.

"Oh Sam," I cried, "What happened? Did you collapse? Did you fall? The floor is *freezing!*"

"I thought I'd lie here awhile," he said, smiling at me—then, "I'm on the floor?"

His eye was beginning to blacken. *He must have fallen and hit the dresser*, I thought, *maybe that's what woke me.*

Unable to help him up, I called 911. The rescue team took him, confused but alert and smiling, to the emergency room. He was admitted for observation and within twenty-four hours developed a raging fever from a urinary tract infection that I had seen no sign of, and that he had never complained of.

Then he developed pneumonia. When a nurse asked if I wanted to sign a DNR form (Do Not Resuscitate, which Sam and I had chosen for each other years before), I signed it, Holly by my side. Day after day he was barely conscious. I both longed for him to live and prayed that he would die, knowing the dreadful end that Alzheimer's would bestow.

Then one day when I was alone with him he opened his eyes, looked at me and said, "You're Aunt Hazel," (his Aunt Hazel had been a nurse).

"No, Honey, it's me, Marian," I told him, relieved that he was conscious.

"Well then you're *Aunt* Marian," he replied emphatically, and went back to sleep.

A morning or two later—early, probably 8 A.M. or so—a nurse called from the hospital and said, "Your husband is asking for you."

Just that suddenly, Sam knew who I was and that I belonged with him.

After ten days of hospitalization, unable to walk without help, Sam was discharged to a nursing home for physical rehabilitation. I expected him to be confused, afraid, angry, when he found himself there, instead of at home, after leaving the hospital. But, as if he understood his need he adjusted to the strange new setting with not one moment of sorrow, anxiety or discontent.

The clinical drug trial at Burke, interrupted by weeks of Sam's hospitalization and rehabilitation, had of course ended for him.

My trial: the eye pain, the anger I'd felt at myself for what I considered poor judgment in risking the return of ICE syndrome (as well as for ignoring what I believe was a flash of intuition shortly before the surgery), had also ended, and I felt not only relief, but release.

Each day of the six weeks that Sam was in the nursing home regaining the strength to walk, I flew out the door, hopped in the car, and drove off to see him, feeling unbelievably youthful, and well—and free.

CLOSER THAN HIS SHADOW

Beauty is life when life unveils
her holy face.
Kahlil Gibran

That hot, dry summer was the kind that a lifetime ago sent Florence, my downstairs friend, and me rushing around our apartments to finish our morning chores, make pitchers of iced tea and lemonade, get our toddlers into bathing suits, fill the kiddy-pool with water, and hurry to the yard while the sun was high so we could sit for hours sunbathing and chatting and watching the youngsters play. On weekends the family might go to the beach at Sherwood Island in Connecticut; days end would find us contentedly carrying sandy, sleepy children up all the stairs to our home. Those summers seemed like one long vacation.

At the beginning of a more recent summer, the last that I would have with my husband Sam, I felt as light-hearted as I had those many years ago, even though Sam was too weak to walk after a fall, illness and hospitalization, even though the Alzheimer's he suffered had progressed considerably during those connected events, and even though—likely *because*—he was in a nursing home for rehabilitation.

Sam was so delighted to see me when I arrived each morning that I felt as if I were dressing for a date: good shirts and slacks, white chinos, a lime-green shell and matching summer sweater that I usually saved for special occasions. On the way home in the evening I would stop to pick up a grilled chicken sandwich or a hamburger or Cobb salad, and eat it in the living room watching the PBS evening news with my feet resting on the coffee table, and the night ahead free from care.

Much of his time, Sam was confined to a wheelchair, but he was free to scoot around his unit at will, and did, often gleefully.

On Thursdays we joined other residents for wine or soda, and cheese and crackers that were served in the rudimentary dining area, a staff member strolling around strumming his guitar and singing familiar old tunes.

Music filled the air on Saturdays, as well, when small groups of musicians gave concerts in a large downstairs room near the entrance, the same room where on Sundays home-baked goodies were served by volunteers for Family Day.

(However when I arrived a quarter past noon on the first Saturday visit, I learned that he would miss those weekend events if I wasn't there to take him.)

Sam was happy. I need to remember that

Before his fall and ensuing illness, Sam had already begun to confuse dreams with daily reality, the first time calmly announcing as we ate our breakfast: "Last night I was a member of Bush's cabinet. I sabotaged him, watch the news." And another time: "Last night I was in Scotland, did you see that guy chasing me?"

In the nursing home he became more delusional, the delusions usually containing a element of triumph:

"Shhhh, come here, hurry," he whispered one day as I arrived on his unit, "I don't want anyone to hear me; I won BIG on the stock market, you can have *anything* you want, anything in the whole world; tell the children they can, too. I won really BIG!"

On father's day he got up late and tired and grumpy, but by afternoon was amusing his visitors, cheerfully declaring to some of the grandchildren, "You know, I'm not retarded, I'm retired," and jubilantly singing a song that my daughter Catherine captured on video, and posted on Facebook so that Heather, my stepdaughter who lives in Texas, could share in the fun. (Even if I took the time to look for the video, I probably couldn't find it, but Catherine assures me that Sam is still there singing away.)

Is it strange to be in love with a man who is fading way? Because it seemed that I loved Sam more every single day.

Maybe it was the freedom of meeting with him, then going home, like when our love was new; or maybe my mind had slipped a cog from the constant stress; or maybe it was because something in the damaged brain of my 'buttoned up' husband allowed him to express emotion as he never had before. Anyway, there it was, I was in love with a broken man. And it made things both easier, and more painful.

Each evening before I left the nursing home, I remembered to whisper in Sam's ear, as I had at bedtime for years, "I love you gladly," and Sam, still able to recall his part of our ritual, would exuberantly reply: "And I love you madly," with an emphasis on 'madly'.

There were intimations that things were less agreeable than I saw through the rose-tinted lenses I donned that summer: One day when I arrived at the home, a resident I'd become friendly with said, "You should have heard him last night! Whew!"

And near the end of Sam's six week stay he was suddenly suspicious of staff. "I don't think they're good people," he told me. That day, unhappy, mildly agitated, he looked at me with suspicion and asked,

"Are you going to leave me here?"

"No, Honey, I promise you're coming home as soon as the doctor says you're well enough," I told him.

"Well then I'm going to keep you closer than my shadow," he responded with no trace of his usual humor.

Around that time, the phone rang at home at about eight o'clock in the morning. Half asleep, I could hardly grasp what the nurse at the nursing home was telling me: Sam had had to have an injection to sedate him; he had "assaulted" another patient, pulling her out of the chair she was sitting on in the day room.

Sam? Sam couldn't move fast enough to assault anyone, I thought. *Where was the aide? Where was the supervision in that day room?*

I asked that question, and got no explanation, but was told the woman whom Sam had accosted was unhurt. Thank God. But it was an ominous development; Sam was scheduled to return home soon.

Mind spinning, I hastily dressed and drove to the nursing home afraid that I would find him heavily drugged. He was in the day room, as usual, and as alert and glad to see me as on any other day. Forgetting that he couldn't remember, I blurted,

"Why did you attack that woman? Why did you pull her off a chair? How could you *do* that?"

"I would *never* do such a thing!" Sam's replied indignantly, looking both bewildered, and shocked.

At a staff meeting to plan for Sam's discharge, my stepdaughter Holly asked for a copy of the report of the assault. (I was particularly anxious to know what had triggered it before I brought him home.) She was told there would be an in-house investigation, that incident reports do not go outside of the facility.

"He needs twenty-four hour care," they told me then, "Are you sure you want to take him home?"

"We can't afford twenty-four hour care," I told them, and "Yes, I do."

I wasn't worried about Sam being up at night, he had been up throughout the night for years, it was the assault incident that gave me pause, and about that no information was given, other than that it had happened. So, yes, I would keep my promise and bring him home, and, yes, I would be sure, at first, that I had made a mistake.

Perhaps two or three weeks before the assault incident, there was an astonishing day when I gladly slid into the rabbit-hole with Sam, landing in time far out of the ordinary.

It was one of those hot, dry, summer days, the sky perfectly clear except for one or two white clouds that looked like cotton puffs pasted against the vivid blue. An unfurled flag fluttered lightly at the top of its pole outside of the nursing home—a post card picture. Pink begonias and red and white geraniums in full bloom nestled among decorative shrubs in front of the building, and along bordered paths in the lovely park-like area where I sometimes took Sam for walks.

Several residents sat in wheelchairs or on benches to each side of the shaded entrance. "Hi, Bert, Hi Harry," I called to two whom I knew, as I rushed into the quiet lobby and up to Sam's unit. As soon as he spotted me he scooted over in his wheelchair, visibly excited.

"There you are! He said, "I won, you know."

"You won? What did you win?" I asked.

"The match!" he exclaimed as if I should know.

"That's *wonderful*," I told him (without a clue).

I followed Sam as he headed for the day room where the results of the Wimbledon Tennis Tournament in England were being announced on television. *Ah, of course*, I thought. As often happened in Sam's reality he was *there* and had won a match.

I helped him from the wheelchair to a couch and sat down beside him. At the far end of the rectangular room, wall to wall windows framed a view of sun-stippled leaves that seemed to sparkle against the vibrant blue sky as a soft breeze stirred them.

"Look," Sam said with pride in his voice, "They gave us the *best* room." A minute later he laughed out loud.

"What?" I asked, wondering what had tickled him so.

"Only in England," he gasped through his laughter, pointing to a taped up notice, "It says, 'Door is *alarmed*."

Then he leaned toward me to whisper, "I'm on my best behavior."

And when I looked puzzled, "*You* know. An American in London?"

Now I was laughing, too, enjoying the fantasy of being with Sam in a hotel in England, amused by a sign that 'only the English' would post, stuck on a door in an American nursing home. The few people in the room paid no attention to our hilarity.

Then suddenly the television station changed, and the poignant, somber melody of *The Last Time I Saw Paris* drifted toward us. Instantly Wimbledon and London and laughter were forgotten, and Paris was a city lost to Sam who was now softly weeping.

"I really miss Paris," he said, as if he had been there last week, and World War II were raging, and the Nazis had occupied the city so he couldn't go back.

"Sam, let's go outside," I said, putting my arm around his shoulders, "That song is making you cry."

"It's alright to cry," he responded in a tone that conveyed

185

surprise at my ignorance.

In all of our years together, Sam had been a chin-up, stiff-upper-lip, men-do-not-cry kind of guy. For too many of those years, I had grieved as more and more of him was lost to Alzheimer's. This new ability to express emotion, to accept it as a natural part of life, to share it with me, made me feel as if that thieving disease had given something back, whether the emotion he shared was based on reality, or not.

But I did want to get him outside; it was far too beautiful to stay in. So I helped Sam back into his wheelchair, put the footrests in place, and wheeled him to the elevator, where we went down, and out into brilliant sunshine that instantly erased his sorrowful mood.

We moved through the crowded area in front of the entrance, then down the sidewalk to where I had spotted a couple getting up from a bench in the shade of a tree. I helped him move from the chair to the bench, and sat beside him. For awhile—ten minutes, maybe twenty—we quietly watched other residents being wheeled down shaded paths, watched the ruffling flag, the cotton-puff clouds, the cars coming and going.

Then I noticed that Sam had a strange expression on his face' as I was about to ask him if he was alright he said,

"See that man in the blue shirt?"

"Where?" I asked.

"There," he said, pointing to a man sitting on a bench near the front of the building, "He's my brother, you know. And that pink flower?"—now pointing to a begonia—"We're *one*, we're *all one!*"

He was awed, astounded, and fully aware of how unusual his experience was, because he quickly added, "Don't tell *anyone* I said that, they'll think I'm crazy."

After a moment, his face glowing with joy, tears streaming down his cheeks, he said,

"I have never felt so complete in my entire life."

I couldn't speak. I just leaned my head against Sam's, and tightened my hold on his hand, feeling a blissful sense of peace.

I don't know how much later it was that he said,

"I'm a brave, you know."

"You're brave?" I asked, not sure that I'd understood.

186

"No, I'm *a* brave," he answered, and after a minute or two as if he had been thinking about it, and was worried:

"That makes you a squaw, are you okay with that?"

"Yes, I'll be your squaw," I told him, half-laughing, half-crying.

In *The Grapes of Wrath*, John Steinbeck's book about the Dust Bowl migration of the 1930s, an unnamed itinerant worker who is sheltering in the Weedpatch camp tells a story that ends:

> "...And the stars come down so close, and sadness and pleasure so close together...and I have joined the brotherhood of the worlds. And everything's holy, everything, even me."

In the book, the worker's stunning mystical experience is induced by overindulgence in alcohol.

But who can say—as Sam and I sat in the shade beneath that intense blue sky, surrounded by flowers at the height of their beauty, a slight breeze brushing our faces—who can say that his unmoored mind didn't experience mystical knowledge that some philosophers, theologians, spiritualists only contemplate.

Sam was an agnostic. Yet for a few moments on that hot, summer afternoon, everything was holy to him, *everything* was closer than his shadow.

If he had died at the end of that day, I would have been at peace with it for the rest of my life.

WHAT SHE REALLY WANTED

Solitude, my mother, tell me my life again.
O. V. de Milosz.

In the villa there was a wing chair by the window, where my sister Jeanne sat watching Hudson River scenes unfold as if solely for her pleasure—the quickening melt of spring, summer's inscrutable shadows, autumn's brilliant pallet, and winter's iced river surrounded by trees dusted with snow soft as confectioners' sugar.

The villa was actually Saint Joseph's home for the aged in Catskill, New York, but to my sister it was always, "The villa." Her room was one of the best, a corner room, its walls and the walls of the short hall leading to it, displaying oil paintings by her daughter Patricia, an artist.

When Jeanne first began to fear her shaky limbs would give way to the floor beneath her feet, and wanted not to be alone, Patricia and her husband, an architect, had converted their basement into a comfortable and safe apartment for her. *Any* of her seven sons and daughters would have given her a home; but Jeanne would have none of them, or their dogs and cats and her many grandchildren, though she clearly loved them all.

It was a time, I think, when she longed only to be cared for, to have someone see that she took her vitamins and medicine, to have a quiet life of peaceful days and daily Catholic Mass. And she had that at her villa.

She raved about the meals the nuns prepared: "Excellent," she said, and the cakes and pastries baked each day, "extraordinary."

Evening dinners were served in a way that delighted her, too (I imagine, starched linen, polished silver, candles, flowers). There was no smoking allowed, of course, but who smokes these days? And no wine was served with those agreeable dinners, but, since her husband Bill had years ago joined Alcoholics Anonymous, she seldom indulged in that pleasure. (Bill, like many who returned from the chaos of World War Two, had succumbed to, and recovered from, the false solace of alcohol, decades before his death.)

When Jeanne's children took her to restaurants to celebrate one or another occasion, she worried away their enjoyment of wine with dinner as if seeing trouble in every glass of sparkling red or white. To me she would confide her fear for them (my steadfast nephews and nieces), as if alcoholism were as contagious as a twenty-four hour virus and they had all been exposed to it, which in a way was true, I suppose.

Anyway, Jeanne was wonderfully happy at her villa, until she fell and shattered her hip. After a long surgery she told me, "I thought I would die, and then I woke up," sounding wistful, as if she would have welcomed that quiet release from her failing body.

The "villa" held her room while she was in a rehabilitation facility after the surgery, but St. Joseph's was not a skilled nursing facility, and I can't remember if she was ever able to return there.

In my recollection, everything happened at once: Jeanne's increasing problems that had not yet been diagnosed as Parkinson's, her fall and shattered hip, surgery, and the sale of St. Joseph's to real estate developers who would construct high-priced condominiums on those park-like acres overlooking the northern reaches of the Hudson River, land having become so valuable during the real estate bubble that the Church, always in need of money, surely could not resist selling.

Jeanne was sent to Teresian House, a nursing home in Albany, New York, and in truth, with her body increasingly oblivious of

189

her will to move it, she needed to be there.

At first she was able to move to a chair, which again was placed near a window. It no longer framed the exquisite changing scenes of the Hudson River, as her window at the villa had, but that no longer mattered because the scenes that interested her now, the only ones she talked about, were those from our shared life—many of which were framed by a bay window in a home across from Long Island Sound in Northport, New York, where she had lived for fifty years.

It was in Northport, when I vacationed with her and Bill long ago, that my sister had firmly schooled me in matters both practical and personal (unlike our mother, who was primarily concerned with our comportment, and comfort).

Thirteen years older than I, and in my memory, always busy with a baby, Jeanne had mothered me as well:

Once, when a sweater I was wearing had a spot on it, she said, "You need to take better care of your things," and immediately made me take it off so she could teach me how to gently hand-wash wool in cool water.

The summer I was fifteen, and arrived at her door twelve pounds heavier than I'd been several months earlier, she took one disapproving look at my burgeoning body, and quickly introduced me to hard-boiled eggs, lightly dressed salads, and cottage cheese with pineapple.

"You'll be sorry," she warned, "if you keep eating Mom's potatoes, and gravy, and that awful bread fried in bacon fat. Bacon fat!"

(I loved that bread fried in bacon fat.)

I remember the last time I vacationed alone with Jeanne and her family as if it were yesterday. I was a young married woman six months pregnant. One afternoon Jeanne went shopping while I babysat my nephews. She arrived home smiling happily, and handed me a bag from Sears Roebuck. Inside were yards of cotton fabric in a tattersall pattern of red and blue lines on a white background, and a Simplicity pattern for a maternity outfit suitable to wear to the beach—shorts and a sleeveless top.

"I can't sew these! The pattern's too complicated. I haven't sewn anything since my home economics class in high school," I told Jeanne.

"Of *course* you can," she replied, impatient and annoyed with me for my defeatist attitude. "Just let me put these things away and I'll show you how."

So while she supervised, I stood at a bridge table, pinned the pattern to the fabric as instructed, then cut the odd-shaped tissue pieces for the maternity shorts, the more normal ones for the top, and sewed them together on her old Singer sewing machine, reading each direction before moving on to the next, as I'd been told to do. "Don't read ahead," Jeanne had warned, "It's too confusing. Just do one thing at a time!"

(A lesson that would be invaluable when applied to other areas of my life.)

I wore the maternity outfit that summer, and through three more pregnancies during the next twelve years, the fabric slowly fading, but remaining serviceable.

Jeanne sewed everything: clothes, curtains, drapes, slipcovers, she even converted Bill's suits into small versions for her growing sons. She refinished furniture, and hung wallpaper, and I watched, and learned, and modeled my behavior on hers.

Until my life turned upside-down, visits with Jeanne and my Northport family were an integral part of my life. For years, we took turns preparing Thanksgiving dinners, and at Christmastime there was an annual trip to Long Island to exchange gifts. Often, Jeanne and I unwittingly bought identical Christmas cards, or Christmas wrap, our similar tastes delighting us.

When my first two daughters were small, John and I would pack a few things, and we'd all pile into the car for the drive to the Island, and one of Jeanne and Bill's parties. I love remembering that: I see the our children playing with their cousins until they were tucked in for the night;

I see Jeanne and Bill's friends arriving, cocktails and wine and hors d'oeuvres being served; I hear warm laughter and soft music drifting on air hazy with cigarette smoke; I recall candles casting light that made the room seem magical.

Many years later, when I divorced John and remarried, Jeanne, devout Catholic, that she was, hugged me, and welcomed Sam, my new husband, into our family.

"But I'll continue to pray for John," she said.

And now Jeanne was living in Teresian House, a Catholic nursing home.

"Do you like it? Is it okay?" I asked the first time I visited her there.

"No!" she answered, quickly and emphatically.

Then, looking at me with an expression that seemed to combine frustration and acceptance she said,

"But I *have* to be here. Life's just a series of surrenders."

"Well, is the food good?" I asked, "I know it's not as good as at the villa but..."

Before I finished the sentence she began laughing like the young Jeanne I still remember, laughing until I couldn't help but laugh with her. Finally, still bubbly, still giggling, she leaned toward me and I learned what the joke was about:

"Never mind the villa," she said, "What I *really* want is a cigarette and a glass of wine!"

A cigarette and a glass of wine, and all that went with them—the lovely lively parties, the lost vitality, the vanished years.

Jeanne would become completely paralyzed by the type of Parkinson's she suffered from.

The progress of her disease was excruciatingly slow, yet as days slipped through our fingers it seemed just overnight that talking on the phone became difficult for her.

It was how we kept in touch now, talking on the phone, reminiscing about life with our mom and dad; life when our children were young. Laughing at the memory of standing in her kitchen with bread laid on every surface for the twenty peanut-butter and jelly sandwiches we were making to take to the beach.

We rued how busy our lives had gotten when the kids were suddenly teenagers.

I rued the days when I was working, going to school, having an affair, too busy and distracted to think of picking up the phone to call Jeanne, except sometimes about our mother, when she lived with her or with me.

Too soon, Jeanne needed to be lifted from the bed to the bathroom with the help of a large metal contraption; needed to be fed, and was able to swallow only with difficulty.

One day, thinking she was near her end, my nephew Bill drove me to Teresian House to see her while Catherine stayed with Sam (by then Alzheimer's had stolen his years from him, and like a young child he could not be left by himself). That day Jeanne could speak only in the faintest whisper that I tried to understand, putting my ear close to her mouth, but none of us were sure that she was really present.

Near the end of the visit I said, "It's cold in here." and almost missed the wisp of words Jeanne managed to expel,

"We're both *always* cold," she said.

Locked in that petrified flesh, she was still with us and knew exactly who I was—she and I had often complained to each other of feeling cold.

There were other visits when my daughter Laura, or my nephew Bill, took me to Teresian House, but exactly when, and what arrangements were made for Sam's care, are lost to me. I know that during one visit I met great-nieces and nephews, and a great-great niece and nephew, a sorrowful-joyful reunion.

And I know Bill took me to say goodbye to my sister when her release was actually, blessedly upon her, and that there was a day—maybe the same day—when my niece Patricia brought a bottle of cabernet sauvignon, poured the wine into small Dixie-cups, and handed me one. I don't remember raising a glass to Jeanne, but we must have.

What I clearly recall, and the memory gives me pleasure, is Patricia picking up a small stick with a sponge at its tip, the kind used to moisten the lips of the very ill with water; a nurse had left some in the room.

I see her dipping the sponge into the Dixie cup full of wine, and moistening my sister's lips.

I like to think Jeanne heard the warm laughter of friends, the sound of ice clinking in cocktail glasses, soft music drifting on air glowing with candlelight and hazy with cigarette smoke.

I like to think that she smiled.

HOMECOMING

People who have not been in Narnia
sometimes think that a thing cannot be good
and terrible at the same time
C. S. Lewis

I think of how I delighted in Sam's triumphant delusional fantasies when he was in the nursing home, how romantically close to him I'd felt, dressing each day as if for a date.

Denial, I suppose, desire to recreate a trace of what we once had. I hadn't realized, or hadn't wanted to, the extent to which his Alzheimer's had progressed in the eight weeks he'd been gone. Staff had warned me that he needed twenty-four hour care, but I brought him home anyway.

Holly came with me to pick him up, and surely stayed that afternoon until she had to leave to care for her own family, and surely Catherine, who had no small children to worry about, came and stayed the night. But my memory of the first day that Sam was back home is of being alone, and afraid, and as tense as a rubber band about to snap in two.

Others must have experienced it: the shock of bringing home a loved one who has been in a nursing home for rehabilitation after injury or illness, only to find that he needs far more care than he did the last time you saw him there, which was yesterday. In a rare moment of paranoia I was sure they—the proverbial 'they'—

planned it that way: prostate surgery for Sam just before he was released to my care. I was with him when he had that procedure, there was no complication. He went back to the nursing home for a day, or maybe two, and, since I didn't hear otherwise, I never gave a thought to possible consequences.

Does surgery for an enlarged prostate always cause a need to urinate every fifteen minutes? Or was that true only for Sam, who needed help to stand up and grab his walker, to find the bathroom, and to manage things when he got there. It made caring for him so much harder.

The first personal essay I ever wrote began with that homecoming. "Can you be happy here?" Sam had asked, as he walked into our small apartment. He didn't even recognize his favorite leather chair.

I wrote about that, and about the second day when I was disoriented almost beyond sanity as the Medicare nurse, the home care agency nurse, the physical therapist, descended all at once (it seemed to me), and I had to sign forms, write a large check, try to help Sam, and try to stay out of the way while a nurse removed scatter rugs that Sam might trip over (one quickly replaced when I found the floor next to his bed slick with urine and slippery as black ice.)

Most of that first story, though, was about how much easier life got as soon as William, Sam's wonderful aide, arrived, which it did; about unexpected joys, which there were; about how thankful I was for those last weeks with Sam, which I was, and am. Sam had just died, and our last best weeks together were all that I wanted to write about, all that I wanted to remember. They're still all that I want to remember.

But today I lifted from a shelf above my computer desk a small purple journal that I began few days after Sam came home on July 13th of 2010, and kept until a few days after his death, and it shows a woman full of fear, sorrow, frustration, and more self-pity than I like to acknowledge. It also reminds me of the reason Sam ended up back in the long-term-care unit of that nursing home.

"Can't even take a walk around the parking lot; can't even get the mail," I wrote on Saturday, July 17th, the first 24 hours that I was alone with Sam. That day he sat in his chair like a visitor; I didn't know what to do with him. Finally I played favorite CDs: *The Fantasticks, Camelot,* Pete Fountain's New Orleans jazz, and he perked up and was suddenly a famous conductor about to leave on a concert tour.

"You'll always be with me, though," he said, "That's if you want to."

About that I wrote, "Breaks my heart."

More Journal excerpts from July 17th
- Music used to make me dance around, today it made me cry
- I don't think I can do this. God, please take him, please.
- I feel what I think is sorrow welling up again and again, tears without sound, hidden from him.

The following week William and I took Sam to see our doctor in Hartsdale, and Sam seemed to remember him. Again the weather was lovely so we stopped for coffee and doughnuts at a sidewalk table outside of the bakery. When Sam said, "Isn't this a place we liked?" I felt great relief, as if things might go back to how they were before his illness and rehabilitation, after all. Even bathroom trips were less that day.

Journal excerpts, August 9th:
- I am going through savings but as the Elder Law lawyer reminded me [in a condescending tone of voice I *hated*] I *am* responsible for Sam.
- I'm very tired of always being responsible.... I have to get together years of bank statements, find a different lawyer, get Sam to the podiatrist, to the dentist, and out for a haircut.
- Disgusted. Going to bed."

Journal excerpts, August 10th, (a day without William)
- I just thought (as I sat here on the couch in a pure funk), 'There are lots of things you could do to make yourself feel better'. I answered: "Yeah, I just did—I cleaned up the urine all over the bedroom floor, and bathroom floor, and washed my husband as best I could so the house (apt.) will smell good!
- Sam doesn't forget who I am lately, but in the bathroom asks,

"Is that where I sit?" or "What do I do now?"

That was my question: *What do I do now?* But in fact I was beginning to handle minor crises with more aplomb, and I'd wised up, withholding liquids from Sam after 6 P.M. except for a sip so he could swallow medication, which made our nights, and early mornings somewhat more manageable.

And as Sam settled in, he began to beam joy at just about everything but those hard bathroom trips

Then, on Saturday July 24th, there was a televised program about the BP oil spill disaster in the Gulf of Mexico, where an oil well had finally been capped. By then a great amount of oil had polluted the waters along the coast. Interested, I watched avidly, never noticing Sam's increasing agitation until he exploded: "I'm NOT going to be responsible for all those dying people! I'm leaving!" "I'm not going to be responsible!"

I was urging him to drink a lot of water to offset the diarrhea he'd had that morning, "Here, Honey," I said handing him a glassful that I thought might distract him. He pushed it out of my hand, the water sailing clear across the room.

"Liquids are NOT good for you," he shouted, "they're lying!"

That night I wrote: "I don't deal with these fits well...I feel instantly, totally drained."

Then I got Sam settled and went to bed myself, earlier than usual, which did nothing to help since we were up about an hour later, and an hour after that, and an hour after that.

Our days never ended until 2 or 3 A.M. when one of us, maybe both (I never knew), simply went unconscious for a few hours.

That particular day never ended at all; at 2:00 A.M. I sprayed Clorox on a small puddle Sam had made in the bathroom, and bent to wipe it up with paper towels. When I stood, black spots covered the ceiling and walls—one looked like a fish about two inches long and a half inch wide. Almost instantly I realized they were not on the ceiling, or the walls, but inside my eye—my only sighted eye.

"My eye, oh my eye!" I cried, and then somehow calmed myself enough to reassure Sam that I was alright, and get him back to bed.

Almost of its own accord, my mind searched for options: *I'm going blind; I have to get to the emergency room. Call 911? But I can't leave Sam alone. But I* have *to get to the emergency room; My God, I won't be able to read! Can't leave Sam, Can't leave Sam, Call Holly? No, none of our daughters. A neighbor? No, not at this hour.* (Nights were when Sam had trouble controlling himself. I knew an unfamiliar face might tip the scale in favor of a temper-tantrum, particularly in the bathroom).

Finally I called my daughter Catherine. I didn't know how she would, or could, help—her vision had become too impaired for her to drive, and there were no trains, cabs, or buses available at that hour in Poughkeepsie, where she lived. Desperate, I called her anyway; having struggled with illness for many years, she is patient and at ease with others' health problems, even with a mother who calls in the middle of the night, even with a stepfather in the bathroom in his pitiful nudity.

As soon as she answered the phone I cried, "Oh Cass, I think my good eye has hemorrhaged," and explained what had happened.

"Don't lie down, Mom, sit up straight, sit still, I'll think of something, I'll call you right back," she said.

A few minutes later she called back to tell me her friend Jill would drive from Mahopac to Poughkeepsie to pick her up, then back down to Mt. Kisco to take me to the emergency room while Catherine stayed with Sam. I was too frightened that night to realize what an astonishing gift Jill gave us.

Jill and I got home around seven that morning, and, though it was a Sunday (of course), my local eye doctor saw me in her office. A large 'floater' (the "fish") had broken away from the retina, causing the slight hemorrhage. On Monday a neighbor drove me to a retinologist—the tear was small, there was no further leak, I could not bend or lift anything heavy for a week, but the eye would be fine. By Friday it had healed and I was released from care.

According to the retinologist, the floater might have broken away causing the hemorrhage when I was bending to pick up a dish that fell, or a grandchild's toy. But it had happened at 2 A.M.

when I was taking care of Sam, and I didn't want to take care of him anymore.

As soon as I could, I called the nursing home that Sam had left just twelve days earlier. There was no room available in their long term care unit, so I had his name added to the list of those waiting for one.

The week my eye was healing, Catherine, who worked per diem at that time, stayed with me. I watched as she got Sam settled in the bathroom, angled the mirrored door on a tall cabinet I'd placed there, and kept her eye on him from the bedroom, giving him privacy until he needed her help. When he became frustrated she would say, "You're really helping me here, Sam," praising him, reassuring him, her encouraging words cooling his agitation better than my soothing ever had. I would use those words often in the weeks to come.

For a long time, afraid that my eye would hemorrhage again, I refused to bend and clean bathroom puddles, instead spraying Clorox then dropping paper towels, wiping with my foot, and kicking them into a corner of the bathroom to wait for William, who scrubbed both bathrooms whenever he came, and often the bedroom as well since Sam, hating Depends, sometimes took them off after I'd collapsed into sleep, and thought him safely there as well.

I wouldn't even help Sam up from his chair or bed, and every time the phone rang I ran to answer it, hoping it would be the nursing home—then I forgot about it, forgot to be afraid.

After three weeks, Medicare would no longer pay for half of what Sam's aide cost, so instead of five days, we had William only Monday, Wednesday, and Friday.

Now there was no nurse stopping in to check up on Sam, no physical therapist coming two or three times a week. And I liked it. Home was more peaceful, even Sam was more at ease.

One day he looked at me and asked,

"Are we legal?"

"Yes, Honey, we've been married almost twenty-five years."

"Oh, oh how lucky I am, he said.

Moments like that happened regularly, often making me laugh, and always warming my heart.

Bright colors now made Sam happy, in fact they thrilled him—hot pink, Kelly green, royal blue, orange, yellow, the brighter the better. He even complimented a neighbor on her "wonderful pink blouse" as we were walking through the lobby. "Beautiful," he told her.

It was a term I began to hear all day, "You're so beautiful," he would say looking at me (gray hair, baggy bloodshot eyes, wrinkled skin).

Long ago Sam had been ultra-conservative, wearing only grays, beige, or navy, with white or blue long-sleeve button-down shirts.

Once when we were at the Poughkeepsie Mall, and I was trying on a fleece jacket with swirling colors of vibrant blues and aquamarines against a white background, I asked,

"What do you think, Sam?" .

"Well they'll certainly see you coming," he replied in a slightly critical tone.

"I think she looks lovely in it," a man standing nearby with his wife said.

So of course I bought it. (He would have loved that jacket now, if I hadn't given it away.)

By mid-Augusts, I had found ways to make life easier when William wasn't here—no jeans or chinos with that bothersome belt that delayed us at crucial moments in the bathroom, and no morning shave, just supervision while Sam brushed his teeth, then a sponge bath, a pair of fresh pajamas. It saved time and I felt more in control and, quite often, happy.

There was one dreadful day at the end of that month, a Saturday of course, with no William here, when Sam had a serious diarrhea episode (but that's a story in itself).

There was also a superb afternoon when Sam and I sat in the living room holding hands for three hours, entranced by a new production of South Pacific being presented on television's Public Broadcasting System; it was a Sunday afternoon, August 23rd, I believe. I recorded the play and we watched it again the next night.

That afternoon, I realized musicals: the one I recorded, our DVDs of *Caberet*, and *Les Miserables*, would give me hours to do whatever needed doing; Sam would watch them and never move, even to go to the bathroom. But I never did anything anyway; drawn by the music, like those fairy-tale children were drawn to follow the pied piper, I would sit on the couch near Sam, who was in his favorite chair, he would reach to hold my hand, and we'd lose ourselves in delight.

Sometimes I sat by him for no reason other than to be close—that's how much things had changed for the better. Once he asked, "Can I always sit in this chair?" And my heart clenched when I answered, "Yes, always," knowing it was a lie.

William took Sam outside for walks, and I took him up and down the hall outside of our apartment, but even with daily exercise it became increasingly difficult for him to get around. With a snail-like pace, he would cling to his walker while moving down the short hall from the bedroom to the living room, either William or me beside him, then he'd sink into his chair with a deep sigh, saying, "There!" as if he'd climbed Mt. Everest and could finally rest.

Even so, after a late dinner one evening I insisted he get up to see the Wolf Moon that television meteorologists were excited about. I'd gotten a glimpse of it when I went to close the drapes, and knew he'd love it. I helped him to the patio doors and there it was—huge and bright, and hanging low in the sky above the woods behind our apartment.

"Oh." Sam said, " when he saw it, "Oh, It looks like a great big pearl. If I could, I'd reach up and pull it down for you."

He would give me the moon.

Saul Bellow wrote: *"How rare is simple thought and pure heartedness! Even a moment of pure heartedness I bow down to, down to the ground."*

That's how Sam's love for me was every day that was left to us: simple and pure, and given each moment, without remembrance, or expectation.

There was a most special Sunday afternoon when Sam suddenly wanted to talk, and for no reason other than that everything was good that day, and I felt blessed, I put down the *Times Book Review* I was reading, turned off the television, and listened. He had been thinking about his mother.

"Is my mother alright?" he asked.

"Honey, your mother died a long time ago," I told him gently.

"Oh." he said, somewhat sad, "But was she happy?"

I had never met her, so I made up a stories about how overjoyed she was when her grandchildren came along (I had seen a snapshot of her with them); about how much she loved them; about how proud she had been of Sam. Then I gave him stories he had given me years ago—about the pleasure she gotten from having married a doctor; from her garden club; from her bridge club that sometimes included the renowned Estee Lauder.

"Dead doesn't mean gone," I finally told him, "our loved ones who have died can visit us in our dreams."

"Oh, I know that. They do." Sam declared.

He then told me a story about when he was a very young boy waiting for his mother who had gone into a bank that was being robbed. "I waited and waited for her, I thought she was never coming back," he said, sounding like the small, lost boy he envisioned. (It didn't matter to me if it were a true, or false memory; Sam had felt abandoned, and afraid, and on the day that I left him in the nursing home forever, I would remember that.)

Then, suddenly pensive, Sam looked at me and said, "You were never encouraged to be all that you could be, were you." (It was a statement, not a question, and I wondered where on earth it had come from.)

"But I'm happy, Sam," I responded, "You've been a wonderful father to my girls, they love you, and my stepdaughters love me—how blessed is that? How wonderful?"

He wanted to know about "these daughters," and I told him shortened versions of the lives all had embarked upon, embellishing some things, eliminating others.

"Our life was good, wasn't it?" he asked.

"Yes, *very*." I told him.

I asked him if he remembered anything about our courtship—"It was our second adolescence," I said, joking (though it was more like a first, for me). Of course he didn't.

So I gave him my memories of us walking all over White Plains; of a little hanky-panky behind a haystack on the New York Hospital grounds; of visiting museums in New York City; of a piper playing his bagpipes when we went to the Neuberger Museum at SUNY in Purchase on our first date, and my shock that day when I learned he had rented a car from Rent-A-Wreck.

"No! No, I didn't do that, did I?" he exclaimed.

"You did," I said, and we both laughed.

How glad I am that I brought him home, that we had those moments of intimacy, how glad, every time I recall his voice saying, "So beautiful," to me, to Holly, to Catherine—or when I take a moment to look at the hill behind our apartment through his eyes that saw living, glowing, golden weeds, butterflies dancing ballets. "My God," he once said, "Look at all the living greens!" And now I notice the myriad shades of green.

Our last weeks at home together, it seemed as if tongues of fire had descended on our heads, filling us with love more intense than I ever thought possible, certainly more than I thought myself capable of, especially considering the emotional, and enervating physical toll of caring for him.

Sometime in September, I experienced a moment of intense grief at the thought that we were near the end of our days together.

As if Sam, too, sensed that the end was near, two weeks before the nursing home called, as I tucked him into bed and said my part of our nighttime ritual: "I love you gladly," Sam—who for months had needed me to coach him through his part—astonished me by instantly saying, "And I love you *madly!*"

Then, as I was about to leave the room, reflective, serious, and fully cognizant, he added, "I really do, you know."

I did know. By then I loved him madly, too.

Last Lived Days

This one gray as grief
black like the hawk I see from
my patio, small speck on faded canvas

Thank God for goldfinch feathers
cardinal and jay, and an aide for
him the hue of good dark chocolate,
the stark beauty of black-silk
against my love's shriveled white skin
gently bathed, patiently clothed—

His needs so confine;
now a stately dance down our short hall,
split seconds in spacious time

DINNER CAN WAIT

After the ecstasy, the laundry
Zen saying

I almost went back to bed this morning when William, Sam's aide, arrived, but then decided to get dressed and go out because he's going to a wedding on Monday, and won't be here until Tuesday, so I'll be housebound for three days. I've decided to stock up on groceries and run to Target for new pajamas for Sam. It's a beautiful summer day, so I should get myself out of the house and into the sun, anyway.

Right now William's getting Sam showered in the bathroom that's fitted for disabled persons. I hated that bathroom when we moved here—that reminder of future frailty—but I thank God for it now that Sam's Alzheimer's has caused neurological muscular weakness in addition to the arthritis he's had for years; he's unsteady on his feet, and in that tub can sit on the pull-down bench while he's soaped and sprayed clean.

Sam's not able to lift a leg over the rim of the tub, now, but must be half-lifted in and out. Only William, our blessing from Ghana, can do this.

On Monday, Wednesday, and Friday, he dresses Sam in chinos or jeans, and a nice shirt, and gets him ready for bed in the evening before he leaves. The rest of the week I sponge-bathe Sam in the

205

morning, and dress him in a cotton pajama bottom and a long-sleeve matching tee-shirt. This has simplified life considerably—there's no belt to frustrate and delay us on bathroom trips, he looks great, and (barring unforeseen accidents), he's ready for bed at breakfast time.

I'm amazed that I've become comfortable with this constantly transforming life of ours, at least emotionally. Physically I'm bone tired, which is why I almost went back to bed when William got here. But for the most part I'm quite happy, as is Sam. The other night he heard people arguing on television—a comedy program meant to be humorous—and said, "Why can't people just love each other?" Then he looked at me with an expression on his face that could melt the North Pole and said, "Like we do."

At Target I buy another set of pajamas for Sam, and a DVD of *Chicago*, then I go to the A&P for groceries, put them in the trunk of the car in a cooler I've filled with a layer of ice-packs, and head for Borders book store. It's convenient that all three stores are in the same shopping center because shopping is my least favorite activity, and stopping at Borders is my reward. If you buy two paperback books, one is half price, so I buy two and go downstairs to the café for a cup of coffee, sipping it while I begin reading one of the books.

But it's really hot today, and soon images of ice-packs melting in the cooler, and milk curdling, fill my mind, urging me away from this relaxation.

On the way home I notice an empty parking space across from The Pastry Corner bakery, and impulsively park and run across the street to pick up pastry for tomorrow's breakfast. Since Sam's gall bladder was removed I serve low-fat food, but now I imagine a Saturday morning like those we used to have, and I buy two Danish shiny with buttery sugar, and thick with dense, rich cheese.

When I get home Sam is watching an old *Mayberry* program on television, William, always careful to choose a program that doesn't upset Sam, is sitting with him. He tells me I don't give him enough work to do, but he changes sheets, scrubs bathrooms, and cares for Sam with patience and compassion, and that is more than enough. Today I let him leave early. I'm looking forward to being alone with Sam—something I feared and dreaded just a few short weeks ago. Since then the days that I'm alone with him have become pleasantly manageable; it's the nights that drain us.

This night (early morning?) it's nearly 3 A.M. when, frustrated beyond endurance, hating the Depends he must now wear, and highly agitated because he needs to put a clean pair on, Sam slams his walker up and down, over and over so hard I think the bathroom floor-tiles will crack. I stand out of his reach, and, half asleep, recite the litany that usually sooths him:

"You're doing fine Sam," "That's alright, you're doing good, Honey."

Suddenly Sam stops, looks at me and says,

"How did someone like you end up with a bad tempered old man like me?"

I melt. Every day Sam says or does something that makes me melt; I think he's forgotten that I'm his wife, I think he's even forgotten my name, but he doesn't forget that he loves me. I've become his North Star, the center of his universe, and it is terrible, the responsibility, and it is wonderful, the love.

I don't know when we finally get to sleep, but we're up again about 11 A.M. on Saturday, and Sam is soon sponge-bathed, and dressed, and waiting patiently for his weekly poached eggs on buttered toast. He used to look forward to this weekly treat (being on a diet that limits eggs), but now it's become *my* habit; he wouldn't miss eggs, I don't think he'd miss eating at all, if the food didn't just suddenly appear before him. Sometimes he doesn't know what's in the glass in front of his plate, "Is it safe to drink?" he asks. But today orange juice is not a mystery, and is quickly gone.

Orange juice is usually my whole breakfast, so I sip it, and sip coffee while he eats, then I bring out those luscious, large, cheese Danish, and Sam lights up like a child looking at a longed for double-size hot-fudge sundae. We devour the pastries, and are relaxing with second cups of coffee when he tells me,

"I have to go."

"Okay," I say, and get up to get his walker.

"No, you don't understand. I have to go NOW!" he exclaims in a panicked voice.

I hurry, and Sam tries to, but for him to hurry anywhere, for any reason, is no longer possible.

Half way down the hall he's in despair. "It's too late, it's too late," he tells me.

In the bathroom I get him on the toilet and peel his depends and pajamas off. When my children were babies I learned to breathe through my mouth, not my nose, so I wouldn't gag when changing dirty diapers. I can do this.

I reach in the linen closet and grab a handful of washcloths. When Sam is finished I help him stand, and, having wet and soaped a washcloth, begin on one of his legs. Then I notice his slippers, even they are soiled—and the seat, and the floor. It is impossible to describe the extent of this accident. Washcloths are useless. Every towel we own would be useless.

My mind begins to spin: *I'll call the agency. But is someone there on Saturday? Should I call one of our girls? No, I can't ask them to help with* this. *Anyway, Sam won't stay put until help comes. Can I get him in the tub? No, we'd both break our necks! Oh my God! William isn't even coming again until next Tuesday!*

Now I'm in a panic equal to what Sam must feel. He's standing nearby gripping his walker so hard his knuckles are white. Then I have an idea—and it comes to me so suddenly that if this were a comic strip you'd see a light-bulb turn on in a bubble over my head—there is another walker in our storeroom. It's been there since I broke my leg three years ago, if I can get it in the shower. . .

We are in the bathroom off of our master bedroom because the toilet here has been fitted with a safety-surround for Sam.

There is a walk-in shower, but the door is only twenty-three inches wide, the shower only thirty inches square. There is no seat, and no bar for Sam to hold on to, and across the bottom of the stall is a small step with a metal strip protruding from the top that he will have to lift his feet over. But maybe. . .

"Sam, don't move!" I practically shout, running for a small bowl on the kitchen counter, rummaging through it for the storeroom key, which is jumbled among other keys, paper clips, safety pins; rushing to the storage area, grabbing my walker, running back—the whole time thinking Sam's going to try to follow me, he always does, and dreading what kind of mess I'll find.

But Sam, my poor Sam, as if stuck to the floor with crazy glue, is standing exactly where he was when I flew out of the bathroom.

"It's going to be alright, Honey, it's going to be alright," I tell him.

He doesn't answer, and doesn't move as I struggle and finally manage to get my walker (which doesn't slide easily, like his) in the shower stall. I'm careful to set the water temperature just past lukewarm. Sam's skin has become sensitive to hot and cold—even one cold finger on his arm causes him to react as if he's been electrically shocked.

I warm my hands in the sink and gently place them on his shoulders. "Oh no, oh no, oh no," Sam says, but he lets me guide him to the shower, hesitates for a moment, reaches a hand in to feel the water, and suddenly is eager with anticipation, and following my instructions without objection:

"Okay, let go of your walker now, and hold on to the one in the shower. That's right. Now lift your leg over this metal strip, see? No, higher, higher. That's right. Now the other one. Good Sam, good."

Once he's under the warm spray, Sam closes his eyes, his face blissful. He looks as if he's stepped into a heavenly parallel reality. I pour shampoo on his head and, smiling, eyes still closed, he reaches up and works it through his hair by himself.

When I begin to soap and rinse him free of effluent, he opens his eyes and looks at me with a wicked, wicked grin, as if he's thinking: *Mmmm, what is my lady up to?*

He calls me "My lady," now," as if he's my knight; but when he's finally as clean as a bathed baby, and delicately scented from the herbal shampoo, it's as if he's become my child.

I'm soaking, *everything* is soaking. I help Sam out of the shower, wrap a fresh towel around him, and grab two more from hooks on the back of the bathroom door to throw on the wet floor, terrified that both of us will fall. That's what happened when I broke my leg.

209

But Sam is careful now, and listens when I tell him to slowly lift his walker, and lift his feet high over the towels on the floor while I hold a dry towel around his shoulders.

When we're back in the bedroom, I choose the brightest of Sam's pajama sets: navy-blue and yellow plaid bottoms, and a buttercup-yellow tee shirt. His perception of the beauty in ordinary things has heightened, bright colors thrill him, "they shimmer," he says, and we need something to brighten this day.

Once he's settled in his chair in the living room, he is almost instantly asleep.

I hurry to the soiled bathroom, put the filthy washcloths and slippers in a plastic bag, throw them away without a twinge of guilt, scrub everything down, throw the wet towels in the washing machine to take care of later, and rush to the other bathroom (which is closer to where Sam's sleeping), hoping to get myself showered and dressed before he wakes.

It's almost dinnertime when—finally clean, and in old soft jeans and a tee-shirt that have never in my life felt so good—I collapse on the couch next to Sam's chair, take a deep breath, and exhale. Sam wakes and, as always, reaches for my hand.

With no memory of what has transpired, he seems to have an unconscious recollection, for he doesn't gently smile, as he usually does when I sit by him, but instead looks directly at me with that *wicked, wicked* grin.

I begin to laugh, and then Sam laughs, too, madly, giddily—the two of us acting like children who—complicit in a bit of naughty intimacy—have escaped discovery.

Strangely, as tired as I am I feel totally triumphant, as if I've won a prize, as if I might sprout wings and fly. For a moment, or maybe just a second, I feel delight so intense that it can only be called ecstasy.

Dinner can wait.

IT'S NOT OKAY

I carefully number the bricks of my heart
For later reconstruction
Jeff Silva

When the call came, I had forgotten that I'd ever put Sam's name on a waiting list for long term care. It was one of those beautiful Indian summer days, a Friday, and I was particularly happy, having lunched with my daughter Beth in White Plains. When she went back to work I walked to Macy's to do some shopping, and then to Nordstroms, which is where I was when I answered my cell-phone.

I expected to hear William, Sam's aide, but it was the man at the nursing home asking if I was still interested.

As soon as I said, "Yes," to the now available room in their facility, I began sobbing. I was standing on the checkout line, and had to put down the items I was holding, and walk out. I almost called back to cancel the room, but Sam's frailty had become dangerous for both of us, and Alzheimer's is progressive, and how long would it be before a room became available again?

Our daughters and I had discussed how it might affect Sam to be taken to the nursing home for long term care. We'd agreed it would be like the first time you left a child at a daycare center, outrage at first, and then adjustment, friends, some sort of acceptance. We'd thought—since using his walker had become a precarious adventure—that Sam would soon be scooting around his unit in a wheelchair, as he had when he was in that same facility for rehabilitation the previous June and beginning of July.

We would soon learn that the nursing home's long-term-care unit was as different from the rehabilitation unit, as week old fish is from fresh lobster.

When I took Sam there, William and Catherine with me for support, he looked at the twenty or so poor souls sitting in front of the television like unclaimed luggage, shook his head with a sad expression on his face, and said, "I don't think I can help these people."

The next day he was one of them.

That day I dreaded the questions I expected to hear: *Why am I here? Why didn't you come back? Where is my helper?* (He called William, whose name he couldn't remember, "my helper," and when seeing a black commentator on television, once said with affection, "That's the man who took me under his wing"), I thought he would say something to me like, *You don't ~~you~~ love me anymore, do you.*

But I guess he didn't remember how he'd gotten there, that in effect I had abandoned him. All he said was, "Nobody smiles around here. Nobody talks to me. Something's up."

The third day a gas leak caused the fire department to block the road to the nursing home. Frantic, I tried to find another way there but couldn't. I never knew what to call it, that unknowing-knowing Sam seemed to have those days, certainly not memory, but when he saw me the day after the gas leak, he was clearly anguished.

"Oh, I *waited* and *waited* for you," he said, grabbing my arm as if he were afraid I'd disappear before his eyes. Eyes that told me he'd been crying or awake all night, probably both, and likely screaming or fighting as well, for he had clearly been drugged with more than the Seroquel and Depakote that I gave him when he was at home.

I took him outside that day, and seriously considered kidnapping him, just wheeling him to the car and leaving the wheelchair in the parking lot. But I didn't know if I could I manage to get him in the car, what if he fell and was injured? And if I did get him home, what would the nursing home staff do? Would they call the police? Would they say I was a danger to Sam and forbid me even to visit him?

I was sitting on a bench in the beautiful park-like area when those thoughts flew threw my head. Sam was sitting right next to me in his wheelchair, "I like it here," he said, "*But not in there!*"

I wish I had been brave enough to at least *try* to bring him home when it might have been possible. But I took him back inside.

The medication that Sam had been given was Haldol. Thereafter, each day he was more heavily drugged, and more confused than he'd been the day before. When I took him to the nursing home's Saturday concert, he nodded his head to the music, or tried to, fighting to keep his eyes open. I recalled us happily singing along with a small band when he was there just two months earlier, and began sobbing. There were plenty of aides at the concert, so I hurried to the ladies room, unable to stop the tears, unable to gain control for what seemed a long time.

The following week, Ativan was added to Sam's drug regimen. One day I arrived to find him trying over and over to get up from his wheelchair, which was now placed right next to a young aide (she looked about fifteen), who was responsible for Sam and all the others parked in front of the television. "Thank you, Jesus!" she said when she saw me, poor girl.

I wheeled Sam over to the couch so I could sit down. "What is it, Honey, what do you need? Why do you want to get up?" I asked.

He could hardly speak. "B'dh, B'dh," he finally got out. *Bed.* I went to the nurse's station and told them Sam needed to lie down. Not possible, the nurse told me, not enough aides. "But *I'm* here, I said, I'm not going anywhere."

Begrudging permission was granted for Sam to stretch what must have been his sore, arthritic, bones flat on a mattress for a couple of hours.

The next day when Holly and I met with Sam's caregivers (a meeting we requested as soon as we saw what was happening to him), a staff member complained that he was up all night because I had insisted that he be allowed to lie down the previous afternoon.

I was enraged. How could staff of a long-term-care facility not know that Alzheimer's patients are *always* wakeful at night? I tried

213

to tell them about Sam, how we had soothed him at home, what he had been like, what things would trigger an outburst, for example, cold hands on his skin. Holly showed them photos she had taken with her smart-phone that clearly illustrated the rapid decline in Sam's well-being.

"Do you want him to fall and break a leg?" someone asked, trying to justify the use of those potent drugs. "Yes!" I said vehemently.

Holly reached over to quiet me; she understood that I thought a broken leg would be Sam's ticket out of there.

Someone said, "He's a danger to himself and others," as if Sam were a criminal.

"He wasn't when I brought him here," I countered.

"They're stonewalling us," said Holly.

By the next week Sam was so heavily drugged that he couldn't find his mouth with a spoon. When I tried to feed him the vanilla ice cream he loved, his tongue moved uncontrollably and he began to choke, so I stopped. He couldn't distinguish the paper napkin on the table in front of him from the food, and began to eat the napkin; couldn't keep his eyes open; couldn't lift his head from his chest for more than five seconds, and so couldn't get a decent breath if his life depended on it, which of course it did.

Even in that state, when he managed to see me, or Holly, or Catherine, he said, "Boo-fl, Boo-fl." He saw us as beautiful.

I asked to talk to the doctor who was prescribing the heavy psychotropic drugs. The nurse would not give me his name or telephone number, but told me the doctor would be signing patient records the next morning, and I could talk to him then, if I got there before he left.

Catherine came with me that morning, both of us bleary-eyed, exhausted, tense, and ready for an argument. To my surprise, the doctor was a kind and compassionate man who patiently explained that he was not on staff, but was called when the nurse thought it necessary, and had to prescribe according to what he was told over the phone. He agreed (perhaps because I had three photos of Sam with me, one taken the day he arrived, one a week later, and one just a few days earlier), that Sam was definitely overmedicated, and suggested that he be sent to a hospital in New York City where there was a special wing for disturbed geriatric patients. There Sam would be weaned from the deleterious drugs, and put on an appropriate regimen.

There are no words to describe the relief I felt.

Since the doctor wasn't sure how long it would take to arrange for Sam's transfer, and thought it might not happen that day, Catherine and I, drained, left after lunchtime.

Sam was transported to the hospital in New York later that afternoon. I don't know if they (the nursing home staff, the ambulance people), would have let me go with him even if I had known beforehand.

Holly visited him that evening, a Thursday, and was told Sam had thrown a chair at someone as soon as he got there. I can't bear to think of the fear he must have felt—not one familiar, trusted face near him; no understanding of where he was being taken, or why; an ambulance ride during which he must have had to be restrained; the usual commotion upon arrival at the hospital.

So Sam had thrown a chair—which he would not have done if I'd been with him--and had had to be sedated yet again. "He's pretty much out of it," Holly told me when she called, "but he's comfortable." He was lying in a nice recliner, she also told me, instead of having to sit for hours in a wheelchair as he had done at the nursing home.

I didn't go to New York with Holly the next afternoon because I had a consultation with a new lawyer who I hoped could help me make better plans for Sam's care. I didn't go on Saturday either, nor did Holly. We knew Sam was being cared for with kindness, and that he was probably still too drugged to miss either of us. And we desperately needed the respite.

I tore the apartment apart that day, cleaning it from top to bottom, my heart light—if too much damage had not been done to Sam's psyche, he might be coming home again. At the very least he would *never* go back to that nursing home.

On Sunday, my daughter Laura was going to drive down from Tillson, New York, where she lives, and then come with me to visit Sam by train, both to see him, and so that I would be comfortable making the trip by myself in the future. But early—I don't know, eight or nine o'clock?—a doctor at the hospital phoned. Sam was comatose. They had suctioned his lungs several times. Did I still want the Do-Not-Resusitate order honored?

"Yes," I said, and then called Holly, who picked me up and drove us down as quickly as she could. We got there ten minutes before Sam died. Pneumonia.

That was October 10th, 2010.

In a photograph Catherine took of Sam and me just 19 days before I took him to the nursing home, he is glowing with health, and smiling that great broad smile that brightened any room I walked into. I couldn't look at it the day he died, I felt so responsible for everything that subsequently happened to him. But that feeling quickly passed—the photo shows Sam as he was when he was home with me, and I love seeing him that way.

It was the long-term-care unit at the nursing home that shattered his smile, and shattered me, as well, for by then, as the Talmud saying goes, "When he cried, I tasted salt."

Recently I read that 'shattered' is a word too often used by writers, but I can't think of another that so well describes what it's like to feel emotional cracks from top to bottom, and side to side, and to sense those broken pieces of yourself lying about your feet so you can't move.

For a long time after Sam's death I could barely walk across my living room.

Sam's death was a mercy, of course it was—but the *way* he died was a violation. His days in that nursing home—with no intent to harm on the part of nurses, or aides, or anyone, I understand that—were torture, nothing less.

To have to sit all day in a wheelchair and not be able to move it away from a television broadcasting programs designed to assault you're psyche, to have to sit there when your joints are probably screaming, to have to sit there when you're so exhausted, so drugged, that you can't hold your head up—what is that but torture?

That first week in the nursing home, when Sam was distraught because I had been gone so long, and I was still able to help him

216

get on the couch to sit next to me, I held him close and told him, "It's going to get better, it's going to be okay, Holly and I are meeting with the staff soon."

"No, it's not okay! It's not okay!" he said, fighting tears.

And he was right.

It was *not okay* to drug Sam out of his mind.,

It was *not okay* to treat his loved ones as if they were interfering nuisances/

It is *never okay* to extinguish a spirit still capable of laughter, capable of love, as Sam was.

It is shattering.

That all happened five years ago.

Today I'm sitting on my patio, sipping coffee and watching birds on the wing, or hopping among the trees on the hill—cardinals, a mocking bird, jays, a goldfinch, and the seemingly ubiquitous sparrows.

A hummingbird just visited the flower on the table next to me, not finding the nectar to its taste, it flew right off; a woodpecker is drilling a tree somewhere out of sight; Monarch butterflies—not as many as years ago, but two—are dancing in the air right in front of me, a ballet, Sam would have called it.

The sun is bright, the sky cloudless, and I sense Sam's spirit with me, or maybe dancing in the air with the birds and butterflies. It is a peaceful day, and I am at peace.

I think of Jeff Silva's beautiful words, "I carefully number the pieces of my heart for later reconstruction."

The only possible happy ending, for a story such as this, is my reconstructed heart.

'GETTING TO THE BEACH

For all your ills, I give you laughter
Rabelais

"Baby Brother," she called him, though Sam was seven years older than Toni, and as protective as any big brother of a much loved younger sister. He made that clear, and it worried me. "She's exactly your age," he told me, "She has four daughters, just like you do. You're going to love each other." Or he would say, "Toni's going to love you," or, "You're going to love Toni." What if we don't even like each other? I thought.

"I can't wait for you two to meet," Sam said for the umpteenth time as we left for Bradenton Florida, where he and Toni had inherited a house from their father. He was in a cloud of happy anticipation that I tried to share, quelling my unease.—Do things ever go the way we expect them to? Would Sam see me through different eyes if Toni didn't approve of me?

I don't remember arriving in Bradenton. Did Sam and I get there first? Or did Toni and her husband Ed? I only recall feeling awkward when we were finally introduced (as I still sometimes do in new, or tricky situations), and I remember Ed's strange comment as we sat together at the table in late afternoon, while Sam and Toni walked through the house discussing what they would do with some of their father's possessions.

218

"You sure you want to do this?" he asked with a grin, referring to my upcoming marriage to Sam, "These Rogers are a different species, you know."

"Different how? I asked, uneasy.

But Ed, still grinning, just got up to make another highball.

He was joking of course, but it gave me pause. Were his words a gentle nudge to get me out of Sam's life?

What I next remember is Sam and Ed arguing over the merits of Genghis Kahn, whom Ed extolled, in part to get a rise out of Sam. Both men were clearly enjoying themselves so Toni and I, tired of listening to them, headed for the supermarket to pick up enough food to stock the refrigerator for the week, and plenty of snacks to offset the effects of the gin and tonics we would drink in the evenings.

The supermarket was fairly empty at that hour, and seemed unusually immaculate, the floor glowing as if it had been waxed and polished right before we walked in. I think that's what made me think of a neat trick I'd recently discovered to clean my ancient bathtub. Eager to be friends with Sam's sister, who, I assumed, also cleaned her own home, I enthusiastically shared my discovery:

"You just squirt toilet-bowl cleaner in the tub," I told her, "use a Scrunge with a handle to scrub it around, and rinse. You don't even get your hands wet! You *have* to try it. It will change your life!"

Toni stopped in her tracks, looked at me deadpan, and said, "Only if I *drink* it."

I laughed so hard she must have thought I'd lost my sanity. I couldn't stop. And then she was laughing too, in that way that you just can't help when someone you're with is laughing like a lunatic.

Of all things I might have enthused about: a book, a play, a movie, I had chosen toilet-bowl cleanser, an *Eloise* household tip. *Who is this ditsy woman my brother is marrying?* Toni might have wondered. But I think that laughter did it—her wit, my semi-hysterical response—for Toni, highly intelligent and with a marvelous, wry, Dorothy Parker sense of humor that could always erase the sober streak I was born with, did end up loving me, and I her.

There are photographs from that week in Florida—of me holding a baby goat at a farm, Ed by my side; of Sam standing on a bridge, a double rainbow painting the sky behind him (a good omen, we said); and my favorite, of Toni and me in our bathing suits (having just left the beach), sitting on two parked motorcycles we had impulsively climbed on, women in our fifties, sitting on strangers' motorcycles, giggling like silly teenagers. The photos are in a carton in my storage room, but the images are clear in my mind.

For thirteen years Sam and I got together with Toni and Ed often. Our last vacation was to be at Wrightsville Beach in Wilmington, North Carolina. That year, 1998, Sam and I first drove to Pittsboro, where Toni and Ed lived, so we could visit with Ed (who would not join us on this vacation), and so that Sam and Toni could participate in a study on arthritis at Duke University. After their Duke appointment, we stopped to eat at a café in Chapel Hill. By afternoon Sam was deathly ill from something he ate (or so we believed).

Instead of driving to Wilmington, we stayed with Toni and Ed. Sam crawling in bed and refusing to see a doctor or go to an emergency room, which we were urging him to do. Near the end of the week, much recovered, and knowing how much Toni and I had looked forward to the beach, he insisted he was well enough for us to go there for the last two days of our vacation.

In Wilmington, we ate our evening meal at a nice restaurant. Sam ordered clams. And the trouble began all over again. He was so sick that Toni and I were afraid to leave him alone—but we did, for about fifteen minutes right before we left for home, walking on wet sand at the edge of the ocean, promising ourselves we'd be back next year. "And no clams for Sam!" one of us said.

As often happens, life took us in a different direction. The next year Toni flew to New York for my daughter Bonnie's funeral. After that there was the illness of another daughter; the progression of the Alzheimer's Sam had developed; Lyme's disease (mine); a fractured hip (Toni's), and then Ed became seriously ill.

We kept in touch by phone, preferring the personal sound of each other's voice rather then email. We talked about our writing, about books we were reading—our taste in books so similar that one of us would say, "You have to read ...." And the other would answer, "I just finished it!". As our lives became difficult, we consoled each other, sometimes complaining about our husbands, often talking about all the things we wished we could do together: go to writing workshops; drive around the Carolina countryside looking for interesting things to photograph (photography being another of our interests), or walking around Manhattan, where Toni had worked years and years ago.

We sent each other stories and poems we'd written. "There now," Toni wrote at the bottom of one that she sent, "I've shown you mine, now show me yours."

The following funny, and sad, poem that she wrote arrived when her life, like mine, was becoming even more arduous.

A Little Ditty

When I was young I spent my time
Trying to find a word to rhyme
With orange
And now I'm old I spend my time
Thinking that I will die and go to hell,
Oh well
Sometime between the then and now
There must have been a time of bliss
I missed.

And we talked, and talked about our love of the ocean, promising ourselves salt-water swims, white sand, waves breaking near our feet, a big umbrella, a good book, a glass of wine.

Next year. Next year.

We would not see each other again until Sam's funeral in 2010. When he died in October, and Ed in December (a double loss for Toni), she and I telephoned each other constantly.

After the strain of caring for our husbands for so many years, each of us had expected to feel a degree of relief, as well as grief, at their deaths. Instead we felt as if chasms had opened at our feet. We each became ill, Toni far more seriously than I. She was hospitalized with pneumonia once, and then again, and still we talked of getting to a beach when we were both well enough, even if all we could do was sit under an umbrella and watch the waves roll in.

During a telephone call on a Sunday afternoon, we visited for more than an hour. Toni was feeling much better, she said, and so was I. We discussed a possible trip to a North Carolina beach in September, when the tourists have left and the weather is still gorgeous. I imagined the smell of sea and suntan oil, lunches in trendy little cafes, Toni's wry humor, which had been gone for awhile, back in full swing.

When the phone rang a week or so later I saw Toni's number on the display on my phone and picked up the receiver expecting to hear "Hey, Marian."

But it was her daughter Julia. "Mom asked me to place the call," she said, her voice thick with sorrow, "She wants to tell you goodbye."

I fell apart. I can recall only snatches of that last conversation: "You're the sister I never had and always wanted," Toni told me, and I know I told her, while sobbing uncontrollably, that I loved her like a sister, too, that we will meet again in another lifetime. She agreed. We will, yes.

About an hour and a half later Toni died. Her 'goodbye' call was one of the greatest gifts I've ever received.

When Sam died six months earlier, and even, to some extent, when Bonnie died, I had robotically continued doing small chores as natural to me as breathing: beds were made; dirty dishes put in the dishwasher; counters wiped; memorial services arranged; the home prepared for guests. Family came from all over, friends brought meals.

When Toni died I phoned Sam's daughters, and mine, and then there was nothing to do.

For two days I left the apartment in disarray, bed unmade, dishes, if I bothered to eat, left in the sink, mail half-opened and left scattered on the dining room table.

Because, unlike Sam and Ed, and my sisters, Toni was just my age; because she was my strongest link with Sam; because she was my pal and we had grand plans for what we would do with what was left of our futures—I walked around my apartment crying and mumbling, "Not fair, not fair, not fair." like a child who got the smallest slice of the pie.

That was in June, 2011. Toni's daughters arranged to have her ashes scattered in the ocean from a beach on a small North Carolina island in September—a beautiful idea, absolutely perfect.

Near the end of August, my sister Jeanne died, and I didn't feel up to traveling to North Carolina with my stepdaughters in September.

But Heather called me from the island beach where Toni's ashes (and some of Sam's that I had sent with Holly), were being dispersed, and kept the line open. She described everything for me: the gorgeous evening, the children's participation, the cloud of ashes sailing over the ocean—they look like silver sparks in the photographs Holly gave me—and in that way I was with them, and with Toni, for the whole moving ceremony her children created.

And now it is 2015. I miss them, Toni, Ed, Sam (my sisters and so many others, too), but oh, the memories I have:

I invite to mind a hot southern summer night, a chill supermarket, a basket holding nacho chips and salsa, chocolate and soda, I see a younger self *so* eager to be liked, sharing her big discovery: a caustic cleanser that "…will change your life!"

I hear Toni's sardonic reply, "Only if I drink it." And then we are laughing.

And so am I, now.

———

ACKNOWLEDGEMENTS

When Joan Potter, author and memoir workshop facilitator, called a week after Sam's death asking if I was still interested in attending a workshop she was leading, I grabbed the opportunity like a drowning person jumping onto a raft. I haven't stopped writing since. At first it was healing, now it's fulfilling. Many thanks, Joan.

Heartfelt thanks to Debra Bloomgarden, Gail Burlakoff, David Gitelson, Philippa Perry, Sylvia Perugini, Irene Smith, and Lisa Zumar, friends and fellow writers who encouraged me to publish my stories. Without them this book would not exist. And special, special thanks to Melvin Perry for getting it into print once, and then again (when I inadvertently undid computer work that he had completed).

Always, love and gratitude to my large and wonderful family for their encouragement and fearless acceptance of whatever I wanted to write about, and to my friend, Estelle Austin, for her encouragement forty years ago when I tiptoed into the 'outside' world—and still.

I'd also like to acknowledge The Sun publications for their wonderful Sunbeams and Paper Lanterns books, compilations of aphorisms from which I gleaned most of the quotations that begin my stories.

ABOUT THE AUTHOR

Marian Armstrong Rogers lives in Mt. Kisco, New York. Her work has been published in *The Sun* magazine and *The Writer's Journal*. She studied at Pace University and worked for the County of Westchester, NY for many years, her last position being assistant to the crisis team at the Psychiatric Institute, Westchester County Medical Center, from which she is now retired.

Not incidentally, she is mother/stepmother of six, grandmother of eleven, and great-grandmother of one. She is currently working on a second collection of stories.

Create Space

Valentine's

The Coun

Made in the USA
Middletown, DE
03 December 2015